36443000534677

TOWN OF PELHAM PUBLIC LIBRARY

TOWN OF PELHAM PUBLIC LIBRARY
BRANCH
W9-BKA-998

CANADA'S STORY
BOOK TWO

The STRUGGLE for a Continent

BY
ROBERT J. FOLEY

ILLUSTRATED
BY
GEORGE BALBAR

THE HAUNTED PRESS
NIAGARA FALLS, ONTARIO

Copyright © Robert J. Foley 1999

All rights reserved. No part of this publication may be reprinted, stored in a retrieval system, or transmitted in any form by an electronic or mechanical copying system without the written permission of the publisher.

ISBN: 1-895528-06-2

Foley, Robert J. 1941-
Canada's Story Book Two
The Struggle for a Continent
by Robert J. Foley
Includes index

Illustrated by:
Balbar, George 1930-

The Haunted Press,
A Division of 314340 Ontario Limited
4219 Briarwood Avenue,
Niagara Falls, Ontario
L2E 6Z1
(905) 374-7245
E-mail: hauntedp@caninet.com

Printed In Canada
by Peninsula Press Ltd.
St. Catharines, Ont

Canadian Cataloguing in Publication Data

Foley, Robert J., 1941-
    Canada's Story

Includes index
Contents: Bk. 2. The Struggle for a Continent
ISBN 1-895528-06-2 (bk. 2)

1.Canada - History. I Balbar, George. II. Title.

FC164.F64 1999   971.   C97-932381-9
F1026.F64 1999

Respectfully dedicated to
Les Canadiens Français
Whose ancestors endured unspeakable hardships
To open up this continent
And, with their blood and sweat,
Laid the first bricks in the foundation
Of this great nation we call Canada

CONTENTS

PREFACE

With the destruction of the Hurons in 1649 the balance of power in Canada shifted dramatically. The Iroquois ranged freely over the St. Lawrence Valley shutting off, for a time, the life's blood of Canada, the Fur Trade. Despite this, Canadians struck out into the unknown to reveal the expanse of a continent. **Canada Story, Book Two** reverberates with the fortitude of great explorers such as La Salle and La Verendrye. At home too was the courage of Canadians who defended their homes against overwhelming odds. The names of Adam Dollard, Sieur des Ormeaux and the petite Madeleine de Verchères echo down through the annuals of Canadian history.

This era in Canadian history also saw the beginnings of the great struggle for control of the North American continent. France claimed everything west of the Allegheny Mountains and it was Canadians who enforced their sovereignty over the vast territory from Quebec to New Orléans. We will meet the man who, more than anyone since Champlain, helped shape this country, Louis de Buade, Comte de Frontenac.

Robert J Foley
Niagara Falls, Ontario
September 25, 1999

CHAPTER ONE
Scourge of the Nations
"There has been yet another great clash between the French and those barbarians in an encounter near Trois Rivières, when our men went in search of nine Frenchmen that the Iroquois had carried off."-Marie de l'Incarnation, 1650

The devastating attack on Huronia broke the will of the Hurons and they ceased to be a cohesive nation. Some fled west and north begging their Petun neighbours to take them in. Many, under the guidance of the Jesuits, settled on St. Joseph's Island at the tip of Nottawasaga Bay. The missionaries moved all their possessions from Ste. Marie including surplus stocks of corn and vegetables before setting fire to the buildings.

The Huron settlement on St. Joseph's Island seemed ideal for the refugees that had survived the Iroquois onslaught. The Jesuits had moved all their supplies and livestock to the island and confidently predicted that they could keep the settlement going for at least three years if not longer.

All the good fathers' help would be needed if the remnants of the once mighty Huron nation were to survive. The Hurons had lost all energy and initiative and the Jesuits found them living on acorns and garlic on their arrival at St. Joseph's. There were plenty of fish in the bay, but the Hurons had few boats and no new ones were under construction.

The missionaries provided the necessities of life and immediately set about building a strong fort against the possibility of another raid. They named their palisade Sainte Marie II. The one unforeseen result of the tragedy that had befallen the Hurons was that in their misery they turned to the teachings of the missionaries for comfort. In that time period fourteen hundred were baptized.

Some of the refugees who did not go to St. Joseph's fled to the land of the Neutrals and sought sanctuary in the villages of this nation of traders. The victorious Iroquois demanded that all Hurons within their palisades be sent out. At first the Neutrals refused reminding the Iroquois of the custom of sanctuary for all in their villages, but the warriors would not be denied and the Neutrals protected them at their peril. Needless to say many Hurons were dragged off to Iroquois towns to an unknown fate.

During that first summer stray parties of refugees continued to make their way to St. Joseph's Island. With the onset of winter the population of the settlement numbered seven thousand. The situation soon became so critical that the resources of the island were overwhelmed. Despite the hard work of the Jesuits starvation became a problem and epidemics swept through the lodges killing the disheartened, disorganized Hurons. Many pulled up stakes and headed further west linking up with the Wyandots while others drifted north seeking refuge with the Ojibwa.

It was during this winter that it was decided to move as many of the Christian Indians as possible to Quebec. On June 10, 1650 a party of sixty Frenchmen and several hundred Hurons began the long trek to Quebec and safety. Enroute they met Father Bressani and a relief party of thirty Canadians and as many Indians. They all proceeded together to Quebec, which they reached on July 28th.

On their arrival they were encamped near the Hotel Dieu where the religious houses and the more affluent citizens provided for them for the coming winter. Another group soon joined them under the Huron Chief, Étienne Annaotaha.

The Iroquois now ranged the lower Ottawa Valley and the St. Lawrence with impunity. On August 30, 1650 Marie de l'Incarnation wrote the following to her son in France:

" . . .There has been yet another great clash between the French and those barbarians in an encounter near Trois-Rivières, when our men went in search of nine Frenchmen that the Iroquois had captured and carried off. Today they have the intention of storming Trois-Rivières and you will note that with them they have several Hollanders that are helping them. One was recognized during the battle and a Huron that escaped has assured us of it."

"They are resolved (so we are told) to come, after they have taken Trois-Rivières, to attack us. Although in appearance there is not so much reason for fear in our houses, which are strong, still what has happened in all the Huron villages, which were laid waste by fire and arms, should make the French apprehend a like disaster if prompt help does not come to us . . .."

"This help can only come to us from France, for there are not enough forces in all the country to resist them. If France fails us, then, we must shortly either leave or die. But because all the French, who are in the number of more than two thousand, will not be able to find means to withdraw, they will be forced to perish, either through poverty or through the cruelty of their enemies; and, also, the fact that they would have to leave the goods they have acquired in this country and be deprived of all means of support in France will make them choose death in this country rather than misery in another."

The Iroquois grip on the upper St. Lawrence Valley grew tighter as the year progressed and the lucrative fur trade, once the domain of the Hurons, ground to a halt. Marie de l'Incarnation's plea to her son was not without foundation. Without the fur trade ships would cease to come to Quebec in large numbers. Quebec depended on France for all of its manufactured goods and that supply would be severely impacted by a drop in traffic on the St. Lawrence. The eventual evacuation of the colony would be a real possibility. The result of the constant harassment by the Iroquois was described in the Jesuit Relations of 1652-53:

"Never were there more beaver in our lakes and rivers, but never have there been fewer seen in the warehouses of the country. Before the devastation of the Hurons, a hundred canoes used to come to trade, all laden with beaver-skins; and each year we had two or three hundred thousand livres' worth. That was fine revenue with which to satisfy all the people, and defray the heavy expenses of the country . . . .."

"The Iroquois war dried up all these springs. The beavers are left in peace and in the place of their repose; the Huron fleets no longer come down to trade; the Algonquins are depopulated; and the more distant nations are withdrawing still farther, fearing the fire of the Iroquois. For a year, the warehouse of Montréal has not bought a single Beaver-skin from the savages. At Trois-Rivières, the little revenue that has accrued has been used to fortify the place, the enemy being expected there. In Quebec warehouses there is nothing but poverty; and so everyone has cause to be dissatisfied, there being no means to supply payment to those to whom it is due, or even to defray a part of the most necessary expenses of the country."

With the coming of spring a decision as to the resettlement of the Huron refugees had to be made. After much deliberation the Île d'Orléans was given to them as their new home. It was close enough to fall under the protection of the citadel at Quebec and fertile enough to support its inhabitants. While the women tended the crops the men could engage in the fur trade bringing in much needed income and helping in the long-term survival of the colony.

The only missionaries left in the field were those among the Algonkins and the Petun on the north shore of Georgian Bay. The Petun were at peace with the Iroquois and so felt safe from the wildfire that burned around them. There were three missions set up among the Petun; St. Matthieu, St. Jean and St. Mathias.

The Iroquois decided to end the neutrality of the Petun. In the early dawn of a summer's day the Iroquois struck at St. Jean. The surprise was so complete that no defense was given and the entire population was slaughtered including the Jesuit, Charles Garnier. Another missionary of St. Jean, Father Chabanel, was escorting a group of homeless Hurons to St. Joseph when they were overtaken by a war party and, as his companions scattered, one of the Hurons killed him. The Petun fled west and ended up in Wisconsin.

The great council of the Five Nations met at Onondaga and came to momentous decision; all the tribes within reach of their war parties must be destroyed. The Eries living on the south shore of the lake that bears their name were the next victims of the warriors of the longhouse. Unlike other Indians of the time, the Iroquois always had a plan and they usually stuck to it. For their conquest of the Eries they developed a new strategy. Carrying their canoes as shields the warriors stormed the Erie towns and using them in turn as scaling ladders poured over the walls carrying all before them. In a single day of blood and fire they wiped the Eries from the face of the earth.

The Andastes proved to be a more troublesome problem. They quickly organized a stout defense of their lands and villages, inflicting heavy casualties on the Iroquois. The war with them dragged on for a few years before they also ceased to exist as a separate nation.

The Iroquois: Scourge of the Nations

On the surface the Neutrals, once considered indispensable in the survival of the Five Nations, as they were the corner stone of the great trading system that covered the continent, should have felt reasonably secure. Their ancient position as a port of trade in the complex trading network made them of some value even to the aggressive Iroquois. However, with the destruction of the tribes to the north and the position of the Dutch and English to the south and east, the very reason for their being allowed to exist was now in question. The port of trade was already shifting to Albany and European goods were supplanting the need for furs and utensils of native manufacture. The chiefs of the Neutral villages knew that it was only a matter of time.

In 1652 the Seneca came out of the morning mist and attacked. They swept through the Niagara Peninsula destroying villages, killing or burning what they could not carry off. The Neutrals were dispersed to the four winds. Many were taken prisoner and either tortured at the stake or, as often happened, adopted into the tribe. Others fled west to be absorbed into other tribes, while many others fled into the woods where most died for lack of shelter and food. The Neutrals, long the peaceful island in a sea of war, ceased to exist.

Curiously the Seneca did not claim the fertile Peninsula that was the home of the Neutrals. Perhaps the ghosts of those slain stood guard against the claims of the Iroquois. Whatever the reason, the Peninsula eventually came under the sway of the Mississaugas, but it was to remain unsettled for a hundred and thirty years.

All fell before the onslaught of the warriors of the longhouse, but it came at a great price to the Five Nations. Although some victories were swift and decisive, others were achieved in a sea of warriors' blood. The Andastes especially fought with cunning and bravery selling their nation dearly to the unrelenting Iroquois. This drain on their strength was to prove the undoing of the confederacy in its war with the Canadians.

In the meantime they continued to harass the growing community of Ville Marie de Montréal. The great council was hatching a plan to drive the French from North America.

While the Canadians in the St. Lawrence Valley struggled with the ever present Iroquois threat, another struggle was taking place in Acadia. As we have seen Samuel Argall of Virginia raided Port Royal in 1613 burning the town and carrying off a good portion of its inhabitants. Biencourt, son of Jean de Biencourt, Sieur de Poutrincourt, was left behind and took charge of those whom the English could not catch or deemed too insignificant to remove. Biencourt and his followers spent a miserable winter among their Indian friends and waited for the spring and the sight of a friendly sail on the horizon. None came. The Acadians lived with the Indians, adopting their way of life just to survive. They finally succeeded in building a small fort at Cape Sable, which Biencourt named Fort Lomeron. The tiny garrison spent a number of years there impatiently waiting for relief from France.

Although they resided within the walls of their fort they continued to live off the land like the Indians, raising just enough crops to supplement their diet of fish and wild game. Out of necessity they learned to co-exist with the New Englanders who prowled the Atlantic coast in search of trade.

Biencourt died in 1623 leaving command and all of his possessions in Acadia to his lieutenant, Charles St. Étienne de la Tour. La Tour was an ambitious Norman who was cunning enough to survive in a world where the Fleur de Lys and the English flag might be changed with the bedding. Indeed there was some concern among the ministers in Paris that la Tour was negotiating with the English, who still claimed the entire eastern seaboard as their domain. The fact that King Charles I of England had seen fit to make la Tour Baronet of Nova Scotia did little to allay their suspicions.

The English occupied Acadia in 1628 along with Quebec, but la Tour continued to rule his little fiefdom and managed to even expand his operations under the nose of the British. He built another fort at the mouth of the St. John River on the far side of the Bay of Fundy. Fort St. Jean was located at a very strategic point in the bay and secured la Tour's hold on the region.

Despite everything, la Tour kept France appraised of the situation and when, in 1632, Acadia was officially ceded back to France in the Treaty of St.-Germain-en-Laye he fully expected to be confirmed in his position. But, the government, unsure of la Tour's loyalty, sent out Charles de Razilly to take formal possession of the territory. La Tour was understandably furious at the snub and one of the most curious episodes in Canadian history began to unfold.

Razilly died within three years and nominated his chief subordinate, Charles de Menou d'Aunay Charnisey, as his successor. D'Aunay, as the records call him, was courageous, devout and dealt with everyone in a courteous manner. He was also staunchly loyal to the French government. For all his courage d'Aunay was grandiose to the extreme, trumpeting his importance to the world. He set himself up at Port Royal as a potentate, bringing out his wife and barrels of possessions that would not have been out of place at the court at Versailles. D'Aunay entertained lavishly, an island of aristocratic pursuits in an untamed land. Port Royal was d'Aunay's feudal stronghold complete with a garrison and a seminary that boasted twelve Capuchin monks. The harbour was always crowded with the masts of trading ships and the comings and goings of Indians bring their furs in to barter. The fertile fields of the Annapolis basin once more felt the plow as new settlers cultivated their crops.

La Tour, who had upheld the French presence in Acadia during a long, bleak ten year period with no help from home, refused to acknowledge d'Aunay's authority. Thus began the first civil war in the history of North America.

The two sides raided each other, plundering possessions and destroying crops. In France the two antagonists had their backers and a bitter war of words swirled about the capital as each lobbied in their champion's favour.

La Tour could not have possibly carried on a war against the better armed and supplied d'Aunay without help. For that help he turned to the hardheaded Puritans of New England. He convinced them that it was in their best interests to help him get the better of his rival. They went so far as to send ships and men to aid him in his battles.

D'Aunay holds
court at
Port Royal

He also brought out his wife whose name was Marie Jacquelin, the daughter of a barber in Mans. Marie proved to be an able and courageous fighter and la Tour did not hesitate to leave her in charge at Fort St. Jean while he went to Boston to consult with his allies.

D'Aunay took advantage of his absence and besieged the stronghold. True to her reputation she fought to the last, encouraging the men when they showed signs of weakening. When the fort finally fell d'Aunay hanged part of the garrison and kept Madame de la Tour prisoner until she died. In his report to Paris he stated that Marie "died of spite and rage."

Shortly after the death of la Tour's wife things took a dramatic turn. While crossing Annapolis Basin d'Aunay's canoe upset immersing him in the icy wa-

ter. He died of hypothermia. During his long struggle with la Tour, d'Aunay enjoyed the full support of the authorities in France, however, after his death the same authorities decided that perhaps his rival should reign supreme in Acadia. After a hasty trip to France la Tour took possession of Port Royal as governor. Madame d'Aunay, who had brought the aristocracy to the new world suddenly found herself in trouble. A merchant of Rochelle claimed that the d'Aunay estate owed him 260,000 livres. He sued and won leaving the widow and her eight children penniless.

Next came the most ironic twist of all. D'Aunay's widow, perplexed, unhappy and desperate, married Charles de la Tour. la Tour died in 1666 bringing to an end one of the most colourful vignettes in Canadian history.

CHAPTER THREE

Montréal faces the onslaught
"The Iroquois grip on the St. Lawrence Valley became so tight
that communications with Quebec became almost non-existent."

Ironically the decision by the Iroquois to destroy the Hurons and attack their neighbours brought a period of peace to Montréal. One of the Iroquois' principles of war was to never fight on two fronts. This illusion of peace spawned dreams of a normal life and settlers, tired of being cooped up in the fort, solicited grants of land from the governor, Maisonneuve. Soon land was cleared for planting, albeit near the stockade. It was even hoped that the mill, now loopholed for muskets would soon serve a more peaceful purpose. The more trees that were felled the farther from the settlement the forest receded making cover for marauding Iroquois harder to come by.

But as the warm summer of 1651 pushed on toward fall the illusion was shattered. The Iroquois renewed their attacks on the St. Lawrence Valley with more determination than ever. Montréal lay exposed and was kept alive only by the heroism of its people, Ailleboust, the governor of New France, deployed a flying column of soldiers who rushed to the danger spots to throw the enemy back, while he sent urgent requests to France for reinforcements.

The stories from Montréal in those critical times were tales of horrible deaths and miraculous survival. A Huron woman working in the fields was carried off with two of her children. A Frenchman tending cattle close to the settlement was killed and a woman nearby received six wounds. She somehow survived. Jean Boutard was killed trying to rescue his wife, Catherine, from fifty warriors. She was burned alive after her captors cut off her breasts, her ears and her nose.

Needless to say the colony was in a panic. Maisonneuve ordered everyone to leave their homes and take shelter in the fort. Jeanne Mance was alone at the hospital when a band of 200 Iroquois stormed the building and attempted to set it on fire. Sixteen soldiers under Lambert Closse, the town major, rushed to the rescue. The pitched battle lasted all day and in the end the Iroquois were forced to withdraw.

Jeanne was forced to abandon the hospital, which became a fortified post with soldiers always on duty. Loopholes were cut in the walls and the chapel became a magazine for the cannon mounted outside.

For the first time there was open talk of abandoning the colony. Jeanne Mance came to the fore in defence of maintaining the settlement. She reminded Maisonneuve that her benefactor in France, Madame de Bullion, had set aside a large sum of money for the hospital. If Montréal were abandoned there would be no Hotel Dieu, and no money. She proposed that Madame de Bullion be persuaded to allow the money to be used to bring more men from France. Further she urged Maisonneuve to go to France in pursuit of both the funds and recruits. The governor promised that he would not return until he had found a hundred men. If he did not return Jeanne was to take all the colonists back to France leaving the island to the Iroquois.

No sooner had Maisonneuve departed then Ailleboust was recalled and the original owner of the island, Jean de Lauzon, a callous man, was appointed by the king in his stead. He assured the colonists that he was well disposed to them, but immediately stopped the flying column that had kept many of the settlers safe. However, at Montréal, Lambert Closse was an inspiration to his men and he was able to maintain a vigorous defence. At the sound of a single shot all the inhabitants rushed to the spot in defence of their neighbours.

The Iroquois' grip on the St. Lawrence became so tight that communications became almost non existent. Lauzon dispatched a pinnace from Quebec to determine if Montréal was still in French hands. They were under strict orders to stand clear of the fort unless they were certain that the French were still in possession of it. Upon their arrival they anchored in midstream in a thick fog, which made visibility almost zero. They listened and waited. On hearing nothing and fearing capture, they sailed away to Quebec with the sad news that all was lost. In the meantime some of those manning the fort swore that they saw a boat, but when the fog cleared the river was empty.

The Onondagas picked this time to send a peace delegation of sixteen chiefs to Quebec. Their inability to wipe out the settlement at Montréal was a major factor in their decision. They arrived with but one proposal, a proposal that took the French completely by surprise. The Onondagas wanted the French to show their friendliness and good faith by establishing a colony among them as they had done with the Hurons. We can only imagine the shock of the French officials. They feared that there was some sinister purpose behind it. To send colonists into the heart of

Jeanne Mance,
The heroine of
Montréal

Iroquois country might be a death sentence, but to refuse would be interpreted as an insult and the Iroquois had made it clear that they did not need much of a reason to make war. The decision was beyond Lauzon and he procrastinated, putting the chiefs off with several excuses.

In the meantime Maisonneuve's stay in France dragged on past the twelve months he had planned. His interview with Madame de Bullion went well and she readily agreed to the diversion of the funds. She even contributed more. Of the 75,000 livres provided for the expedition, she contributed 42,000.

In the signing on of men he was less successful. The right combination of skill and piety was hard to come by in mid 17th century France. Stories of harsh winters and cruel Indians dampened the adventurous spirit of many a young Frenchmen. He finally was able to recruit one hundred and eighteen men, but on their terms. They were to come out under five year contracts, their room and board to be paid by the company and they were to receive full wages, according to their trade. A mixed company of sixty labourers and plowmen with an assortment of carpenters, masons, shoemakers and even a pastry chef set sail for the New World. Among them was Marguerite Bourgeoys, a teacher, who was to have a profound affect on the history of education in Canada.

While the Onondaga chiefs waited, the governor of New France, Jean de Lauzon, pondered the advisability of sending French settlers into Iroquois country. The Jesuits urged acceptance of the offer as it meant the establishment of a mission. They argued that the motives of the Onondagas may well have been peaceful. A strong French fort would be a rallying point if they were attacked by an enemy; they would learn how to repair their firearms and if the French Indian allies followed they would be adopted into the tribe boosting the Iroquois population reduced by the constant wars waged against the tribes on their borders.

It was finally decided to send someone to look over the situation and report back. The Jesuits offered to send Father Simon le Moyne, who had spent some time among the Mohawks and was well respected by them. His report was favourable. Still Lauzon hesitated and decided to send two more delegates. This time Fathers Dablon and Chaumonot, the latter known for his ability as an orator, went to face the lion in his den. The headmen listened with delight to Chaumonot's harangue, however, they now punctuated their invitation with threats, come to the Valley of the Onondagas or know our anger. Father Dablon returned to Quebec to report while Chaumonot remained to keep the warriors happy with his oratory.

The decision was finally made and the bravery and determination of the Canadians was exemplified when fifty men volunteered to accompany the party into Iroquois country. On May 17, 1657 two large boats and twelve canoes left Quebec under the command of Major Zacharie Dupuy

Strangely, this expedition created an unforeseen problem. The Mohawks became jealous. If the French were to have a settlement why not in Mohawk country? They immediately sent off a war party of three hundred warriors who slipped passed Quebec in the night and mounted a surprise raid on the Hurons at Île d' Orleans killing a few and carrying off eighty prisoners, most of them women.

The following morning the Mohawks paddled past Quebec in broad daylight raising their paddles in mock salute. Terror stricken Hurons screamed for help, but Jean de Lauzon watched passively from the safety of the citadel. The Mohawks forced their captives to stand and sing as a final insult.

No shot was fired. Nothing was done to save the helpless Hurons. Inhabitants along the shore rushed to the citadel for protection and the Mohawks sent parties ashore to ransack the houses and still the governor refused to give the order. French prestige was dealt a crippling blow that day. The Mohawks went away with the knowledge that the French were not to be feared and that they could raid the St. Lawrence Valley with impunity.

In the meantime the mission to the Onondagas pressed on. They changed to canoes at Montréal and went forward under a banner containing the word JESUS. Soon, however, their path was lined with Mohawks with death on their minds. The Onondagas restrained their brothers and they had to be content with killing a few Hurons every day, clubbing the women and dragging the men off to be burned alive.

The flotilla crossed the eastern end of Lake Ontario and entered the Oswego River into the valley of the Onondagas. They found a rich land centred around long lakes, teeming with fish, that stretched out like human fingers.

Father Chaumonot had chosen a site on high ground for the settlement in the midst of salt springs and a commanding view of the surrounding country. They marched there immediately under the escort of French soldiers in their blue coats with Indian drums adding to the din.

The Jesuits went on to Onondaga to begin their work only to find the confederacy gathered in council. Warriors and their families stretched out on every side. Although the welcoming speeches were friendly many a face was turned away to hide the hatred in their eyes.

Back at the settlement it soon became apparent that the Iroquois were preparing for the greatest blood bath in their history. Pure terror drove the axemen as they cut the logs for the fort. They dared not stop until the walls closed them in. Inside they built a house big enough to accommodate all as well as a chapel and smaller buildings as needed. They named their mis-

Escape from Onondaga

sion Ste. Marie de Gannentaa.

Death lay siege to the little settlement almost from the start. Slaves would whisper to the French about secret meetings that plotted the when and how of their demise. The only thing that held back the tomahawk was the departure of Lauzon and the appointment of Louis d'Ailleboust in his place. He had seized twelve Mohawk warriors and was holding them hostage against the safety of the mission.

With the arrival of winter a dying slave gave the fifty Canadians the truth about the Iroquois plan. They would survive the winter, but as soon as the ice broke up on the lakes and rivers, by which time Quebec would be tricked into freeing the hostages, they would be slaughtered.

As the winter gripped the country the French made and discarded plan after plan. The nearest sanctuary was Montréal. What chance would they have in a race for safety?

Finally a plan emerged, put forward by a young man from Trois Rivières, Pierre Esprit Radisson. He had been captured by the Mohawks and adopted into one of their clans. He managed to escape and sailed from New Amsterdam to France and subsequently back to the colony.

In the loft of the main house, away from prying eyes, two large boats and four elm bark canoes were constructed, ready for March and the promise of open water. It was then that the second part of the plan was executed.

The Iroquois were to be invited to a great feast and stuffed with so much food that they would fall into a deep sleep. Feasts held a great significance for the Iroquois and such an invitation could not be refused even if the guests were going to kill the hosts shortly afterward.

Every male in Onondaga showed up and sat around huge fires just outside the walls. Every pig in the colony had been butchered becoming the base for the feast. The parade of food seemed endless. Corn and mincemeat came first followed by pots full of broiled bustard, chicken and turtle. Next came eel, salmon, carp and a stew of thickened flour filled with vegetables. This was the mother of all feasts and the warriors didn't let a dish pass them by. As Radisson noted in his diary,

"they eat as many wolves, having eyes bigger than bellies."

It was customary at such feasts for the hosts to abstain from eating, and so the French beat their drums and played their instruments to hide the noise of the back wall of the fort being dismantled. Soon nature took its course and one by one the warriors toppled over in slumber.

Boats and canoes were pushed to the waters edge and axes and poles chopped a channel to open water. The warriors awoke in the night cold and bewildered. The gates of the fort were closed and it was not until the end of the day that they broke down the gates to discover their quarry gone.

On April 3rd the flotilla reached Montréal. After resting themselves they pushed on to Quebec arriving there on April 23rd. The young man, Pierre Radisson disembarked at Trois Rivières to rejoin his family. There he met a man ten years older than himself who was to be his partner in one of the most fascinating stories in Canadian history. That man was Médard Chouart des Groseillers.

On his return to Trois Rivières the young Radisson regaled his family with the tales of his experiences at Onondaga. One member of his audience knew quite well of what Pierre spoke. His brother-in-law, Médard Chouart, had spent part of his life in the shadow of the Iroquois torture stake.

Médard Chouart was born July 31, 1618 at Charly-sur-Marne in France and came to Canada at an early age. He was employed by the Jesuits and went on a mission with Father Gabriel Dreuillettes to Lake Nipissing. From there he went to Huronia assisting the Jesuits at Ste. Marie and the other missions that dotted the shores of Georgian Bay. He lived through the horrific days of the massacre of the Hurons in 1649 and went with the missionaries to St. Joseph's Island to minister to the dispirited refugees. He left St. Joseph's with the last party and landed at Trois Rivières shortly after Radisson had left for Onondaga.

At Trois Rivières Chouart purchased a small bit of land overrun with brambles and gooseberry bushes. As a joke he was dubbed Sieur des Groseilliers, a name that was to be honoured in the annals of Canadian history. Shortly after his arrival he met Marguerite Hayet Veron, the widow of the Sieur de Grandmesnil and Radisson's half sister. He married her and settled down with her and her three children content, for once, to stay in one place.

In the long winter nights the two adventurers compared notes on the tales they each had heard about distant tribes and forests thick with beaver. Stories told by the Algonkins of a great lake called Ouinipeg and tribes of wandering hunters called Christinos (Crees) and a tribe of mighty warriors to the south who were the Sioux. The two friends soon had a bad case of itchy feet and began to plan a journey into the unknown.

A serious obstacle immediately raised its head for Radisson and Groseilliers. The governor had promulgated a law that restricted French participation in the fur trade. No one could trade without a permit and they were hard to come by. They would have to slip out of Trois Rivières without anyone knowing.

Unfortunately they were not the only ones with their eyes on the west. Thirty young Frenchmen came down from Quebec ready for adventure. It was obvious that they had little or no experience and looked on the trip as one big party. Two Jesuits also planned to go west in search of souls to save.

Late one night in June 1658, accompanied by Algonkin guides, the two paddled down the the St. Maurice River in search of fame and fortune. They traveled at night to avoid detection by the Iroquois and arrived in Montréal three days later. Gathered there were the thirty Frenchmen, the two Jesuits and one hundred and forty Indians from the northwest all ready to embark. No gun was fired at Montréal lest the Mohawks be forewarned of their departure. Sixty canoes silently glided across Lac St. Louis constantly on the alert for signs of the enemy. Three days journey and the hard work had damped the enthusiasm of the thirty French adventurers as they paddled with bleeding, blistered hands. There was no sign of the Iroquois.

Apparent safety bred carelessness. Canoes began to scatter some as much as ten miles from the main body. Guns were fired breaking the silence. They were ambushed at a portage by the Iroquois who had thrown up a log barricade from which they fired musket volleys into the canoes as they landed. The French threw up their own barricade to cover the canoes as they came in. As darkness fell the Algonkins made a mad dash for the boats. The French got away as best they could with all but Radisson and Groseilliers turning back to Montréal.

The two adventurers and their guides traveled at night for fear of the Iroquois. Supplies dwindled to the point that they were surviving on green moss boiled into soup. Only when they were beyond the Iroquois did they dare to shoot game and replenish their larder.

After a series of sixty portages they reached Lake Nipissing where the Indians from the northwest always kept caches of supplies. They were not out of danger however, for here Iroquois footprints were found in the sand. They finally reached Lake Huron where the fleet split up. Radisson and Groseilliers crossed the lake to Green Bay on Lake Michigan. News reached them there that the Iroquois were on the prowl. Before fear took hold among the Algonkins

Radisson & Groseilliers prepare to leave Trois Rivière

the two Frenchmen offered to lead a raid against the marauders. They ambushed the war party and killed everyone in it. From that point the Indians could not do enough for the two voyageurs.

Before the spring of 1659, Radisson and Groseilliers saw the upper reaches of the Mississippi, the first white men to do so. They were received well by all the tribes of the region. They marveled at the lush land that was Wisconsin and the plains beyond.

In late spring they were still among the tribes of the Mississippi who told them of the warlike Sioux who lived by the hunt and made constant war on a tribe to the north called the Cree. Between these two were the Assiniboin who used clay pots for cooking and boiled water by dropping heated rocks into the water.

Radisson wrote, "We desired not to go to the north till we had made a discovery in the south." Their guides refused to go further so the two pushed on alone across the high ground separating the Mississippi and the Missouri. Radisson gives us a description of that journey,

"all amazed to see us and very civil. The further we sojourned, the delightfuller the land became. I can say that in all my lifetime I have never seen a finer country . . . Being among the people they told us . . . of men that built great cabins and had knives like the French."

They showed them a string of beads of European design. Radisson knew that these natives were speaking of the Spanish.

Turning back north they visited the Sioux and may have come in sight of the foothills of the Rockies. This is only a guess from the evidence given, but given that evidence the two could have visited Iowa, South Dakota and Montana returning through North Dakota and Minnesota to the head of Lake Superior.

The Cree told them of a great salt sea to the north, Hudson Bay. Loaded with furs the two prepared to return to Quebec. Five hundred Indians from the Upper Country chose to accompany the two explorers down the Ottawa to the St. Lawrence. As they made their preparations couriers came from the east, more than a thousand Iroquois were on the warpath boasting that they would exterminate the French and all their allies. Despite this the fleet set out.

Meanwhile in Montréal there was about to be displayed an act of courage that must remain unsurpassed in the annals of North American history. In Texas they say "Remember the Alamo." In Canada we could say "Remember the Long Sault."

CHAPTER SIX
The Battle of the Long Sault
"The position of the small remnant was desperate. They had no water and what little they could get
by digging in the earth did not slake their thirst. They could only man their loopholes and pray."

While Radisson and Groseilliers were wending their way home, the Iroquois met in council and decided to exterminate the French once and for all. They gathered a thousand warriors for the purpose and there seemed little doubt but they would achieve their goal. Two hundred wintered on the upper Ottawa River and in April eight hundred Warriors stood ready on the Richelieu to join their comrades for an all out assault on New France. The plan was to destroy Montréal and Trois Rivières, sweeping on to Quebec to break the back of the French presence in North America.

In the meantime Montréal, unaware of the Iroquois concentration, was preparing for another season of harassment from the warriors of the longhouse. Among those present was a young twenty-two year old soldier, Adam Dollard, Sieur des Ormeaux, who was eager to prove his courage. Although there is no documented evidence, the story goes that he left France in 1657 under a cloud. Dollard approached Maisonneuve with a plan. Arguing that the best defence is a good offence he offered to recruit a small party of French soldiers to meet the Iroquois on the Ottawa and perhaps put a dent in their war party before they approached Montréal. Maisonneuve agreed and preparations began.

Dollard was eager to get started and the small party of seventeen French Canadian soldiers began the arduous canoe trip to the Ottawa. To reach the Ottawa and beyond was a task that challenged the strongest of men. After crossing Lac des Deux Montagnes they encountered the Carillon Rapids then the rapids of La Chute à Blondeau before reaching the most formidable of all, the Long Sault. Here the river roared down a long narrow passage requiring three portages to reach the far end. It was at these rapids that one could expect an Iroquoian ambush or conversely the Iroquois could expect to be ambushed. It was here that Dollard decided to await whatever war parties might come their way.

A short distance from the rapids the French discovered an abandoned Indian stockade falling into ruin. It was merely an enclosure of logs meant as temporary protection for some small hunting or trading party.

Dollard was thankful as the heavy work of raising a fort was already done, however, still ignorant of the odds against them, they did little beyond clearing bush to prepare for the battle to come.

Meanwhile a large party of Hurons under the chief, Anahotaha, hearing of the expedition, arrived to lend support. The forty Hurons were a welcome addition along with four Algonkins from Trois Rivières led by Mitewemeg. All was ready.

They did not have long to wait. Soon the scouts placed at the head of the rapids reported two elm bark canoes with five Iroquois braves were in sight. Dollard concealed his force at the likely landing spot and waited. As the warriors landed the French and their allies fired a volley killing four of them. Unfortunately the fifth got away to warn the main party.

To Dollard's dismay forty or fifty canoes came into view filled to the gunwales with Iroquois warriors bent on revenge. The small force quickly withdrew to the safety of the stockade with the war whoops of the enemy close behind. Without taking time to organize themselves the Iroquois stormed the little fort. The French and their allies poured volley after volley into the charging warriors throwing them back time and again. The evidence of the savagery of the fight lay before the fort in the number of dead and wounded Iroquois strewn about the approaches.

The Iroquois chiefs called a council. This delay in their plans had come as a surprise and a delegation was sent forward to parley with the defenders. A nervous member of the French party fired a shot and the rest, equally as nervous fired a volley killing several of the emissaries. The rest scrambled back to safety of the woods. It is reported that the Huron chief, Anahotaha, shook his head and said to Dollard,

> "Ah, comrade, you have spoiled everything.
> You ought to have waited the result of the council our enemies are holding."

The Iroquois were on the horns of a dilemma. If they delayed too long they would miss the rendezvous with the Richelieu contingent. However, the sight of their dead comrades won the day. After a long debate

The Battle of the Long Sault, May, 1660

they built their own stockade further up the river.

Dollard immediately set his men to work strengthening their own enclosure. Gaps were filled and the walls braced with sturdy branches. As they worked they could see bands of Iroquois moving up and down the river smashing canoes and destroying the kettles left hanging along the shore. The French knew that now there was no escape.

The next attack came from all sides with a suddenness that took even these vigilant defenders by surprise. The enemy came forward and tried to set the logs ablaze using the scraps of birch bark from the French canoes. Musket balls smashed into the closely packed warriors. Dollard coolly directed the fire of his little band. The Iroquois failed to fire the walls and fell back in disarray. Their chiefs rallied them and they came on again with the same result. A third charge fell back leaving the dead in heaps before the

muskets of the defenders. The Iroquois retreated to their own fort for another council of war.

The stout resistance displayed by the French left the warriors bewildered. Never had a group of French and Hurons stood against the warriors of the longhouse. It was decided that they could not defeat this enemy alone and messengers were sent off to the Richelieu for reinforcements.

For five days there was a break in the fighting, but the Iroquois were not sitting back. They kept close watch on the stockade giving the defenders no chance to rest. The Hurons adopted by the Iroquois kept up a constant verbal assault on the followers of Anahotaha urging them to save themselves and join them. Soon the Hurons began to slip away. Those left jeered their comrades while edging up to the palisade themselves to accept the offer of clemency. Before long only Anahotaha and the four Algonkins remained.

The position of the small remnant was desperate. They had no water and what little they could get by digging in the earth did not slake their thirst. It was so bad that they were unable to swallow the dry rations which remained. They could only man their loopholes and pray.

On the fifth day the Richelieu contingent arrived, five hundred strong, their war whoops ringing in the ears of the weakened defenders. Dollard knew that the end was near. The only bright light was the fact that the Iroquois would pay dearly for the lives of his men. The fort was well sighted and despite the numbers only a relative few could charge the walls at any one time. The difference now was that this time the replacements for those that fell were virtually unlimited.

The first attack came like a giant wave only to break on the walls of the little fort. Incredibly the warriors of the longhouse went reeling back before the onslaught of the tiny knot of defenders. A council was called and the prospects of abandoning the siege was considered, but the reputation of the unbeatable Iroquois was at stake. Dollard and his men staggered about from lack of nourishment and they could barely hold their places at the walls.

Preparations were complete and the warriors moved forward with blazing torches. The attack came from all sides and the smoke from the torches and blazing fuel blocked the sun. It was impossible to be heard above the war cries of the Iroquois. Even then the palisade held. Ironically, it was Dollard himself who inadvertently gave the enemy his opening.

Dollard had stuffed a musketoon with powder and ball intending to throw it over the wall to explode among the close packed attackers. When he launched his missile it caught on a branch and fell back among the defenders killing several outright and temporarily blinding the rest. In the confusion some of the Iroquois gained the loopholes and fired in among those left standing. Dollard was killed and four Frenchmen were captured. Three were so badly wounded that they were killed immediately. The fate of the fourth can only be imagined.

A few days later Radisson and Groseilliers came on the scene, grim witnesses to the aftermath of the gallant stand of Adam Dollard, Sieur des Ormeaux.

As for the Iroquois, their losses were so great that they abandoned their master plan and headed home. Dollard and his little band had saved Montréal from certain destruction and perhaps the very existence of the French in Canada.

Remember the Long Sault!

CHAPTER SEVEN
Le Moyne of Longueuil
"For years the old women of the longhouse had been gathering wood
to burn Charles le Moyne at the stake. Akouesson they called him . . .."

With Dollard's stand at the Long Sault the Iroquois threat to Montréal, for the summer of 1660, was at an end. It is remarkable that the little settlement was able to sustain itself much less grow under the constant harassment of the warriors of the longhouse. Of course the explanation is really quite simple; the pioneers refused to be driven from their homes and were prepared to defend them with their lives.

One of the leaders of the community and the patriarch of one of New France's greatest families was Charles le Moyne, the young Norman who came to Montréal with the first contingent when he was only seventeen years old. After a stint as an interpreter with the Huron missions on Georgian Bay, he came and settled down, becoming a guide and a fearless fighter in his defence of the settlement. His part in the fight against the Iroquois was such that a story began to circulate, which always began,

"For years the old women of the longhouse had been gathering wood to burn Charles le Moyne at the stake. Akouesson, they called him . . ."

The Iroquois finally captured le Moyne on the Richelieu River and triumphantly began their journey back to their own country. What a prize they would bring back to the stake. The excitement mounted as they dipped their paddles drawing them closer to the matrons and their stake.

As the journey progressed, however, their ardor cooled somewhat. Le Moyne, familiar with the language, played on their feelings. He told them of the misfortune that would befall the people of the longhouse should they kill him. The French would come in canoes, which were higher than the highest trees and with guns so big that they would silence the thunder. He repeated this over and over until the warriors began to have second thoughts.

While camped one night they held a council debating the wisdom of inviting such a disaster on their people. The following morning they paddled back to where they had captured him and turned him over to some of his Indian allies.

When le Moyne came of age he was granted land on the south shore of the St. Lawrence opposite Montréal, which he named Longueuil. It was to become one of the most prosperous seigneuries in New France. It had a river frontage of fifty arpents and a depth of one hundred arpents (1 arpent = approximately 1 acre). His grant was in the most vulnerable in the area as the Iroquois passed there on their way up from the Richelieu River. Despite this the young le Moyne began to clear his land and build a house. In 1654 he married Catherine Primot and as a concession to her safety and that of his growing family he moved into a house on the Rue St. Joseph in Montréal.

On the occasion of his marriage le Moyne received a further ninety arpents of river frontage. With his brother in law, Jean le Ber, he entered the fur trade, building shops and warehouses along the Rue St. Joseph. Le Moyne's fortune was made. With his growing wealth also came a growing family. Catherine eventually gave birth to eleven sons, ten of whom lived to adulthood, and two daughters.

The first son arrived in 1656 and was named for his father, Charles. In 1659 a second son, Jacques made his appearance. In 1661 a third son, Pierre, was born. We will run into the sons of Charles le Moyne de Longueuil again in our journey through the story of Canada. The eldest was to make Longueuil paramount among the seigneuries of New France. He was created Baron de Longueuil after his father's death. The third son, Pierre, was to become the great Canadian fighter on land and on the sea. He is known in Canadian history as Pierre le Moyne d'Iberville. The eighth son, Jean Baptiste le Moyne de Bienville became the founder of New Orléans and the life long governor of Louisiana.

The saga of Charles le Moyne nearly ended prematurely. But for the urgency of getting the spring planting done he would have been at the Long Sault with Adam Dollard des Ormeaux.

In the meantime the ordinary citizens of Ville Marie de Montréal went about their daily routine with one eye on the forest. Life was precarious at the best of times. Jeanne Mance and Marguerite Bourgeoys struggled to keep the colony healthy and educated under deplorable conditions. For four years the hospital

18

Charles le Moyne at Montréal, 1660

was turned into a defensive position forcing the patients to move to a low ceiling building near the fort. Bourgeoys used the attic as a classroom and the lower floor was the hospital. The edifice had been constructed of green wood and as it dried out large cracks appeared in the walls allowing the cold drafts to whistle through and the snow to create tiny drifts along the floors. Food had to be kept in front of the fire to keep it from freezing.

The situation was unbearable and the two women decided to sail for France to plead their case for more funding for the colony. The first thing Mance did was to insist on the reorganization of the Montréal Company. It conveyed the ownership of 200 arpents to the hospital on condition that it be divided into parcels of thirty arpents for individuals to cultivate.

Jeanne Mance was able to convince her wavering benefactor, Madame de Bouillon, to continue her support of the colony. As a first installment she carried

22,000 livres away with her. She kept 2,000 livres to take back to Montréal and left the balance with the Sieur de la Dauversière for investing.

Finally, three young nuns were selected from a community of nursing sisters to come and work in the New World and Marguerite Bourgeoys managed to recruit three teaching nuns to face the rigors of the wilderness and they sailed for home. Unfortunately Dauversière was ill and in debt. He misappropriated the remaining funds and they were never recovered. As a result Jeanne Mance and her helpers lived in poverty for years not being able to even afford new gowns.

We cannot help but admire the bravery and persistence of those early French Canadian pioneers of Montréal who persevered through seemingly impossible condition to hand down to us the Canada we have today.

CHAPTER EIGHT
Laval comes to Quebec
"For in addition to the happiness that returns to the whole country at having an ecclesiastical superior, it is a consolation to have a man whose personal qualities are rare and extraordinary." -Marie de l'Incarnation. June, 1659

With the reorganization of the Company of Montréal it became apparent that the original founders were no longer capable of providing for the growing community. The newly created religious order of St. Sulpice was invited to take on the task. On the surface this may seem an odd decision, a religious order taking on the temporal affairs of Montréal, but the Sulpicians were secular priests and each one a gentleman of some wealth. Although they retained their property, they lived simply and used their resources to help the people they served. Unlike the Jesuits, who were rather austere in their preaching of the gospel, Les Messieurs de St. Sulpice, as they were called, looked on the service to mankind as a joyous mission to be celebrated by all.

The arrival of the Sulpicians in Canada in 1657 coincided with an evolution in the organization of the Canadian church that was to cause a clerical war of words to erupt on both sides of the Atlantic. There was a growing realization that the colony was in need of its own bishop to run the affairs of the church in the new world. To this point Quebec was under the control of the Diocese of Rouen based on the fact that the majority of the ships sailing for the colony left from ports in that diocese. Since the vows of the Jesuits precluded them from accepting a bishopric, the Sulpicians reasonably expected that one of their number should be chosen. They sought and received the approval of the Assembly of French Clergy to have the Abbé de Queylus appointed. The Jesuits realized the great disadvantage of having another order in command after their extended service and sacrifices for the colony and they quietly used their influence at court to block the appointment.

On the surface Queylus was an excellent choice for bishop. He was wealthy, generous and of high moral character. However he was also aggressive, ambitious and lacking in the diplomatic skills necessary to pull the various factions together at Quebec. Unable to be confirmed as bishop, Queylus arrived at Quebec armed with letters from Archbishop François de Harlay de Champvallon, Bishop of Rouen appointing him Vicar-General of Canada. He immediately antagonized the Jesuits by lashing out at them from the pulpit for their opposition to his appointment. The Jesuits replied in kind declaring that the Abbé was warring on them more savagely than the Iroquois.

Meanwhile in Europe Pope Alexander VII was persuaded to confer the new post on François Xavier de Laval-Montmorency, Abbé de Montigny. He was also created Bishop of Petraea. Laval was a young man of thirty-six when he was appointed, and although his family was quite wealthy, he lived a rather simple life having renounced all his titles in favour of his younger brother. The Queen Mother was delighted by the appointment and set aside a pension of 1,000 livres a year for the new head of the church in New France. She wrote a personal note to Governor d'Argenson at Quebec,

"I wish to join this letter to that of the King, my son, to let you know that, according to his inclination and to mine, you must have the Bishop of Petraea acknowledged as vicar-apostolic all over the country of Canada under the power of the King."

Laval arrived at Quebec in June of 1659. It was six o'clock when his ship was warped to its moorings and he stepped ashore in all the vestments of his office. The governor, Le Vicomte d'Argenson, officially greeted the new vicar-apostolic and must have had some apprehension on seeing the stern, exacting dark eyes of the new head of the Canadian church. His noble bearing combined with those thin lips, which signaled an unbending will, foretold of clashes to come in relations between the secular and clerical realms.

The superior of the Ursulines, Marie de l'Incarnation, gives us a glimpse of the reaction to Laval in one of her letters to her son,

"For in addition to the happiness that returns to the whole country at having an ecclesiastical superior, it is a consolation to have a man whose personal qualities are rare and extraordinary. Without speaking of his birth, which is very illustrious - for he is of the house of La-

Laval arrives at Quebec, June, 1659

val - he is a man of high merit and singular virtue."

The arrangements for his accommodations speaks somewhat to his character. After staying briefly with the Jesuits he rented a small house owned by the Ursulines. The tiny, two room stone house was no more than seventy-six by eighty-four metres and he shared this with three priests, two male servants, a valet-cook and a gardener.

Another indication of his character came in his dealings with Queylus, who had installed himself at Montréal. He firmly held on to the belief that his letters from the Bishop of Rouen made him the head of the Canadian church. Laval summoned him to Quebec and when he got no reply he persuaded the governor to send a squad of soldiers to bring him there by force.

There were a number of clashes between these two strong willed men but in the end Laval, armed with the authority of the Pope and the King, won out. Queylus was sent off on the next ship to France. The incident created waves on both sides of the Atlantic. The Sulpicians protested and began a campaign in France, but Laval's influence reached into high places and the king wrote a letter to Queylus.

"My will," he declared, "is that you remain in my kingdom, enjoining you not to leave it without my express permission."

The good abbé disregarded the royal command and set out for Rome where he received a cool reception, however, he was able to extract bulls from the Vatican

21

confirming the independence of the Sulpicians at Montréal. Armed with these he set sail for Canada arriving triumphant and belligerent on August 3, 1661.

To say that Laval was angry would be an understatement. He ordered the Abbé to remain in Quebec until the authorities in France could be told of his illegal entry into the colony. The governor was supposed to put Queylus in close confinement, but was reluctant to get into the middle of the dispute. He procrastinated and before he could act Queylus and his servants obtained a canoe and headed out for Montréal.

Laval was livid. He sent orders suspending the abbé from his priestly duties. The orders reached him before his arrival at Montréal, but, unpreturbed, Queylus ignored them. In time orders came to the governor instructing him to support Laval and d'Argenson had no choice but to bring Queylus to Quebec and send him back to France on the first available ship.

The papal bulls were withdrawn and the Bishop of Rouen renounced all claims to any supervision over the church in Canada. Laval had won a complete victory. He could now turn his attention to the spiritual and temporal well being of his flock.

As the decade of the 1660's began events on both sides of the Atlantic were to leave their stamp on Canada. On March 9, 1661 the able first minister of the king, Cardinal Giulio Mazarin, the Sicilian churchman who had served the French Crown for nineteen years, died leaving Louis XIV to ponder the future of his kingdom. He had dearly loved Mazarin and replacing him would be difficult task. Louis closeted himself in an anteroom for two hours while he thought out his next move. The courtiers waited patiently for their master's decision.

Silence fell over the assembled nobles as the king emerged and called his closest advisers to his side. He handed the heir apparent to Mazarin, Nicholas Fouquet, Intendant of Finance, a paper on which he had recorded his decisions. The announcement drew a gasp from the crowded room. The king would act as his own first minister. He pledged himself to a life of hard work. His day was divided up so that not a moment was left free. So many hours for sleep, so many for meals, this much for recreation and these for prayer. The most important was the six to eight hours a day allocated for work. These did not include official receptions and appearances.

The young king was true to his word. He rose each morning at eight o'clock, dressed himself except on special occasions when hereditary rights to assist the king had to be taken into account, gave interviews, went to Mass, and then met with his council of advisers until noon. He took his lunch alone at a small table after which he went for a drive before going back to work, not finishing until dinner, which often was not until ten o'clock.

This is what Laval faced on his arrival in France to attempt to consolidate his power and improve conditions in the colony. It was clear from the beginning that he enjoyed the favour of the king and the admiration of the Queen Mother, Ann of Austria.

Laval came armed with a list of changes, which he wished to see implemented. First he asked that the governor, Baron Dubois d'Avagour, Argenson's successor, be recalled using his obstinacy regarding the trade of brandy to the Indians as the reason. Not only did the king readily agree, but told Laval to select the successor himself. As it turned out the young vicar-apostolic already had a man in mind. When he was studying under the Jesuits at Caen he made the acquaintance of the commander of the citadel, Saffray de Mezy. He struck Laval as being a very pious man as well as being of humble origins and thus devoid of the haughty pretensions of the aristocracy that so frustrated him in his dealings with d'Avagour.

His second request was more problematic. He vigorously pushed to be named Bishop of Quebec. The king was willing, however questions arose, would he be subject to the authority of the Archbishop of Rouen or to the direct control of the pope? The old Gallican controversy surfaced with the French church split into two camps. It was to be ten years before Laval was named Bishop of Quebec.

On his third point Laval was completely successful. It was very apparent that the mechanism set up by Cardinal Richelieu to govern the affairs of Canada was a total failure. The Company of One Hundred Associates still nominally controlled the colony, but the monopoly of the fur trade had been transferred to the leading citizens of New France. The company received a portion of the profits while doing nothing to earn it. No supply ships were provided, no colonists arrived under the auspices of the company. The provisions set out by Richelieu were cast aside even as its directors schemed to get more from the New World.

In 1660 the company sent out an agent named Peronne Dumesnil to investigate conditions there. Dumesnil found plenty of evidence that the leaders in

The Court of Louis XIV at Versailles

Quebec were doing quite well while giving the company but a token payment. Charges flew on both sides with arrests being made including Dumesnil himself.

Laval placed these facts before the king and asked that the charter be revoked. By royal proclamation in April, 1663 the company was dissolved. To replace it a council was set up with the governor and Laval as co-chairmen. They were to select five councillors from among the citizens of Quebec and a new civil official with the title of intendant was to round out the new authority in Canada.

Laval and Mezy sailed for Quebec the picture of harmony and understanding. Soon after landing, however, their relationship changed. Laval made the appointments to the council himself making Jean Bourbon, who had risen from barber, painter and chief gunner of the citadel of St. Louis to collector of customs

for the One Hundred Associates, attorney general. The council consisted of Royer de Villeray, Juchereau de la Ferte, Ruette d'Autueil, Le Gardeur de Tilly, and Matthieu Damours.

The council immediately seized some incriminating papers of Dumesnil that he intended to use on his return to France against some of the council. He raised such an uproar that he was arrested. The plan was to hold him until the last ship left for the season, but Dumesuil got wind of the plot and got away on a ship bound for France.

Mezy felt that some of Laval's choices for council were ill advised and he implored him to drop Bourbon, Villeray and Autueil and call an election to have the people select the remaining councillors. Laval refused.

Here Mezy made a fatal error. He posted placards

23

around Quebec calling for the election of councillors. The king would be furious at the thought of picking councillors by popular vote. He was the authority who appointed members of government. Mezy prevailed temporarily getting his new council by a vote of the people, however, as predicted the king flew into a rage and immediately recalled the governor to give an account of his actions.

Mezy was relieved of the necessity of facing his king. He fell ill and died before his return to France could be arranged.

Meanwhile d'Avagour, the deposed governor, was also busy. He had prepared a statement of conditions in Canada that was to have a far reaching effect on the colony. It was an in depth appraisal that caught the attention of the king's adviser, Jean Baptiste Colbert and in turn the attention of the king. D'Avagour stated that the country along the St. Lawrence had the potential to be the greatest state in the world. To realize the full potential of this crown colony it would be necessary to establish a permanent peace, first by defeating the Iroquois. To insure the continued security such a victory would create, strong forts would have to be built both on the St. Lawrence and on the Hudson giving the French a new outlet to the sea. It would also restrict the growth of the English colonies along the Atlantic seaboard.

D'Avagour included a detailed plan with his report. Three thousand soldiers were to be sent out immediately to begin offensive operations against the Iroquois Confederacy. After three years service the soldiers were to be discharged and given land to settle on. This would give the colony three things; an increase in the production of food, a vital link in the fur trade with the Indians and a trained force of veterans to call on in the case of a military emergency. D'Avagour even had the plan costed out. Four thousand francs per year for ten years would turn the struggling colony into a new French empire.

At last New France was to have the full support of the king. A new era in the affairs of Canada was dawning.

CHAPTER NINE
In Search of an Iroquois Peace
"Since the Italian affair was happily terminated to the King's satisfaction, His Majesty
has resolved to send to Canada a good regiment of Infantry."-Colbert, March 18, 1664

On March 18, 1664 the king's minister, Jean Baptiste Colbert, wrote to Laval at Quebec,

"Since the Italian affair was happily terminated to the King's satisfaction, His Majesty has resolved to send to Canada a good regiment of infantry at the end of this year or in the month of February next, in order to destroy the Iroquois completely; and Monsieur de Tracy has been ordered to go to confer with you on the way of succeeding promptly in this war."

Alexandre de Prouville, Marquis de Tracy, was to be lieutenant general of all French dominions in the New World. Tracy was a tall, rather stout man of sixty-four. He spent the year 1664 in the West Indies restoring order there before sailing to Quebec.

The unit selected to come to Canada was The Carignan-Salières Regiment. The regiment had distinguished itself in the Turkish war and against the rebel nobles in the Fronde in France. Their reputation was not one of garrison troops, but of fighting men who sought out the enemy and brought him to battle. Of the twenty companies expected four arrived in June of 1665 and Quebec was in for a gala summer never seen before in its history. On June 30th Tracy himself landed and Quebec was treated to a spectacular show of pomp and circumstance. Up Mountain Hill from the harbour came twenty-four guards wearing royal colours. Four pages led their splendidly attired commander who was in turn followed by his entourage of equally well dressed officers. He was so racked by shipboard fever that he could barely drag himself up the hill.

The regiment's discipline was perfect. The troops in their blue coats piped with white, plumed hats, buff leather bandoleers, muskets carried on slings over the shoulder, some with long leather boots turned half way up the calf, marched up the hill to the sounds of the fife and drums, and the flourish of trumpets. The citizens lined the route cheering and waving at this magnificent show of French power. Church bells peeled and at the entrance to the church Laval waited in his episcopal vestments to greet the saviour of the colony. After formal introductions he led him into the church for Mass and the singing of the *Te Deum*. Surely now the Iroquois threat would be silenced forever.

The ships carrying the balance of the regiment were delayed with eight more companies arriving in August and the balance not dropping anchor until September. With this last contingent came the new governor, Daniel de Remy, Sieur de Courcelle, and a man who was to leave his mark on Canada, the new intendant, Jean Talon. Sickness was so prevalent among the troops that offensive action against the Five Nations in 1665 was impossible. However, in July work was begun on forts on the Richelieu River with three being completed that year. Two more were planned for the following year.

One of Courvelle's first acts was to order Maisonneuve home to France installing Zacharie Dupuy as acting governor. Dupuy had commanded the Onondaga Mission in 1656.

The Iroquois viewed the build up along the Richelieu and the presence of so many soldiers at Quebec with alarm. In December of 1665 they sent a peace delegation under the Onondaga chief, Garakontie. Tracy grew impatient with the long harangues that accompanied negotiations and when the Oneidas were about to offer fifty-five belts of wampum and the oratory that would come with each, he wanted to refuse them. Of course, this was not an option.

The Mohawks were still a problem. They had always been the most ardent enemies of the French. On January 9th Courcelle himself led six hundred men into Mohawk country. A combination of the inexperience of the recent arrivals from Europe plus the alternate freezing and thawing that occurred combined to make the expedition a disaster. The Indian guides abandoned them and the wretched force struggled on to Schenectady where they were surprised to find the English in command. Although they saw no Mohawks the fact that they had penetrated their territory in strength induced the Five Nations, including the Mohawks, to send peace emissaries the following summer.

The negotiations began with the usual round of

The Carignan-Salières Regiment marches into Quebec, June, 1665

speeches and gift giving, but the whole process came to a grinding halt with word that a party of Mohawks had attacked some French hunters on the Richelieu killing a nephew of Tracy and taking the rest prisoner, including Tracy's cousin. The twenty-four delegates were immediately clapped in irons and a rescue mission launched under the command of Captain Pierre de Saurel of the Carignan-Salières Regiment. A short distance from the borders of Mohawk territory they met a party of Mohawks on their way to return the prisoners. The attack was called off, but, Courcelle refused to resume the negotiations.

On the 14th of September Tracy led an army of fourteen hundred, including Canadians from Quebec and Montréal and one hundred Algonkins and Hurons into Mohawk country. They moved up the Richelieu in three hundred small boats, crossed Lakes Cham-

plain and George, then continued on foot to the Mohawk villages. The five villages in the area were all deserted. The French marched into them one by one and burned them along with their granaries and the the crops growing in the fields. The army was back at Quebec by the 5th of November, having lost only eight men by drowning and not having fired a shot. It is estimated that four hundred Mohawks died of starvation that winter.

Delegates from among the prisoners held at Quebec were sent to the council at Onondaga in the summer of 1667 and a general peace was concluded that was to last until 1684. Tracy returned to France, his mission completed and the colony was now free to expand under the able direction of Jean Talon, the great intendant.

CHAPTER TEN

Jean Talon, the Great Intendant

"Since he has been here as Intendant, the country has accomplished more and practical affairs have advanced further than they have ever done since the French have lived here."-Marie de l'Incarnation, 1668

With the defeat of the Iroquois and the subsequent peace the grand design of Louis the Invincible, King of France, could at last be implemented. The ground work was laid in 1664 with the reorganization of the way the French overseas possessions were administered. The Company of the West was set up by the king's minister, Colbert, to take control of all French possessions in the New World and Africa. As with the Company of One Hundred Associates, they were to have a trade monopoly and in turn they were to build forts, bring out settlers, appoint and pay administrators, and provide priests. With Canada some adjustments had to be made. The new company began operating in the same fashion as the old with the same disastrous results. A compromise was reached. The company would pay the cost of administration with no control over the officers or their appointments. They would recover their costs by taxes on beaver pelts and moose skins. The tax on beaver was called *le droit du quart* and the moose tax *le droit du dixieme*. The company's expenditure each year amounted to 50,000 francs. To implement the Grand Plan the king set up an extraordinary fund. The expenditures from this fund in 1665 was a staggering 358,000 francs caused in part by the dispatch of the Carignan Regiment and a thousand other persons to the colony. It was hoped that this was a one time cost, but large sums continued to be paid year after year to maintain the royal plan.

An ongoing expenditure of this magnitude demanded careful supervision. No longer could the control of the colonial purse strings be left to chance and the landed aristocracy who had served as governors or the churchmen whose main interest was the saving of souls. Fortunately France had, in Jean Baptiste Colbert, the consummate administrator. He was determined that New France would have the same. Of the first man selected little is known other than his name, Sieur Robert. For some reason he never assumed his duties. Casting about for a replacement Colbert chanced on a kindred spirit in the brilliant controller of Hainault, Jean Talon.

Jean Talon was born at Chalons-sur-Marne circa 1623 and began his career in the commissariat of the French Army. His grasp of the accounts was so rapid that he quickly rose up through the ranks to the post of chief commissary. In less than a year after that he was promoted to intendant of the Province of Hainault, an appointment of major significance. When approached by Colbert he jumped at the challenge to transform Canada into a vibrant part of the French Empire.

His first priority on taking up his duties was to increase the population. He conceived a plan to have the Dutch holdings, which had been taken over by the British, transferred to France. When the time came for the three countries to negotiate a permanent peace, France would insist that those possessions be returned to the Dutch. By secret agreement the Dutch would then cede the territory to France. Talon pointed out that once this was accomplished the British would be hopelessly hemmed in as France would control the majority of the Atlantic seaboard. As an addendum to this plan he suggested that five hundred settlers be brought out each year ensuring Canada of a thriving population. Colbert cautioned Talon to go slow and the plan went nowhere.

Undetered Talon began improvising plans of his own within the colony. The most ambitious was the establishment of new settlements around Quebec City. Selecting the area around Charlesbourg. He had forty houses erected in three separate villages called Bourg-Talon, Bourg-la-Reine, and Bourg-Royal. The forty houses were snatch up quickly and to show his faith in the scheme Talon bought a tract of land in the neighbourhood and built himself a large house, barn and other out buildings.

Despite the peace with the Iroquois those moving out to the Charlesbourg development were extremely security conscious. To alleviate their fears he had the tracts of land divided into pie shaped lots with the houses built at the narrow angle and the fields becoming broader as one moved to the rear of the farm. Thus the houses formed a small village for mutual defense.

The settlers who moved to Charlesbourg were given a supply of food to see them through the first season while they cleared the stipulated two acres. They were paid for their time and given the necessary

Talon inspects the shipyard at Quebec

tools to complete their task. The money came from the king's extraordinary fund. One other stipulation was placed on the settlers, they had to participate in the clearing of two acres on the unoccupied lots so that those following could become self sufficient that much quicker. Under those conditions the Talon villages filled up quickly.

Talon next tackled the problem created by the increase in population. An industrial base was needed to supply the necessities of life while at the same time providing non agricultural employment. He had farmers growing hemp and then created a demand for the crop. This was done in a very arbitrary way, which fortunately worked out well for everyone. Hemp seed was distributed free to farmers on the condition that they plant it immediately and replace the seed the next year from their own crop. In the meantime Talon had

all the thread seized from the shops ordering that thread could only be exchanged for hemp. Thus wives ensured that their husbands planted hemp or went to market to buy it. This highhanded method was only necessary for a short time as soon the laws of supply and demand took over.

Talon also established cod fishing stations along the lower St. Lawrence where seals and white porpoise were taken along with cod. The oil was in demand in France thus helping create a balance of trade between colony and mother country.

Another of his ambitious projects was the creation of a shipbuilding industry at Quebec. He contended that the colony needed to be in a position to take advantage of trade opportunities with French possessions in the West Indies. The first ship was built by Talon from his own resources. The cost of the sec-

28

ond, a bigger vessel costing some 40,000 francs, was borne by the King. The building program gave employment to three hundred and fifty men. In 1667 six vessels of various sizes were built and commissioned at Quebec.

The brandy trade was a sore point in the colony. Despite laws prohibiting it many independent traders still used it as their main item of barter. The colonists liked it as much as the Indians and Talon thought hard and long on how to tackle the problem. He finally built a brewery with his own money in the St. Charles section of Quebec in 1668. Fresh beer was an instant success with large amounts being produced within three years of its establishment. Demand for brandy fell accordingly.

Talon continually begged Colbert for livestock to put agriculture on a firmer footing. Colbert complied and soon cattle, sheep, and hogs were sent out regularly. This led to the establishment of tanneries. The farmers' wives were given looms on which carpet weaving began and is a fixture in Quebec society to this day.

Jean Talon, from his tiny office at Quebec, was determined to succeed in making Canada a jewel in the crown of France. The world looked on with envy as Spain grew rich from the easy gold of Peru and Mexico. Canada had beaver and great stocks of fish, but hard work and risk was ever present in the recovery of these resources. It was hoped that there would be natural resources that could be mined and shipped to France to add to the treasury of King Louis.

Any rumour of the discovery of a potential mine was followed up immediately at Talon's order. When a report of a lead deposit in the Gaspé surfaced a team went to investigate, but nothing was found. Iron ore was discovered at Baie St. Paul 150 km up river from Quebec and mining operations were begun.

The rumours of the discovery of coal sent a wave of excitement through the colony. The discovery was made right at Quebec City itself. The evidence came from the cellar of a house in the lower section of town. Talon wrote to Colbert,

"The coal is good enough for the forge. If the test is satisfactory, I shall see to it that our vessels take out loads of it."

Talon's excitement was justified. An ample supply of coal meant fuel for heating homes, industry would thrive and they would no longer have to buy coal from England. His last letters to France on the subject indicated that the coal was of a sufficient quality at least for industrial use.

Talon's letters on the coal deposit in the great rock of Quebec stopped suddenly and no further reports were sent. It can only be surmised that further testing proved disappointing and the idea of a mine was abandoned.

One metal that was in evidence in large quantities was copper. Missionaries brought back stories of great mines with samples of ore to back their claims. The intendant was fascinated by these reports and saw that copper could provide the king with the wealth needed to continue his dream of a great empire.

The most exciting find was among the islands in the Lake Huron/Lake Superior region. One in particular, Île Royale, held large deposits of copper and Talon sent his engineers to investigate. They reported that its hills were rich in high grade copper ore. The problem was how to get this vast resource to market. Talon dreamed of smelters built on site with fleets of flat bottomed boats being towed through the Great Lakes to Quebec. He envisioned great foundries casting guns to support the military efforts of the king. Alas, Talon was a man born one hundred years too early. As it was New France had but a precarious hold on a new continent and the ways and means of achieving his dream were just not available in the Canada of the mid 17th century.

All this energy and hard work on Talon's part eventually drew the wrath of the governor, Daniel Remy, Sieur de Coucelle. More and more the king directed his orders to Talon. Courcelle's rash invasion of Mohawk country and the heavy losses that resulted had left him in disfavour at the court. Also Colbert realized early that communiqués sent to Talon were acted upon quickly while those to Coucelle languished for months in bureaucratic red tape. Coucelle often lashed out at the intendant when they met to discuss business and his letters to France showed his displeasure with Talon.

Despite this Talon pressed on. One problem was the lack of women in the colony and therefore the lack of suitable wives for the hard working farmers. The solution was the sending out of, what was known as, the King's girls. These were young ladies recruited to come to New France to provide husbands for the men of the colony. This was not a new idea. The English

Talon greets Les Habitants

had sent such women out to Virginia and the Spanish had done the same in Central and South America.

On landing the girls were directed to one of three halls where the selections were to be made. It is not known how this choice of halls was made, but it is possible that they were divided by social status, height and weight so that the prospective grooms could be directed to the most suitable location for his particular circumstances.

The girls were lined up for inspection much as slaves were shown for auction, but the girl had the right to refuse any suitor. They also were free to ask any questions of a prospective husband. *How many acres have you cleared? How much money have you saved? Have you a horse? How many rooms in your house? Have you a bed and plenty of blankets?*

These were among the questions most asked.

There was nothing romantic about it. Priests were standing by and the wedding took place on the spot once the young lady had accepted the offer of marriage. Each couple received two pigs, a cow, an ox, a pair of chickens, two barrels of salt meat, and a sum of money with which to start their new lives.

In 1668 Talon asked to be recalled to France, partly because of his constant battles with the governor and partly due to ill health and the need to take care of personal business. Reluctantly the king agreed and he sailed for home in November of that year. He was sorely missed as shown by a letter that Marie de l'Incarnation wrote to her son,

"Monsieur Talon is about to leave us finally and return to France, to the regret of everyone and the loss of all Canada, for since he has been here as Intendant, the country has accomplished more and practical affairs have advanced further than they have ever done since the French have lived here."

The new Intendant was one Monsieur Boutroue, but in fact the reins were never out of the hands of Talon. On his arrival the king and Colbert kept him at court with week after week of conferences on the progress and plans for the colony. The King's interest in Canada had grown steadily since he had taken over the complete control of the affairs of state on the death of Mazarin.

Talon accomplished a number of things in his discussions with the king and Colbert. He succeeded in having New France removed from control of the Company of the West arguing that the profit oriented merchants had no concern for the well being of the colony.

It was decided to reinforce the Carignan Regiment with six new companies of fifty men each along with thirty officers. It was understood that they would remain in Canada when their term of service expired. The king also pledged to send out an additional two hundred settlers and a long list of supplies.

Of course the outcome of all this was inevitable. Barely home for three months, Talon was reappointed Intendant of New France. He sailed from La Rochelle on July 15, 1669, but due to adverse weather and ship wrecks, he would not see Quebec until August of 1670.

CHAPTER ELEVEN
Of Furs, Canoes and Voyageurs
"Our fleet, consisting of seven canoes, each with three men, left Montréal on the
6th of July, 1669, under the guidance of two canoes of Seneca Iroquois."-Fr. Galinée

With peace between the French and the Iroquois came a rapid expansion of the fur trade. With the dispersal of the Hurons, the traditional middlemen in the trade, the French were forced to strike out on their own. One of the men sent into the northwest was Nicholas Perrot who more than any other secured the early advantage for the French in the west.

Perrot was born in New France in 1644 of humble origins. He was in the employ of the Jesuits in 1660 as an interpreter until he went with the Sulpicians in 1665. He quickly won the respect and trust of the tribes, which greatly facilitated the increase in trade in the west.

Many of the other tribes from the Georgian Bay area such as the Ottawas and the Saulteurs were driven to the south shore of Lake Superior and the area around Green Bay on Lake Michigan. They came into contact with more remote tribes in the interior and introduced them to European goods. This incursion into their territory also caused new wars to break out as the tribes defended their traditional hunting grounds. The Ottawas crossed from Green Bay to the Mississippi and encountered the Pottawatomi and the Sioux among others. The Ottawas became the new middlemen as the trade pushed west.

The French were quick to exploit these new connections of their allies. The impact on the tribes of the west was enormous. Perrot wrote:

"The Sioux, who had no acquaintance with the firearms and other implements, which they saw among the strangers, for they themselves use only knives and hatchets of stone and flint, hoped that these new peoples, who had come near them would share with them the commodities, which they possessed; and, believing that the latter were spirits, because they were acquainted with the use of iron . . . conducted them . . . to their own villages. . . . The Sioux returned to their country with some small articles, which they had received from the Outaouas (Ottawas)."

In April of 1665 a large flotilla of canoes started northward from Green Bay and made for Sault Ste. Marie where Perrot had managed to gather representatives from several of the tribes including the Miami, Sac, Winnebago, Menominee, and the Pottawatomi. The French raised a cross with the royal coat of arms and the trading began. After the French departed the Indians tore down the standard. The Indians had always had a dislike for the tall crosses that the French liked to put up at strategic locations, realizing that this was their way of laying claim to the land.

The Ottawa who had settled around Chequamegon on Lake Superior learned from the Saulteurs that the Nipissings had settled at Lake Nipigon and there were Crees to the north of Lake Superior. According to Perrot:

"At these tidings [of abundant beaver] the Outaouas went away to the north, and sought to carry on trade with these tribes, who gave them all their beaver robes for old knives, blunted awls, wretched nets and kettles used until they were past service. For these they were most humbly thanked. . . . They assured the Outaouas at parting that they would go on a hunting expedition (to make ready) for their coming; that they would be present without fail at the rendezvous agreed upon."

The demand for European goods among the remote tribes caused a rapid increase in trade. The Ottawas became skilled negotiators and worked every advantage in securing their position in the supply chain. Many of the tribes such as the Sauk, Fox and Illinois had no knowledge of the canoe thus they became the hunters and the Ottawa and Saulteur, with their knowledge of the Ottawa route and their expertise with the canoe, became the traders and the transportation link. Jacques du Chesneau in his memoir on the western Indians dated November 13, 1681 suggested that the Ottawas were in control:

"The Outawas Indians, who are divided into several tribes, and are nearest to us, are those of the greatest use to us, because through them we

Shooting the rapids

obtain Beaver; and although they, for the most part, do not hunt, and have but a small portion of peltry in their country, they go in search of it to the most distant places, and exchange for it our merchandise which they procure at Montréal. . . .

They get their peltries, in the north, from people of the interior . . . and in the south. . . .

Some of these tribes occasionally come down to Montréal, but usually they do not do so in very great numbers, because they are too far distant, are not expert at managing canoes, and because the other Indians intimidate them, in order to be the carriers of their merchandise and to profit thereby."

The relentless search for beaver and the religious zeal of the missionaries inadvertently made French Canadians the great explorers of the North American continent. Their sketches and journals helped fill in that vast territory marked *Unknown* on the maps of the day. Into this milieu came a man who was to become, arguably, the greatest explorer of his day.

René Robert Cavelier, Sieur de la Salle was born at Rouen, France on November 21, 1643 of a wealthy family. At age fifteen he entered the Jesuit novitiate to study for the priesthood and service as a missionary in foreign lands. He left the Jesuits in 1665 and followed his older brother, Jean Cavelier, to Canada. Jean was a member of the Sulpician Order living at Montréal and La Salle arrived in the New World in 1666.

La Salle at Burlington Bay, 1669

La Salle's timing was perfect. The Sulpicians were looking to expand the settlements around Montréal and they saw in la Salle just the sort of man needed to tame the wilderness. He was granted a large tract of land west of Montréal where he set up a trading post to handle the flow of furs that streamed into the colony each season. He was hard working and successful in his new vocation, but he turned his eyes more and more to the west and the vast unexplored tracts that lay waiting for the those brave enough to challenge the virgin forests and waterways.

The winter of 1668-69 brought a party of Senecas to Montréal to spends the winter hunting and trading. Their stories galvanized la Salle into action. He took his plan to the governor, Courvelles, and Jean Talon who immediately gave their blessing to an expedition to explore the country around the Ohio River. To fi-

nance this la Salle sold his lands at Montréal. All was ready.

Just before departure the governor added a wrinkle to the mix. He decided that the efforts of la Salle should be combined with a project dear to the hearts of the Sulpicians who wished to set up a mission among the western tribes. So in July, 1669 la Salle, the explorer, joined with two Sulpicians, Fr. Francois Dollier de Casson and Fr. René de Bréhant de Galinée, to begin his journey. Galinée's journal gives us some insight into that auspicious day:

"Our fleet, consisting of seven canoes, each with three men, left Montréal on the 6th of July, 1669, under the guidance of two canoes of Seneca Iroquois, who had come to Montréal as early as the autumn of the year 1668 to do their hunting and trading. These people whilst here had stayed a long time at M. de la Salle's, and had told him so many marvels of the River Ohio, with which they said they were thoroughly acquainted, that they inflamed in him more than ever the desire to see it."

The party moved quickly into Lake Ontario and held to the south shore until they came to an Iroquois village where they waited for the chiefs to greet them. Gifts were given and the head chief presented la Salle with a belt of wampum to show that they thought of him as their brother. Then began a round of feasting that lasted for days as each clan attempted to outdo the other. Our journalist, Galinée, left us with a description of some of the foods:

"Meanwhile they treated us in the best way they could, and everyone vied with his neighbour in feasting us after the fashion of the country. I must confess that several times I had more desire to give back what I had in my stomach than to put anything new in it. The great dish in this village, where they seldom have fresh meat, is a dog, the hair of which they singe over coals. After scraping it well, they cut it in pieces and put it into the kettle. When it is cooked, they serve you a piece of three or four pounds weight in a wooden platter that has never been rubbed with any other dishcloth than the fingers of the lady of the house, which appear all smeared with the grease that is always in their platter to the thickness of a silver crown. Another of their greatest dishes is Indian meal cooked in water and then served in a wooden bowl with two fingers of bear's grease or oil of sun-flowers or of butternuts upon it."

Here the Seneca guides decided not to accompany the party further, but fortunately there was another Iroquois who agreed to go. They left the Seneca village and Galinée made the following entry in his journal:

"We discovered a river one-eighth of a league wide and extremely rapid, which is the outlet or communication from Lake Erie to Lake Ontario. . . . This outlet may be forty leagues in length, and contains, at a distance of ten or twelve leagues from its mouth in Lake Ontario, one of the finest cataracts or waterfalls in the world; for all the Indians to whom I have spoken about it said the river fell in that place from a rock higher than the tallest pine trees; that is, about two hundred feet. In fact we heard it from where we were."

From here la Salle moved across Lake Ontario to a village near present day Hamilton where a fever laid him low for a few days. They moved on meeting Louis Jolliet on his way back to Quebec to report to Talon on the search for copper mines in the west. Here Casson and Galinée decided to follow Jolliet's route, but la Salle was determined to strike south in search of the Ohio. Little is known about la Salle's wanderings because his notes have been lost, however, it is fairly certain that he reached the Ohio and perhaps beyond. Misfortune plagued him and his men deserted him leaving him to make his way back to Quebec on his own.

Despite these trials and disappointments that would have discouraged other men, we have not heard the last of Réne Robert Cavelier, Sieur de la Salle.

CHAPTER TWELVE
Louis de Buade, Comte de Frontenac
"Children, I have a fire lighted for you to smoke by and for me to talk to you."-Frontenac to the Iroquois, 1672.

The future of New France looked brighter than ever as it entered the decade of the 1670s. Talon had the finances of the colony under control and, with the Iroquois peace, the fur trade was expanding. However, a dark cloud appeared on the horizon. France was embroiled in a war with Holland and the attentions and finances of the King and Colbert were focused there. The edict came forth that the colony was to exist for the enrichment of the mother country, provide a market for French manufactured goods and supply raw materials; furs of course, but also timber for shipbuilding but not ships. The fledgling industries of Quebec soon wasted away and the progress made arrested.

In 1672 both Courvelle and Talon were recalled to France. The new governor would have to be a man of resolve and energy if the French empire in Canada was to survive.

The choice of governor turned out to be one of the most colourful men in Canadian history. The new governor who sailed for Quebec in 1672 was Louis de Buade, Comte de Frontenac.

Frontenac was born at Bearn, Gascony in 1620 the son of a minor courtier. The family fortune fell on hard times and young Louis entered the army when he was fifteen where he distinguished himself in the Dutch Wars of the 1630s. His accomplishments were such that he was made colonel of the Normandy Regiment at age twenty-three. Again he attracted the attention of his superiors for his handling of the regiment in the Italian campaign. At age twenty-seven he was made *maréchal de camp*. With the making of peace he found himself unemployed and, returning to his father's house in Paris, tried his hand at advancement at court. Indications are that he was not overly successful among the élite at the court of Louis XIV. However he did fall in love and married Anne de la Grange-Trianon. The passion was short lived and after the birth of a son they went their separate ways. The child was left with a nurse and died at a young age.

At age fifty-two, finances in a poor state, Frontenac was offered the governorship of New France. He was not the only candidate. A Monsieur de Grignan was lobbying hard for the appointment and called in all favours to acquire it, however, those at court realized that only a man of action could keep things going in Canada and Frontenac was their man.

There is a story that one of the factors in Frontenac's favour was the love interest of the king. One of Frontenac's mistresses was one of the queen's ladies in waiting, Françoise Athenais de Pardaillan, Marquise de Montespan, who had the eye of the king and gossip abounded at court regarding the situation. A song was discretely sung that went like this: *I am enchanted that the king, our sire, Loves the Lady Montespan: I, Frontenac, with laughter I expire.* The song went on with some risque verses before ending, *Tu n'as que mon reste, Roi, Tu n'as que mon reste.* By sending Frontenac as far away as possible the king was assured of the full attention of the lady in question.

We can only speculate at Frontenac's first impression of Quebec. After a life amid the tall spires of Paris and the grandeur of old French towns, Quebec would certainly be a let down with its appearance of a hastily built collection of odd looking buildings. To his credit if he was taken aback he did not show it.

Frontenac arrived with all the splendor that the court at Versailles could muster. They had given him an allowance of 6,000 livres for his equipment and an additional 9,000 livres to provide a bodyguard of twenty horsemen. Frontenac dressed with great care for this momentous occasion. His thin, gray hair was covered by a resplendent wig topped by a tapabord hat with a fine white plume and turned up brim that showed its expensive red silk lining. His coat was of rich, gray levantine cloth, his shoes a matching gray leather. He followed his guard in their splended new uniforms down the gangway with all the pomp and circumstance of a day at court. The people who lined the streets were impressed and it seems that their new governor was as equally impressed with them and their town. In his first letter home he remarked on the location of Quebec, which *could not be better situated as the future capital of a great empire.*

Frontenac called a meeting of the council and wisely turned it into a session of praise for the king.

LOUIS DE BAUDE COMTE DE

Frontenac

He boasted of the victories in Flanders and predicted that peace would bring the king's attention back to the welfare of his colonies.

The reaction from Versailles was swift and hostile. Colbert pointed out that Canada was to be governed in the same way that France was governed. The States-General had been abolished in France and would not be tolerated in Canada. In this Frontenac saw the hand of Talon and if the latter had remained in Canada the smoldering embers would most certainly have erupted into full flame, however, since Talon was leaving on the last boat of the season an armed truce prevailed between them. The council never met again, however, the new governor had met the people and a new era in the history of Canada was about to begin.

Frontenac was determined to put his stamp on New France. The Sovereign Council, which was responsible for the day to day business of the colony, met every Monday morning. It consisted of the governor, the head of the church, the intendant and four councilors chosen for among the leading members of Quebec society. At the first meeting he attended Frontenac listened intently as Talon dictated the decisions to the council with all nodding their ascent to each. The new governor was convinced that the system needed to be overhauled.

Frontenac was a man of action, but he first determined that he would have to acquaint himself with all the workings of the colony before making any changes. To this end he began an inspection of his far flung realm. He visited every office and warehouse in Quebec, made his way to Trois Rivières to see the mines there and to consult with the people. He listened intently to everyone from wealthy merchant to the lowest habitant. After a month of looking and listening he felt he had at least a rudimentary grasp of the problems facing the people of New France.

One of the ongoing problems, of course, was the Iroquois. Although peace reigned supreme at that time, it was clear that war was never far from the minds of the warriors of the longhouse. Partly to secure the eastern end of Lake Ontario and partly to awe the Iroquois, Frontenac decided to establish a fort at Cataraqui, which he named Fort Frontenac. The plan to build a fort at this site was not a new one. However, opposition was strong on several fronts. The king discouraged expansion because he felt that the best defence against Iroquois attacks was in a compact territory where troops could be dispatched quickly to any trouble spots. As well, the merchants of Montréal

Frontenac on his way to meet the Iroquois, 1672

saw in the plan a post that would rival their own in the fur trade. In its defence was the fact that it could defend the trade route to Montréal as well as keep the furs from moving south to the English.

Frontenac decided to meet the Iroquois problem head on. He sent La Salle to Onondaga to convey his wish to meet with the chiefs of the Five Nations in council. They replied that they would be happy to meet the new French leader in their own council house. His reply was a dangerous one. He sent word back to Onondaga,

"It is for the father," he declared, "to tell the children where to hold council. The children must always come to the father. He, Onontio, the father would never come to them."

The Five Nations, impressed by this show of confidence, agreed.

The meeting was first set for the mission on the Bay of Quinte, but on the advice of La Salle it was moved to Cataraqui. Here, Frontenac used his showmanship to great advantage. He decided to have Fort Frontenac built while the council with the Iroquois was underway. He intended to show the power of France to these potential enemies with a display of force and splendor never seen before in their country. And the miracle of the fort being built and finished before their very eyes was to be the piéce de resistance.

Of course the governor did not have the resources to build the fort so he ordered the citizens of the colony to provide him with the necessary materials. Boats and canoes, arms and men, food enough for the job and the skilled workmen and tools were grudgingly assembled for the show of the century. On June 3rd the flotilla left Quebec for Montréal. The citizens of the island gave Frontenac a warm welcome as they were not yet fully aware of his intentions. The local governor, François Perrot, gave a reception and the local military assembled their contingent under Charles le Moyne who was to act as interpreter at the council.

What the Iroquois thought as this imposing armada approached Cataraqui on July 12th we can only speculate. A brisk wind was blowing across the lake and the French banners whipped and cracked in the breeze. In the lead were four squadrons of canoes filled with voyageurs all very noisy, next came two large barges carrying the materials for the fort. Frontenac and his staff came next in the breastplates and swords, a sight that left the waiting delegation in awe.

Following them came the troops, regulars in the centre, the contingent from Montréal on the left and their Indian allies on the right. In the rear was two more squadrons of voyageurs. This display of might had the desired affect on the Iroquois.

On landing they proceeded to set up their tents ignoring the chiefs. Frontenac retired to his tent for a bath announcing that negotiations would begin the next morning.

The conference and the construction on Fort Frontenac began at the same time. One of the chiefs, Garakontie, opened with a greeting to the French and Frontenac gave his reply. Here he made his first move to establish the tone for their relationship. It had always been the custom to greet the Iroquois as brothers, however, to the surprise of the warriors gathered Frontenac began,

"Children, I have a fire lighted for you to smoke by and for me to talk to you. You have done well, my children, to obey the command of your father. Take courage: you will hear his word, which is full of peace and tenderness. Do not think that I have come for war. My mind is full of peace, and she walks by my side."

The council lasted four days and at the end Fort Frontenac was finished much to the surprise of the Iroquois. Gifts were exchanged and the assurances of continued peace given. A period of renewed exploration was about to begin.

CHAPTER THIRTEEN
The founding of the Hudson Bay Company
"The Governor and Company of Adventurers of England, Trading into Hudson's Bay"

While Jolliet and Marquette were exploring the Mississippi and its surrounding territory to the south, there developed a renewed interest in the north, particularly toward Hudson's Bay. To tell this story a prologue is necessary involving the two partners from Trois Rivières, Radisson and Groseilliers.

Upon their successful return from the west in 1660 they had almost single handedly saved the financial health of the colony with their rich cargo of furs. The two immediately planned their next foray into the wilderness. Their destination: Hudson's Bay. The two were certain they could lead the way to this untapped source of beaver and other pelts. However, before they had their expedition organized word came down that another group led by two Jesuits, Fr. Gabriel Dreuillettes and Fr. Claude Dablon, were given permission to make a dash for the bay using the Saguenay River route. A second blow fell when the governor, the Baron Dubois, Sieur d'Avagour, offered to give them permits in return for half the profits. They offered the governor a share if he would accompany them on their adventure. Of course, later this was denied by Avagour, but, whatever the truth, the two slipped out of Trois Rivières in the dead of night as they had done before.

In 1663 they returned to Quebec with furs and a secret of an overland route to Hudson's Bay via Lake Winnipeg and the Nelson River. As the Jesuit expedition had failed to reach the bay there was much interest in what Radisson and Groseilliers had to say, but, the governor, still angry over their unauthorized departure seized the cargo and fined the two almost the value of the furs. Of an estimated £60,000 they ended up with about £4,000, just enough to pay their expenses.

Radisson and Groseilliers were not ones to take such treatment without a response. Groseilliers sailed for France to plead their case with the King's ministers. With the healthy addition that the fines made to the treasury, they refused to intervene on their behalf. This was to prove a grave error on the part of the French government. Upon his return the two adventurers made their way to the English colonies in search of support.

In 1664 they attempted the sea route to the bay and made it as far as Hudson Strait before turning back. In Boston two ships were outfitted and backed by the merchants of that city. When one of the ships was wrecked the crews lost heart and returned to Boston without reaching the bay and the backers sued the two Canadians to recover their investment.

It was at this desperate time that good fortune smiled on them. Sir George Carteret, proprietor of "a certain island and adjacent islets in perpetual inheritance to be called New Jersey" was in the New World on business and met Radisson and Groseilliers. He was immediately intrigued with the possibilities of their plans and persuaded them to sail to England with him.

They arrived in England in 1665 when London was in the throes of the Great Plague. King Charles II was at Oxford and Carteret took the two there to see the King. He was impressed enough to order an allowance of forty shillings a week to be paid to the Canadians while they drew up their plans for the conquest of the north. The king put the entire project under the control of his cousin, Prince Rupert, as a means of getting him out of some financial difficulties. Fortunately Rupert had as his secretary a man of foresight in James Hayes. He became one of the strongest supporters of the plan. He even had Radisson's book published to help sell the idea to the business community.

The first voyage was to be a test. The King ordered his brother, the Duke of York, later King James II, to loan the Eaglet, a ship of the South Seas Fleet for the expedition. Also outfitted for the voyage was the Nonsuch, which, like the Eaglet was forty feet long with a beam of sixteen feet. On June 3, 1668 the two sailed in company for Hudson Bay.

Unfortunately the Eaglet, with Radisson on board, was disabled early in the trip and was forced to return to Plymouth. The Nonsuch, with Groseilliers aboard penetrated the bay and sailed as far as James Bay where trading began in earnest with the Indians. On the advice of the two Canadians the cargo of trade goods contained all the right articles. A half pound of beads or five pounds of sugar was traded for one bea-

HBC 1670

Charles II

Wee Doe Grant into the said Governor and Company and theire Successors the sole Trade and Commerce of all those Seas, Streightes, Bays, Rivers, Lakes, Creekes & Soundes that lie within the entrance of Hudsons Streightts and make ... ate and constitute them ... and absolute and Propietors of the ... ame Territory

NONSUCH

ver pelt. Twenty fish hooks for five pelts, a gun for twenty and so it went. The Nonsuch returned with a cargo valued at £19,000, which, after expenses, left a tidy sum to split among the investors.

On May 2, 1670 the charter of "the Governor and Company of Adventurers of England, Trading into Hudson's Bay" was signed by Charles II. One of the most successful and long lasting companies in the history of the business world was born.

The charter gave the adventurers practically the whole of the north and the oceans around it. There were eighteen charter members listed including the Duke of York, Prince Rupert, Carteret, Sir James Hayes, Sir John Kirke, whose daughter became Mrs. Radisson, and an assortment of peers of the realm.

What about Radisson and Groseilliers? Their names were conspicuous by their absence. It was understood that they were to continue on an allowance and the King gave them "a gold chain and metall" but they were not to share in the fortunes of the company that their vision and knowledge made possible. Ultimately they returned to the service of France.

CHAPTER FOURTEEN

Exploring a Continent

"Monsieur Jollyet arrived with orders from Monsieur the Comte de Frontenac, our Governor, and Monsieur Talon, our Intendant, to accomplish this discovery with me."-Fr. Jacques Marquette, December, 1672

From the days of Champlain the haunting stories of the mighty Mississippi had intrigued the traders and explorers of Canada. The credit for its eventual discovery has been claimed for a number of adventurers. Nicolet likely visited some of the tributaries of the great river in 1640. Radisson and Groseilliers probably crossed the Mississippi about 1660 and La Salle reached the Ohio in 1669. The first recorded journey to the Mississippi, however, was accomplished by Louis Jolliet and Fr. Jacques Marquette in 1673.

The French push to claim the entire interior of the North American continent began in earnest with a pageant at Sault Sainte Marie in 1671. As a follow up to this event Frontenac organized an expedition with the sole purpose of discovering the legendary Mississippi. The man chosen to lead the effort was Louis Jolliet, a Canadian born interpreter and voyageur. Jolliet was born in 1645 at Quebec the son of Jean Jolliet, a wagonmaker employed by the Company of One Hundred Associates, and Marie d'Abancourt. Jolliet studied at the Jesuit College at Quebec and entered the seminary there in 1663. However, the call of the wilderness beckoned him and after taking his minor orders he left the seminary to study in Europe where he majored in engineering and hydrography, disciplines he felt would be useful in his desire to explore the west. He returned to New France and was present at the Sault in 1671.

On all such expeditions it was customary to have a priest along to preach to the Indians that were encounter. Fr. Jacques Marquette was chosen to accompany Jolliet. Marquette was born at Laon, France January 10, 1637. At age 17 he entered the Jesuit novitiate at Nancy and after ordination came to Canada in 1666. He took over the mission at St. Esprit de Chequamegon on Chequamegon Bay and moved his flock to Michilimackinac in 1671 where he founded the mission of St. Ignace.

The great expedition was about to begin. Marquette described the begin this way:

"The feast of the Immaculate Conception of the Blessed Virgin . . . was precisely the day on which Monsieur Jollyet (sic) arrived with orders from Monsieur the Comte de Frontenac, our Governor, and Monsieur Talon, our Intendant, to accomplish this discovery with me. . . ."

"We were not long in preparing all our equipment, although we were about to begin a voyage, the duration of which we could not foresee. Indian corn, with some smoked meat, constituted all our provisions; with these we embarked - Monsieur Jollyet and myself, with five men - in two bark canoes, fully resolved to do and suffer everything for so glorious an undertaking."

On the 17th of May, 1673 the expedition departed St. Ignace de Michilimackinac armed with a map drawn from the descriptions of the country by Indians trading at the post. After entering Lake Michigan they visited the Menominee tribe whom Marquette had evangelized for several years. Marquette informed them of their intention of finding the great river and the Menominee tried to dissuade him from going. He wrote in his journal:

"They were greatly surprised to hear it, . . . They represented to me that I should meet nations who never show mercy to strangers, but break their heads without any cause; . . . They also said that the great river was very dangerous, when one does not know the difficult places; that it was full of horrible monsters, which devoured men and canoes together; that there was a demon, who was heard from a great distance, who barred the way, and swallowed up all who ventured to approach him . . ."

The party continued their journey warnings of monsters and demons notwithstanding. They encountered the Miamis, who Marquette described as pleasant and beautiful, the Mascoutins, a rather uncouth race, and the Kickapoos, a wild and warlike tribe. They descended the Wisconsin and arrived at the junction of the Mississippi on June 17th. Marquette wrote:

"After proceeding 40 leagues on this same

Jolliet & Marquette on the Mississippi, 1673

route, we arrived at the mouth of our river; and, at 42 and a half degrees of latitude, we safely entered the Mississipi(sic) on the 17th of June, with a joy that I cannot express."

Here their Indian guides again tried to dissuade the two explorers from going further, but they would not be deterred. They did encounter monsters, which were in fact huge catfish and sturgeon. They continued as far as the Arkansas River where they realized that the Mississippi did not flow to the Vermilion Sea, but instead to the Gulf of Mexico. They decided to turn back and report their findings. They arrived back at the Illinois River at the end of September and Jolliet immediately left for Quebec to report to Frontenac.

Ironically, Jolliet's must perilous encounter on the journey happened at the Lachine Rapids near Montréal. His canoe was overturned and his two companions drowned. Jolliet was lucky to escape with his life. All his notes were lost in the mishap.

Marquette set out to open a mission among the Illinois in 1674, but the rigors of the previous year had taken their toll and he died on May 20th. Jolliet married Claire Françoise Bissot in 1675 and they raised a family of seven. For his service to the crown he received a grant of the Mingan Islands on the lower St. Lawrence River and later the Island of Anticosti. He moved there where he died in 1700.

Jolliet and Marquette opened the way for French dominance in the interior of North America.

While Radisson and Groseilliers were pushing into Hudson's Bay, plans to further explore the west were in full swing. Daniel Greysolon Duluth discovered the portage routes from Lake Superior to the head waters of the Mississippi and planned to establish a post there among the Sioux. His plans were frustrated by his recall to Quebec that same year.

In the meantime La Salle was preparing another attempt to explore the Mississippi itself. Among his party were two men who were to figure prominently in the expedition; Henri de Tonty, his Lieutenant, was a cousin of Duluth, and Father Louis Hennepin, a Recollect, who was to be the spiritual component of the expedition.

They set out in the fall of 1678 from Quebec arriving at Fort Frontenac on the 2nd of November. On the 18th they embarked on a brigantine of 10 tons and a crew of fifteen under the command of the Sieur de la Motte. They visited the various Iroquois villages along the way and arrived at the mouth of the Niagara River on the 6th of January 1679. Here their ship was wrecked and La Salle decided to return over the ice to Fort Frontenac leaving Tonty in command until his return.

Before leaving La Salle ordered a fort and some buildings to be constructed to hold and protect their supplies. A delegation, including Fr. Hennepin, was sent to reassure the Iroquois as to the purpose of the buildings. Father Hennepin left us this description of the encounter:

"We passed through forests thirty-two leagues, and five days' journey came to a great village, and were immediately carried to the cabin of their principal. The younger savages washed our feet and rubbed them over with the grease of deer, wild goats and oil of bears. They are for the most part tall and well shaped, covered with a sort of robe made of beavers' and wolves' skins, or black squirrels, holding a pipe or calumet in their hands. The Senators of Venice do not appear with a graver countenance, and perhaps do not speak with more majesty and solidity than those ancient Iroquois."

After the traditional exchange of gifts the party set out for Niagara arriving there on the 14th of January. La Salle returned on the 20th with materials and rigging for a ship he intended to build above the Falls of Niagara to facilitate the fur trade on the upper lakes. On the 22nd they journeyed two miles above the falls and set up a dock for the building the ship. La Salle returned to Fort Frontenac on foot with two men and a dog who dragged their baggage over the snow. Tonty was left in command to supervise the construction.

The Iroquois were suspicious of the activity going on and except for the fact that most of the warriors were away on a raiding party might have done something to interfere with the shipbuilding. Fr. Hennepin wrote:

"We made all the haste we could to get our ship afloat, though not altogether finished, to prevent their designs of burning it. She was called the Griffin, about sixty tons, and carried five small guns. We fired three guns and sung Te Deum; and, carrying our hammocks aboard, the same day were out of the reach of the savages."

Fr. Hennepin returned to Fort Frontenac to pick up two of his confréres to assist him in his ministry. In the spring they set out aboard a brigantine and stopped at a river flowing into Lake Ontario (perhaps the Oswego) to trade. Here La Salle caught up to them and they reached the Niagara on the 30th of July 1679. Hennepin took the time to see the falls for the first time. Hennepin wrote:

"Father Gabriel and I went overland to view the great fall, the like whereof is not in the whole world. It is compounded of two great cross streams of water and two falls, with an isle sloping along the middle of it. The waters which fall from this vast height do foam and boil after the most hideous manner imaginable, making an outrageous noise, more terrible than that of thunder; so that when the wind blows from the south their dismal roaring may be heard above fifteen leagues off."

Fr. Louis Hennepin views Niagara Falls, Summer, 1679

Fr. Hennepin described the maiden voyage of the Griffin in his journal:

"On the 7th of August we went on board, being in all thirty-four men, and sailed from the mouth of the Lake Erie, and on the 11th entered a strait thirty leagues long and one broad, except in the middle, which makes the Lake of St. Clair. On the 23rd we got into Lake Huron."

On the 26th a violent storm nearly ended the expedition, but fortunately the ship survived and arrived at Michilimackinac on the 27th. La Salle weighed anchor on the 2nd of September and sailed for Green Bay where he traded with the Indians. Loading the furs on the Griffin he ordered the captain and five men to sail for Niagara. Hennepin recorded this in his journal:

"They sailed on the 18th, with a westerly wind, and fired a gun as taking leave. It was never known what course they steered, nor how they perished; but it is supposed that the ship struck upon sand and was there buried. This was a great loss for M.de la Salle and other adventurers, for that ship with its cargo cost above sixty thousand livres."

The fate of the Griffin has been a source of controversy for three hundred years. Lately a theory has emerged that perhaps the Ottawas, jealous of their position as middlemen to the western tribes, may have attacked and burned the ship to prevent direct French trade with the western tribes. Despite this setback La

Salle was determined to push forward in his search for the Mississippi.

La Salle was building a strong fort, which he christened Fort Crevecoeur, at the site of present day Peoria Illinois when rumours reached him of the disappearance of the Griffin. Leaving Tonty in command, he set out on foot for Fort Frontenac to discover what had happened. When he reached his destination, news of the loss of the Griffin was confirmed. Other bad news awaited him. A ship carrying 22,000 livres worth of goods for his use was wrecked in the St. Lawrence and his supply depot at Niagara was broken into and looted.

The final blow came with the word that most of the men under Tonty had mutinied destroying Fort Crevecoeur and stealing all the supplies stored there. It turned out that the mutineers were heading east for the expressed purpose of killing La Salle so as to prevent reprisals for their actions. La Salle waylaid them on the shores of Lake Ontario, killing two of them and making prisoners of the rest.

The difficulties now seemed insurmountable. His creditors were clamoring for their money, his supply depots rifled and his base in the west burned to the ground. His only hope was to find the unfinished hull of a vessel that was begun on the Illinois River and to find the faithful Tonty.

Somehow he managed to placate his creditors and find some additional funding and on August 10, 1680 he set off with twenty-five men to start again.

Tragedy seemed to plague La Salle wherever he went. On reaching the Illinois country he found their main village on the river had been destroyed and its inhabitants scattered. Only a blackened ruin greeted La Salle's party. The Iroquois had struck with a brutality that shocked even the those hardened by years of warfare with the warriors of the longhouse.

When the Iroquois attacked they found the village practically deserted. After killing the few that were too old to flee, the warriors dug up the burial ground and disinterred the bones. They took the bodies of the recently deceased down from the burial scaffolds and savagely mutilated them. La Salle found the skulls of those long dead nailed to the tops of charred posts, silent witnesses to the carnage wrought there.

Where was Tonty? It was here that La Salle expected to find him. Was he among the victims? If Tonty was dead then this would be the final blow, the one from which La Salle could not recover.

But Tonty was very much alive. He had attempted to reason with the invaders and to negotiate a truce, but the Illinois were suspicious. Was Tonty a spy for the Iroquois? They seized Tonty's supplies and destroyed the tools and forge with which he had hoped to complete the ship under construction. Despite this Tonty stayed beside the Illinois and by some miracle survived and made his way to Michilimackinac where a relieved La Salle found his faithful Lieutenant.

Tonty described his adventures in his journal:

"The desertion of our men and the journey of M. de La Salle to Fort Frontenac made the savages suspect that we were betraying them. They severely reproached me respecting the arrival of their enemies. . . . this embarrassed me and determined me to go to the enemy with necklaces to tell them that I was surprised they had come to make war upon a nation dependent on the Governor of New France, and that M. de La Salle, whom he esteemed, governed these people. An Islinois (sic) accompanied me, and we separated ourselves from the body of the Islinois, who were 400 in number, and were already fighting with the enemy. When I was within gun-shot the Iroquois fired a great volley at us, which compelled me to tell the Islinois to retire. He did so. When I had come up to them, these wretches seized me, took the necklace from my hand, and one of them, reaching through the crowd, plunged a knife into my breast, wounding a rib near the heart. However, having recognized me, they carried me into the midst of their camp and asked me what I came for. I gave them to understand that the Islinois were under the protection of the King of France and of the Governor of the country, and that I was surprised that they wished to break with the French, and postpone peace.

"All this time skirmishing was going on on both sides, and a warrior came to give notice to the chief that their left wing was giving way, and that they had recognized some Frenchmen among the Islinois, who were shooting at them. On this they were greatly irritated against me and held a council concerning what they should do with me. There was a man behind me with a knife in his hand, who every now and then lifted my hair. Tegancouti, chief of the Tson-

The aftermath of an Iroquois raid, Illinois country, 1679

nontouan, wished positively to have me burnt. Agonstot, chief of the Onontagues, as a friend of M. de La Salle, wished to have me set at liberty. He carried his point."

Everything that could go wrong for La Salle did up to this point, but with Tonty back by his side he was ready to try again. He returned to Fort Frontenac to gather his strength for a fresh start. In the late fall of 1681 he set out again to follow his dream of exploring the mighty Mississippi.

La Salle's arrival at Fort Frontenac created a financial storm that threatened to engulf the great explorer. Whatever we can say about his luck in the wilds he certainly was able to talk himself out of tight corners on the fringes of civilization. He not only smoothed out his creditors wrath, but secured additional funding

for his next attempt at the Mississippi. The backing came from an unlikely source. François Plet, a shrewd and rather ruthless investor to whom La Salle owed a great deal of money, advanced the necessary funds. Whether this was an attempt to recoup his investment or the fact that La Salle executed a will in his favour we will never know, however the normally tight fisted Plet opened up his purse one more time.

In the fall of 1681 La Salle set out again on the 3rd of November to join up with Tonty in the west. Tonty, in the meantime, chose twenty-three Canadians and eighteen Mohegan and Abenaki Indians to make up the expedition. The Abenaki insisted on taking ten of their women to cook for them as was their custom. The entire party consisted of fifty-four people including three children. Father Zenobius Membre, a Recollet priest, wrote in his journal:

"On the 21st of December I embarked with the Sieur de Tonty and a part of our people on Lake Dauphin (Michigan), to go toward the divine river, called by the Indians Checagon, in order to make necessary arrangements for our voyage. The Sieur de la Salle joined us there with the rest of his troop on the 4th of January, 1682, and found that Tonty had had sleighs made to put all on and carry it over the Chicago, which was frozen; for, though the winter in these parts is only two months long, it is, notwithstanding, very severe."

The party dragged their sledges and canoes across the frozen Illinois River and proceeded to Lake Peoria where they found the Illinois Indians in winter quarters. They reached the Mississippi on the 6th of February. They continued on and one of their party, the armourer, Pierre Prud'homme, became lost while hunting. He was nine days in the woods without food. La Salle feared that he had been taken or killed by Indians and he had a fort built, which he named Fort Prud'homme in his honour. Tonty's description of their search gives us a glimpse of some of the people they encountered:

"As they were looking for him they fell in with two Chicachas (Chickasaw) savages, whose village was three days' journey from there, in the lands along the Mississipy (sic). They have 2,000 warriors, the greatest number of whom have flat heads, which is considered a beauty among them, the women taking pains to flatten the heads of their children, by means of a cushion which they put on their foreheads and bind with a band to the cradle, . . ."

"M. de La Salle sent back one of them with presents to his village, so that, if they had taken Prud'homme, they might send him back, but we found him on the tenth day, and as the Cicachas did not return, we continued our route as far as the village of Capa, fifty leagues off." (Capa was a village visited Jolliet and Marquette in 1673)

Forty miles down the Mississippi the sound of drums and war cries reached the ears of La Salle and his men. Father Membre wrote:

"We heard drums beating and sasocouest (war cries) on our right. Perceiving that it was an Akansa village, the Sieur de la Salle immediately passed over to the other side with all his force, and in less than an hour threw up a retrenched redoubt on a point, with palisades, and felled trees, to prevent a surprise and give the Indians time to recover confidence. He then made some of his party advance on the bank of the river and invite the Indians to come to us. The chiefs sent a periagua (these are large wooden canoes, made of a hollow tree, like little bateaux), which came within gunshot. We offered them the calumet of peace, and two Indians, advancing, by signs invited the French to come to them."

La Salle sent a Frenchman and two Abenaki who were treated with kindness and soon the whole party was at the village giving and receiving gifts. The village was well stocked with food including flocks of turkeys and other domesticated fowl. They also cultivated fruit trees and vegetables. On the 14th of March La Salle took possession of the land by raising a cross and the coat of arms of France.

Father Membre describes the next part of the journey in his journal:

"On the 17th we continued our route, . . .On the 22nd [or 20th] we reached the Taensa, who dwell around a little lake formed in the land by the River Mississippi. They have eight villages. The walls of their houses are made of earth mixed with straw; the roof is of canes, which form a dome adorned with paintings; they have wooden beds and much other furniture, and even ornaments in their temples, where they inter the bones of their chiefs."

Early in April the expedition came to a place where the river divided into three channels. La Salle sent three parties, one down each channel taking the western most himself with Tonty taking the centre and Autray, the third in command, the eastern channel. It was La Salle's canoe that first broke into the Gulf of Mexico and their paddles first tasted salt water. The mystery of the Mississippi had been solved.

While La Salle was busy exploring the Mississippi things at Quebec were in constant turmoil under the

La Salle at the Gulf of Mexico, April, 1682

fiery Frontenac. The strong willed Jesuits refused to knuckle under and the ongoing battle sent streams of letters back and forth across the Atlantic. The Jesuits and the Sulpicians were instrumental in the banning of the brandy trade with the Indians, whereas the governor and the merchants found it helpful in the fur trade. Frontenac dismissed the missionaries claims of orgies, cruelty and killings that resulted when the Indians became intoxicated as an exaggeration. The Jesuits finally accused Frontenac of engaging in the fur trade using the rumour that he and La Salle were conspiring to gain a monopoly on the trade in the west and south. The king's minister, Colbert wrote the governor a warning letter:

"His Majesty further orders me to tell you in secret that, although he did not believe what was said here that some trade and pelt traffic was carried on in your name, you must beware lest any of your servants or any person who is near you carry on such a trade. It would be impossible for the colonists to be persuaded that you will protect them and render them the impartial justice which you owe them as long as they see a few persons who have private access to trade."

The reference to La Salle, while unspoken, was obvious.

The turmoil in the colony forced the king to make some changes. He finally appointed a replacement for Talon in Jacques Duchesneau who had been the royal treasurer at Tours. Further the king reserved the right to appoint members to the Sovereign Council to himself.

Duchesneau and Frontenac fought from the very beginning and to complicate things further Laval, finally named Bishop of Quebec, returned in 1680 to join the fray. To add to the drama the winds of war were blowing through the longhouses of the Five Nations. Frontenac managed to temporarily dampen the ardour of the warriors, but it soon became obvious that blood would soon run again along the banks of St. Lawrence.

The constant battles with Frontenac pitted against Duchesneau and Laval resulted in Frontenac's recall to France. His replacement and that of Duchesneau was to bring New France to the edge of extinction.

Antoine de la Barre, Sieur de le Febvre replaced Frontenac in 1682 bringing with him Jacques de Meules, Sieur de la Source as intendant. La Barre arrived in Canada with a firm dislike of both Frontenac and La Salle and a resolve to get rich.

La Barre immediately made a number of serious mistakes. On receiving a letter from La Salle informing him of the discovery of the mouth of the Mississippi he wrote the king that the discovery was of little value. Louis replied,

> "I am convinced, like you, that the discovery of the Sieur de la Salle is very useless and that such enterprises ought to be prevented in future."

La Barre took the king's words as carte blanche to act against La Salle. He detained the men that he had sent to Quebec for supplies, seized all of La Salle's goods at Fort Frontenac and refused to send help in deterring Iroquois aggression in the west.

La Barre next set himself up in business with a cartel of Canadian merchants and opened a storehouse at Michilimackinac and began operating a trade network throughout the Great Lakes region. For this he needed peace with the Iroquois. Charles Le Moyne set up a meeting at Montréal with forty chiefs of the Five Nations. La Barre was no Frontenac and made no impression on the assembled warriors. Although the chiefs promised to refrain from attacking the Indians of the upper lakes and to respect the peace with France, future events proved their promises hollow. The Iroquois also complained that La Salle had sup-

plied the Illinois with guns and powder. La Barre promised that he would be punished and left the chiefs with the impression that they were free to attack La Salle's party and his possessions at will.

With his fortune in tatters La Salle returned to France and his humble apartments in the Rue de la Truanderie from which he immediately asked for an audience with the king or his ministers. Louis, ever curious and always looking for something to add to his glory agreed to see La Salle. His plan was no less than the settling of the mouth of the Mississippi and the capture of the Spanish mines in Mexico. The king agreed sending off a scathing letter to La Barre to restore La Salle's possessions and to inform the Iroquois that La Salle was in great favour with the king.

Four ships were outfitted and the expedition to colonize the mouth of the Mississippi by sea was ready to go. The ships were under the command of Captain Beaujeu. The expedition sailed from La Rochelle in the summer of 1684. The smallest vessel, the ketch St. Francois, was captured off San Domingo by the Spanish where La Salle was struck by a fever through which he raved wildly. Many in the crew including Beaujeu wondered if the great explorer was not insane. It was a sick and emancipated La Salle that boarded the flagship and ordered beaujeu to sail into the unknown waters of the Gulf of Mexico.

Finally the lookout sighted land and soon a long stretch of flat islands came into view. At first La Salle was sure that it was the mouth of the Mississippi, however it turned out to be Matagorda Bay on the Texas coast some four hundred miles southwest of the Mississippi. Disaster struck immediately. One of the ships, the Aimable, hit a reef under full sail while entering the bay. Captain Beaujeu returned to France in the ship, Joly and the remaining frigate La Belle was wrecked shortly thereafter.

The new colony was cut off from civilization, surrounded by hostile Indians and with only their meager supplies to sustain the men and women left behind. La Salle was in despair. There would be no Spanish gold, only death from fever and Indian attacks. The only recourse was to find the Mississippi and get word back to France. Accordingly La Salle set out with twenty men including his brother, the Sulpician from Montréal, and his nephew Moranget. As it turned out he would have been better to leave the nephew behind. He was a bad tempered lad who was thoroughly disliked by all. A party, including Moranget, one Duhaut

The death of La Salle, 1684

and a man called Liotot, were sent to retrieve a cache of food left earlier for emergencies. A quarrel ensued, which resulted in the murder of Moranget and two others while they slept. In the minds of the assassins it was now necessary to dispose of La Salle in order to cover the crime.

Two days later La Salle set out to discover what was keeping the party. The conspirators set up an ambush along the trail. The journal of one of La Salle's party gives us this account:

"The first of them, spying M. de la Salle at a distance, as he was coming towards them, advanced and hid themselves among the high weeds, to wait his passing by; so that M. de la Salle, suspecting nothing, and having not so much as charged his piece again, saw the aforesaid Larcheveque at a good distance from him,

and immediately asked for his nephew Moranget, to which larcheveque answered that he was along the river. At the same time the traitor Duhaut fired his piece and shot M. de la Salle through the head, so that he dropped dead on the spot, without speaking one word."

Thus ended the life of La Salle. The conspirators quarreled among themselves and Duhaut was killed. The rest of the party worked their way to the Arkansas where they met up with some Frenchmen sent by Tonty to find his friend. The king refused to send a ship to rescue the lost colony and the last traces were found by a Spanish expedition under Alonso de Leon. The bodies of the last three survivors were still recognizable in the broken down·fort, which had been attacked and burned by hostile Indians.

51

CHAPTER SIXTEEN
The Iroquois Peace begins to Unravel
"Onontio calls us his children, and then helps our enemies to knock us in the head."-Iroquois orator, 1684

With the death of La Salle the French dream of a southern colony at the mouth of the Mississippi faded into the background. However, the voyageurs and their fur trading employers continued to push west to fulfill their driving hunger for beaver.

In the east the political and social climate was in a state of flux. The Dutch colony of New Netherlands fell under the control of the English who renamed the colony New York in honour of its patron and proprietor the Duke of York who later became King James II.

The duke appointed as his governor colonel Thomas Dongan, which was unusual as he was an Irish Catholic who had served in France and was not only familiar with the language; but partial to the French king and the nobility of that country. Despite this he threw his energies and talent into his new job. The Dutch and English traders were anxious to profit from the fur trade and were poaching on territory claimed by the French. Dongan advanced their cause as much as he could while still following the orders of the duke, which was "to give the French governor no just cause of offence."

The Iroquois, in the meantime, although at peace with the Dutch and English in New York, were plundering and killing settlers in Virginia and Maryland. In the summer of 1684 a council was held at Albany where the offending tribes of the confederacy, the Onondagas, the Oneidas and the Cayugas, and the governors of Virginia and Maryland promised friendship and peace. A hole was dug in the courtyard and each tribe threw in a hatchet and the governors did likewise. The hole was filled in and peace songs were sung with pledges of mutual respect and peace. The Mohawks and Senecas showed up a short time later and joined in the accord.

Shortly before the council the governor of New France had sent Dongan a letter informing him that Seneca and Cayuga warriors were plundering Canadian canoes and assaulting forts and settlements and that he was going to attack them. He asked that the Dutch and English traders be forbidden to supply guns and ammunition to the Five Nations. La Barre's communication had two results that were detrimental to Canada; first the Iroquois were forewarned of his in-

tentions and second, Dongan used the opportunity to assert the English king's sovereignty over the Five Nations and possession of all the lands south of the Great Lakes. He told La Barre that if the Iroquois had done wrong he would require that they make reparation as British subjects. He further urged La Barre not to invade British territory and risk war between the two colonies.

Dongan laid the French complaints before the assembled chiefs who immediately defended themselves by accusing the French of supplying their enemies, the Illinois and Miami with arms. Their orator made the following speech,

"Onontio calls us his children, and then helps our enemies to knock us in the head."

They expressed alarm at the prospects of a French attack and Dongan managed to get them to acknowledge the authority of the Duke of York promising to protect the Iroquois from the French in return. The orator did not hesitate,

"We put ourselves under the great sachem Charles, who lives over the Great Lake, and under the protection of the great Duke of York, brother of the great sachem." After a moment's hesitation he added, "Let your friend who lives over the Great Lake know that we are a free people, though united to the English."

Word of La Barre's preparation for war was received with excitement by the Senecas. Fr. Jean de Lamberville, a Jesuit who lived among the Onondagas, wrote La Barre,

"You cannot believe, Monsieur, with what joy the Senecas learned that you might possibly resolve for war. When they heard of the preparations at Fort Frontenac, they said that the French had a great mind to be stripped, roasted, and eaten; and that they will see if their flesh, which they suppose to have a salt taste, by reason of the salt which we use with our food, be

Le Moyne entertains at Longueuil

as good as that of their other enemies."

La Barre visited Charles le Moyne at his palatial manor house at Longueuil to discuss the ongoing Iroquois situation. Le Moyne, knowing the governor's fondness for the luxuries of life, entertained him only as one of the most successful seigneurs of New France could. The banquet room could have easily been in one of Paris' finer salons. Here La Barre asked le Moyne to invite the Five Nations to a conference at Fort Frontenac where he intended to show them the might of the French army.

La Barre embarked his army consisting of three companies of newly arrived regulars who had not had time to get acclimatized to the Canadian summer, seven hundred Canadians volunteers and a few hundred Indian allies and headed across Lac St. Louis determined to end the Iroquois threat once and for all. He made a series of errors on his arrival at Fort Frontenac. He situated his camp on some low swampy ground outside the fort, which resulted in an epidemic of malarial fever that swept the camp killing many. Because of poor management supplies ran low threatening the expedition with starvation. When the

Onondagas arrived La Barre quickly arranged the council for the opposite bank of the river. Taking the healthiest men with him he attempted to bluff his way through. The Onondagas were to shrewd for that and their great orator, known as Big Mouth, stood and after a few moments spoke these words,

"Listen, Onontio. I am not asleep. My eyes are open; and by the sun that gives me light I see a great captain at the head of a band of soldiers, who talks like a man in a dream. He says that he has come to smoke the pipe of peace with the Onondagas; but I see that he came to knock them in the head, if so many of his Frenchmen were not too weak to fight. I see Onontio raving in a camp of sick men, whose lives the Great Spirit has saved by smiting them with disease."

La Barre was forced to withdraw in humiliation. His failure to deal with the Iroquois was not lost on Louis XIV. La Barre was recalled to France in disgrace.

CHAPTER SEVENTEEN

Denonville's Folly

"We began to see the famous Babylon of the Senecas, where so many crimes have been committed, so much blood spilled, and so many men burned."-Abbé Belmont, July, 1687

With the departure of La Barre the era of relative peace between the French and English colonies was drawing to a close. On the surface the new governor of New France was a good choice. Jacques René de Brisay, Marquis de Denonville was an experienced soldier with thirty years of service to his country. He was blindly loyal to his king and this rigidity was to cause him to commit grave errors in judgment during his tenure in Canada. His first mistake concerned the Iroquois. During La Barre's term the French King had decided that one way to control the Iroquois was to capture as many as possible and send them to France as galley slaves. La Barre, although neither astute nor particularly clever, realized the folly of such action and did nothing. Denonville, ever obedient to the commands of his king, decided to implement the policy.

The selection of the Indians for this cruel policy was as faulty as the decision to act. Along the north shore of Lake Ontario were two villages of friendly Iroquois peacefully pursuing a life of hunting, fishing and farming. Denonville sent the new intendant, M. Champigny, to roundup as many able bodied men as he could. By various tricks he managed to lure these harmless people aboard his vessel and when he had sorted out the group he had fifty-one captives for the king. While awaiting passage to the galleys of Marseilles they were tied to stakes at Fort Frontenac where many died of exposure. Some of the prisoners were released, but many were sent to France. Far from teaching the Five Nations a lesson it stirred up the war blood of the confederacy causing Denonville to fire off a letter begging for the return of the prisoners. Even if the prisoners could have been returned unharmed the Iroquois would not forget such treachery. Many a Canadian family suffered for the folly of Denonville.

Denonville was now forced to face an increasingly hostile Iroquois Confederacy. He now made another error in judgment. His solution to the problem was to attack the Seneca in the hopes of destroying their ability to make war on the St. Lawrence Valley. With reinforcements from France numbering eight hundred soldiers, Denonville planned his campaign.

To open the campaign Denonville moved his army to Fort Frontenac and sent word to Tonty, La Salle's former Lieutenant, who was at the Illinois and La Durantaye at Michilimackinac, to meet him at Niagara. By early July they had reached their destination and Denonville was ready to proceed with the humbling of the mighty Seneca. Denonville ordered them to meet up with him at Irondequiot Bay.

Denonville had over three thousand men under his command including French regulars, Canadian militia, Christian Indians and warriors from the western tribes. All was ready. As they camped on the edge of Seneca country three scouts called out from the woods demanding to know what they wanted. A volley of musket fire was the answer to their question. They ran off to warn their brothers of the coming invasion.

It was indeed a perilous time for the Seneca. Most of their best warriors were absent and they could but muster four hundred men many no more than boys. They sent the women and children away, burned their chief town and march out to meet the French army.

Denonville started his march on July 12th. A broad Indian trail showed the way to the Seneca heartland. They marched forward in the oppressive heat passing through two dangerous ravines without incident. They entered a third lead by Tonty and his cousin Du Lhut along with La Durantaye. This vanguard, nine hundred strong, was made up of Coureurs de Bois, the voyageurs of the fur trade, and the Indians of many nations under the command of Nicholas Perrot and two other Frenchmen of Michilimackinac. The main force commanded by Denonville followed them. Scouts returned reporting that they had reached the clearing to the Seneca town and saw only four women in the fields. The vanguard rushed forward leaving the main body behind in hopes of surprising the town before they could mount a defence. They fell right into the Seneca trap.

The Seneca warriors lay in way in the heavy woods that crowded the left side of the trail. On the right a marsh filled with alder thickets and rank grass barred escape to that quarter. Suddenly the air was filled with war whoops and the Seneca, many naked and

Manning the ramparts, Fort Denonville, winter, 1688

swinging swords and hatchets, rushed against the van. But they had made a fatal error. Seeing the size of the advance guard they surmised that it was the entire force. After a moment of confusion and panic Denonville was able to rally the main body who charged into the fray causing heavy casualties among the enemy. Seeing that they were facing an army seemingly without end, the Seneca picked up their dead and wounded and withdrew.

Denonville made no attempt to pursue. He now feared this warfare in the woods and did not relish another ambush. He wrote,

"Our troops were all so overcome by the extreme heat and the long march that we were forced to remain where we were till morning."

In the morning they marched on in battle order. Abbé Belmont wrote,

"We began to see the famous Babylon of the Senecas, where so many crimes have been committed, so much blood spilled, and so many men burned. It was a village or town of bark, on the top of a hill. They had burned it a week before."

The Seneca had fled to their cousins to the east and the only things left were some hoppers of corn and a number of hogs, which were slaughtered by the soldiers. A nearby fort was burned and three other abandoned villages were destroyed. Denonville decided not to pursue the Senecas for fear of bringing the entire confederacy down on his force. He withdrew to Niagara where he built a fort on the site of La Salle's Fort Conde. He named the post after himself, Fort Denonville. Leaving a garrison of a hundred men he withdrew back to Fort Frontenac and hence to Quebec. The garrison left behind was short of provisions and as winter set in the Senecas prevented the garrison from foraging for food. They could do nothing but man the ramparts in the bitter cold and pray for spring. In the spring of 1688 the relief party found only twelve survivors. The fort was re-garrisoned, but soon afterward they took inventory, pulled down the stockade and abandoned the site. Meanwhile the Iroquois planned their retribution.

CHAPTER EIGHTEEN

The Lachine Massacre
"They paddled their canoes up and down the river before the stockade
showing off their captives and shouting in derision, 'Onontio! Onontio!'"

The Denonville raid on the Seneca had no immediate repercussions on the settlements along the St. Lawrence. Denonville was desperate to make peace with the aroused Iroquois and the Five Nations agreed to send a peace delegation to Fort Frontenac. A renegade Huron, wanting to sabotage any peace attempt, ambushed the chiefs killing one of them and wounding the rest. The leader of the ambush party, called the Rat, then professed, to the astonishment of the envoys, that Denonville had asked him to attack this Iroquois war party. He then sent them on their way to tell their tale at Onondaga. Denonville immediately sent his regrets and the Iroquois accepted his explanation of the Huron treachery

The summer of 1688 was deceptively quiet and the settlements around Montréal thrived. La Salle's old stomping grounds at Lachine rapidly changed from a fur trading outpost to a full fledged settlement. Prosperous landowners dwelled in the high peaked, whitewashed houses along the shores of Lac St. Louis. Three stockades garrisoned by soldiers provided protection, La Présentation, Remy, and Roland.

The night of August 4, 1689 was hot and muggy. Thunderheads rolled in with its promise of trouble before the night was out. In the middle of the night the storm broke bringing hail and a torrential downpour. The people of Lachine rose to make sure that all was closed up against the raging elements. Therefore some were awake when a strange but forbiddingly familiar cry rose above the thunder and pelting rain. That cry was the sound of the Iroquois warwhoop. Fifteen hundred warriors had taken advantage of the first downpour to cross Lac St. Louis and now crowded around the houses of the village.

Pandimonium set in as the warriors began breaking down doors and slaughtering the men, women and children in their beds. It is said that some men turned their guns first on their wives and children to save them from the fate that awaited any taken alive. After the initial wave of slaughter the attackers began to round up prisoners to satisfy the stakes that had been raised in all the villages in Iroquois country.

Some managed to put up a defense; but soon all were overwhelmed. But what of the garrisons? Three

miles from Lachine a company of two hundred regulars fresh out from France were camped. Unfortunately the officer commanding, a Lieutenant Subercase, was in Montréal attending a reception for Denonville. The camp was aroused at four in the morning by the ominous roar of a cannon from one of the forts. This could mean only one thing, an Iroquois attack. A subordinate officer gave the order for the men to dress and prepare for action. To confirm his fears, out of the rain came a mud splattered survivor crying that the inhabitants of Lachine were being massacred. The young officer sent him on his way to raise the alarm in Montréal.

Very shortly thereafter more fugitives crashed into the camp hotly pursued by a band of warriors. On seeing the soldiers they turned and headed back to Lachine. In the meantime the first survivor reached Montréal over the ten kilometres of muddy roads.

Subercase immediately rushed back to his command to find his men still in camp along with the garrisons of the three forts and some settlers who had come to see what they could do. Why the soldiers had waited for their commander we will never know, but Subercase propelled his force to Lachine without delay. What greeted them there was a scene of unparalleled savagery. Not content to drag their prisoners away, they had set up stakes in the square and tortured men and women on the spot. The would be rescuers found only broken bodies and smoldering ruins. Miraculously the local surgeon had survived by hiding in the woods. He informed Subercase that the enemy had only gone about a mile and a half down the shore and had stopped in a grove of trees. Another piece of information was received with great satisfaction. Before firing the houses each was searched and a large quantity of brandy was consumed before the rampage was over.

Subercase realized that he must act at once while the warriors were in a drunken state. however, he was under no illusions that his task would be easy. The enemy was out in force and once aroused would give a good account of themselves. His troops were willing to take the risk to save the wretched captives.

At that moment the Chevalier de Vaudreuil arrived

The Lachine Massacre, August 4, 1689

from Montréal with orders from the governor. No unnecessary risks were to be taken. The force must remain on the defensive in order to protect those settlements not yet under attack.

Subercase begged and pleaded with Vaudreuil to be allowed to proceed with his attack. Denonville had no way of knowing that over one hundred men and women were in Iroquois hands and headed for a horrible death at the stake, he asserted; but Vaudreuil stood firm and the moment passed.

For two days the Iroquois roamed the countryside taking new captives and burning houses and barns while the troops stood behind the new palisades thrown up to protect Montréal. Finally they paddled their canoes up and down the river before the stockade showing off their captives and shouting in derision, "Onontio! Onontio!"

The scene now shifted to the south shore of the St. Lawrence where they set up stakes within sight of the soldiers and spent a wild night of torturing men, women and children.

It is said that the scenes of August 1689 plagued Denonville for the rest of his life. He was recalled to France where he became governor to the sons of the king. To replace him they sent the old war-horse Frontenac to attempt to salvage France's North American empire.

CHAPTER NINETEEN
Frontenac returns to Canada
"I send you back to Canada where I am sure that you will serve me as well as you did before."-Louis XIV

The situation in New France was desperate. In Europe William of Orange, an avowed enemy of France and of Roman Catholicism, had ascended the throne of England ushering in a new era of aggression in North America. Louis XIV, patron and benefactor of Canada, was growing tired of pouring money and resources into a enterprise that showed little sign of filling the royal coffers with gold. Denonville's correspondence grew ever gloomier as the years went by. A change was needed and the great king knew just what that change had to be.

Since his recall to France in 1682 Frontenac lived at court penniless and out of favour, because of the many feuds he was embroiled in. One incident that plagued him was in regard to the Governor of Montréal, François Perrot, and occurred just before his recall. Perrot was married to a niece of Jean Talon and came to Canada to improve his fortune. He did little to disguise his intent. Although he did not openly engage in the fur trade he did turn his seigneury, Ile Perrot, situated between Lac St. Louis and Lac des Deux Montagnes into a point of interception for canoes coming from the west. He placed an old comrade in arms, Antoine de Fresnay, Sieur de Brucey, in charge of his estate. Brucey gathered a motley crew of deserters from the colonial forces and with the assistance of a liberal supply of brandy managed to acquire a large portion of the furs destined for Montréal. A group of citizens petitioned Perrot to stop the illegal interception, but he refused placing Migeon de Branssat, their spokesman, under arrest holding him for several days. Needless to say Perrot's involvement soon became common knowledge.

Frontenac could not tolerate such blatant disregard for the law and proceeded in his usual manner to take care of the situation. He kept a close eye on the Montréal governor waiting for him to make a fatal mistake. The opportunity was not long in coming. Charles d'Ailleboust, the judge at Montréal, arrested two men on a charge of engaging in the fur trade without a permit. One of Perrot's officers, named Carion, helped them to escape. Frontenac sent an officer, Lieutenant Bizard, to Montréal to arrest Carion and bring him back to Quebec. He included a letter to Perrot explaining his action of invading his jurisdiction.

Bizard arrested Carion and gave the letter into the care of Jacques le Ber, a merchant, to give to Perrot after he had left with his prisoner. Madame Carion sent word to Perrot and he arrived at the house of le Ber in a towering rage. He immediately placed Bizard under arrest throwing Frontenac's letter in his face without opening it. Several days later he found out that le Ber had sent a message to Quebec and Perrot placed him under arrest as well. La Salle was in Montréal at the time and slipped out of his house at midnight and headed for Quebec to report to his mentor.

Frontenac's reaction was uncharacteristically cool. Although he most certainly was angry beyond belief, his response was measured and cunning. He drafted two letters. One was addressed to Perrot instructing him to release le Ber and inviting him to come to Quebec to discuss the situation and to resolve it to their mutual satisfaction. The second was to the Abbé de Salignac Fenelon, a Sulpician, intimating that he, Frontenac, wished to establish a better relationship with Perrot and settle any animosities that might exist between Montréal and Quebec.

The letters had their desired effect and Perrot in the company of Fenelon set out for Quebec and a reconciliation with the old count. It was in the middle of winter and the two traveled most of the distance on snowshoes, a long and difficult journey. On arrival Perrot made an official visit to the citadel where he was met by Lieutenant Bizard who demanded his sword placing him under arrest. Fenelon protested but Frontenac would not relent. The good Abbé walked back to Montréal and painted a bitter picture of the governor's conduct. Both Fenelon and Perrot were eventually sent to France to face the king. Although Frontenac won, this incident hung over him like a cloud.

Despite all this Frontenac still had friends in high places and his wife was constantly lobbying to help him regain the confidence of the king. So it was that in those dark days in Canadian history, the count, now seventy years old, found himself standing before his king, who began by informing Frontenac that he now believed the charges brought against him seven years

Lt. Bizard arrests Perrot on his arrival at Quebec

before were untrue. Then he looked him in the eye and said,

"I send you back to Canada where I am sure that you will serve me as well as you did before; and I ask nothing more of you."

Although Frontenac was delighted, it was a formidable task that lay before him. With the powers of Europe ranged against him, the Sun King could not send any additional troops to aid him. Alone and unsupported, Frontenac would have only his courage and his reputation to carry him through.

Frontenac made one request of his king, that the Iroquois prisoners in the galleys that were still alive should be freed and sent back to Canada with him. Thus thirteen warriors, all that remained of the hundred odd enslaved, were dressed in the finest French fashions, treated with great respect and sent off with the old count to the homes they had not seen in seven years.

Frontenac sailed from La Rochelle for Canada with two ships of the French Navy and an heroic plan to save the French Empire in North America, the invasion and capture of New York; a scheme that was still born in the autumn of 1689.

Frontenac arrived at Quebec to the news of the Lachine massacre. He immediately set out by boat for Montréal where he found a dejected Denonville among the ashes of defeat. Here Frontenac learned of an incident that made him furious. On the demands of the Iroquois Denonville destroyed Fort Frontenac leaving the upper St. Lawrence to the marauding bands of the Five Nations.

Despite his age Frontenac had not lost the fire that burned within him. He decided that the only way to regain lost ground and prestige was an offensive against the English colonies. The Iroquois and the English would soon know that "Onontio" was back.

CHAPTER TWENTY

The Schenectady Raid
"The gates stood open and only the two snowmen barred their way."

Frontenac moved with his old promptness and energy once he settled into the chateau at Quebec. Despite his advanced years Frontenac was everywhere at once, demanding men and gathering boats ignoring the autumn drizzle that chilled him to the bone.

New France took renewed hope that they would indeed survive the Iroquois onslaught. Among the hopefuls were the people of La Chesnaye, a small community some twenty miles down river from Montréal. At last things were moving, action was being taken. On the 13th of November the people were still excitedly talking about the governor who had passed by on his way to Montréal. Snow began to fall leaving a pastoral scene of tranquility and peace. That peace was suddenly shattered by the dreaded war cry of the Iroquois. Too Late the alarm was given and within a short time the houses were ablaze. Three days later Frontenac was told of the twenty butchered corpse left laying in the snow and the scores of prisoners, men women and children taken away to the stakes of the Iroquois towns.

The time for action had come and Frontenac revived the plan of attacking the English colonies, but with a far less ambitious goal than that of Louis XIV. Before he could put his plans into effect, however he needed to secure the western tribes who were in the process of making peace with the Iroquois. He knew that he would need their help in the raid into English territory. The prestige of the French was at an all time low with the Ottawas and their allies.

What was needed was a miracle. Of course fate provided Frontenac with one. He sent a large force to meet with the western tribes to show that the French were still able to mount a substantial army to face its enemies. While enroute they came upon an Iroquois hunting party, which they overwhelmed after a short fight. They came away with a number of scalps and one prisoner thus arriving at the rendezvous with a victory under their belts. This was not enough to sway the tribes alone, however, the prisoner was given to the Hurons and they were urged to put him in the kettle or lose him. The Ottawas angrily demanded that he be given to them. As a compromise they both tortured the prisoner who did not take his fate as stoi-

cally as he should have. It was decided that he did not deserve a warrior's death and a musket ball ended his ordeal. Of course now negotiations with the Iroquois became difficult to say the least. Frontenac was back in control.

Frontenac proposed a three pronged attack on the English colonies. One, leaving from Montréal, was to assault Albany. A second, departing Trois Rivières, had as its objective the settlements in New Hampshire, and the third expedition, originating at Quebec, was to raid into Maine.

The New York party left Montréal in February amid the most bitter cold in memory. The one hundred and sixty Canadians and one hundred and forty Indians were led by two of the Le Moyne brothers, Jacques de Ste. Hélène and Pierre d'Iberville, the latter being on the threshold of his role as one of the heroes of Canadian history. They moved across the frozen St. Lawrence on snowshoes taking turns pulling the Indian sledges loaded with supplies behind them. It took five days to reach Chambly and ascend the Richelieu. Here the Indians demanded to know where they were to attack. When told it was Albany, they were openly skeptical. "How long has it been," they asked, "since the French grew so bold?"

A warm spell brought a partial thaw and they were soon knee deep in slush. The weather changed again and the bitter cold returned. Eight days into the march they reached the Hudson River. A moment of decision had arrived; to the right lay Albany to the left Schenectady. The force of three hundred had been reduced to two hundred and fifty by the arduous journey. The Le Moynes realized that the Indians might desert at the critical point in the battle should stiff opposition be encountered. The less heavily defended Schenectady was chosen as the objective.

The French movements had not gone undetected and the mayor of Albany, Peter Schuyler, sent a warning to Jacob Leisler in Schenectady of the pending raid. Leisler, an enemy of Schuyler's, scoffed and the local merchants set snowman sentries facing Albany as a sign of their derision.

When the Le Moynes approached the ten foot high stockade in the early morning hours they could not be-

**On the march to
Schenectady,
February, 1690**

lieve their good fortune. The gates stood open and only the two snowmen barred their way. They entered the sleeping town and moved among the houses until the two brothers met at the far end. Only then did the cry of a single war whoop signal the massacre to begin. The guards were killed in their blockhouse and flames soon shot skyward from its loopholes. People ran half dressed into the street only to be cut down in those early moments of blood lust. It was a savage revenge for Lachine and La Chesnaye. Men, women and children slaughtered indiscriminately. Some children were thrown alive into the flames of their burning homes. Amid this savagery some signs of humanity shone through. Iberville, going to the home of Captain John Sander Glen, treated him with great courtesy and to the surprise of Glen spared himself and all his relatives. It seems that Glen had treated French prisoners of the Iroquois with kindness and had arranged to free some of them. Iberville even allowed him to visited the captives and point out any relatives that they might be freed as well. Strangely thirty Mohawks found in the town were spared and treated with great kindness.

When the raiders departed with their booty including fifty horses to pull the sledges the eighty odd homes of Schenectady were in flames and the four hundred inhabitants either dead or prisoners with the exception of Glen's family. Simon Schermerhorn, awakened by the first wild scream, managed to mount a horse and make his escape. He rode to Albany with the news that nineteen hundred Frenchmen and Indians had destroyed the town. Albany made ready for the onslaught they were sure would come their way. However, the Mohawks on whom they would have to depend were not so easily moved. How could a few Frenchmen reek such havoc? The English had assured the Five Nations of their invincibility; could their choice of an alliance been misguided? Frontenac's magic was already at work.

Finally some warriors reluctantly went in pursuit spurred on by fifty young men of Albany. Within sight of Montréal they caught up to a band of stragglers killing or capturing fifteen.

The other two expeditions were equally successful and the prestige of France was on the rise again under the leadership of Louis de Baude, Comte de Frontenac.

Frontenac hoped to achieve two things by the devastating raids on the English colonies. First and foremost he wished to reestablish his mystique among the Indians, both the western tribes as allies and the Iroquois who might think twice about relying on the English for protection. Secondly he hoped to discourage the English from adopting an aggressive policy toward Canada. The western tribes did renew their commitment to the French; however, the Iroquois, although initially disillusioned by the ease of the French victory maintained their uneasy alliance with the English. The colonies, far from counseling prudence, began to plan a combined attack on Canada.

The original idea for an assault on Canada came from the Iroquois. The colonists called a congress and delegates from New York and the New England governments embraced the plan to finally drive the French from North America.

The plan was to launch a two pronged attack. New York was to furnish four hundred men while Massachusetts, Connecticut and Plymouth were to provide three hundred and fifty-five jointly. The Iroquois agreed to bring the bulk of their warriors to the expedition. This force would rendezvous at Albany and march on Montréal. In the meantime the New England colonies would attack Quebec by sea, a formidable and costly task. Massachusetts had no money and were in the process of mounting a less ambitious project. In the winter of 1689-90 their commerce had suffered from French cruisers that found shelter at Port Royal on the Bay of Fundy. They were determined to end this threat before embarking on any other expeditions.

To command the attack they chose William Phips, a native of what is now Maine, but in those days it lay within the disputed land between the St. Croix and Kennebec Rivers claimed by Jean Vincent de l'Abadie, Baron de St. Castin as his domain. Indeed, St. Castin ruled the area like a kingdom, keeping the Abenaki constantly at war with the English settlers on the frontier. William Phips was born the twenty-first child in a poor family at Woolwich on the Kennebec. His father died when he was six and his mother remarried adding six more brothers and sisters to the brood.

He grew up in a cruel and savage world where French and English maintained a bloody existence of attacks and reprisals for over a century. He became in succession a shepherd, farm hand, woodsman and an apprentice in a shipbuilding yard. He arrived in Boston when he was thirty years old and married Mary Hull, the widow of a wealthy merchant. His salvaging of a Spanish wreck in the Bahamas to the tune of £300,000 earned him a knighthood and a £16,000 reward.

On the 28th of April 1690 he sailed from Nanasket with seven ships and five hundred militiamen arriving off Port Royal on the 11th of May. After landing his militia he called on the governor, Meneval, to surrender. Port Royal was garrisoned by only seventy soldiers and Meneval negotiated the terms. Phips agreed that the church would be unmolested, private property respected and the soldiers returned to Quebec. All having been agreed to, the Fleur-de Lys was lowered from the flag pole and Governor Meneval turned his own money over to Phips for safe keeping. At that moment one of Phips officers reported that some merchants had carried off some goods and hidden them in the woods. Although this was private property and thus protected by the agreement Phips considered it a serious breech of protocol and declared the terms void. The looting began. One of the invaders wrote,

"We cut down the cross, rifled their church, pulled down their high altar and broke their images."

Phips called the local inhabitants together and guaranteed them security to life, liberty, and property, on condition that they swear allegiance to King William and Queen Mary, which some did. Those that refused were plundered. Everything moveable, whether private or public, was packed in barrels and transported to the ships. The governor and fifty-nine soldiers were put on board to be taken to Boston.

Phips made no attempt to occupy Acadia although he did appoint a president and council from among those who had taken the oath, to administer the captured territory. The Acadians, long the subject of the ebb and flow of first French and then English domina-

The Fleur-de-Lys is lowered at Port Royal May 11, 1690

tion tried to walk that fine line that would insure their survival.

While he secured Port Royal he ordered Captain John Alden to raid all along the Fundy coast. He succeeded in destroying St. Castin's post on the Penobscot River and continued attacking all the settlements up to the head of the bay and along the east coast as far as Chedabucto.

Phips sailed triumphantly into Boston Harbour on the 13th of May with booty and prisoners in tow. His victory was somewhat tainted by his treatment of the Acadians who had surrendered to him in good faith. Governor Meneval complained to the Massachusetts council regarding his own possessions that he had entrusted to Phips. After repeated orders from the council Phips returned some of the money and the older cloths keeping the remainder for himself.

With this victory the American colonies began to plan the grand assault that would drive the French from America forever.

CHAPTER TWENTY-TWO

The Invasion of Canada
"A man like me is not summoned after this fashion. Let him do his best: I will do mine."-Frontenac to Phips' envoy

With William Phips successful capture of Port Royal the governing council of the Massachusetts Colony began formulating a much grander scheme; the conquest of Canada itself. Simon Bradstreet, the governor, appealed to London for supplies and ammunition for the expedition, noting that the crown would profit greatly from driving the French from Canada. The request was refused. Nonetheless plans went ahead and William Phips was chosen to command.

Humility was not one of the New Englanders' virtues and they entered the project with the notion that God would give them victory over the papists and idolators. A day of fast was proclaimed and as Cotton Mather, a New Englander, observed, "the wheel of prayer was kept in continual motion." The big problem was funding and when private subscription failed the colony stretched its already considerable debt further hoping that the booty from Canada would more than pay for the expedition.

Thirty-two trading vessels were pressed into service, the largest, "The Six Friends" was a forty-four gun West Indian trader. Volunteers were call for and many came forward, but others had to be called out to fill the ranks. With John Walley of Barnstable appoint second command all was ready.

The expedition put to sea on the 9th of August 1690 with twenty-two hundred men and supplies for four months, but with insufficient ammunition and no pilot for the St. Lawrence.

While this was going on the force charged with the capture of Montréal was mustering at Albany. Dysentery and small pox took a grim toll and there were fewer men to march than was planned. They marched to Lake Champlain accompanied by Mohawk, Oneida and Mohegan warriors. The Senecas, Onondagas and Cayugas were to join them at the head of the lake.

Meanwhile Frontenac was busy organizing Quebec for the assault he had no doubt was coming. Through the winter of 1689-90 he had gangs of men in the forest cutting trees to build a palisade. Quebec was naturally protected by cliffs, but was vulnerable from the rear. At the same time he looked to the safety of the outlying settlements by stationing French regulars in the many small forts scattered about the country. Patrols guarded against surprise and watched over the farmers in the fields.

In July Frontenac left Major Prevost in command and went to Montréal where he felt the greatest danger lay. On the 24th of July a messenger from Fort Lachine rushed into Montréal with the news that Lac St. Louis was "all covered with canoes." Nobody doubted that the Iroquois were upon them in earnest. The gun was fired calling the soldiers in from the outlying detachments. The reckoning, long dreaded, was upon them.

They waited behind the palisades that now seemed so flimsy against the might and ferocity of the Iroquois. One could almost touch the hysteria that lay just below the surface. A shout from the wall brought everyone to see what death looked like. A single rider charged for the gate. Could the Iroquois be far behind? The rider plunged through the gate calling for Frontenac. All waited for the news.

The gloom of the defenders suddenly turned to cries of joy and relief. It was not the Iroquois that swarmed Lac St. Louis, but warriors of the western tribes come to trade beaver pelts. The capture of Schenectady had had its desired affect and they came to Montréal as in the old days.

The following day they came down the rapids, all five hundred of them, Ottawas, Nipissings, Crees, Ojibwas, and Pottawatomies. Three days later La Durantaye arrived from Michilimackinac with fifty-five canoes loaded with French traders and furs. At the customary council held before trading began the Indian orators rose and talked of trade and war, when Frontenac did a curious thing. He suddenly snatched up a hatchet and began to sing a war song, dancing about in the fashion of an Indian warrior. Soon the Christian Iroquois joined him and then the others. War to the death was the cry that went up from the entire assembly.

Frontenac sent scouts into Iroquois country and soon word of the Albany march reached him. He moved troops to La Prairie and waited. The English, however, were squabbling among themselves. The Iroquois were cold and restless and the contingent from the Senecas, Cayugas and Onondagas stayed

The Iroquois in Council, 1690

away fearing smallpox. Winthrop, the commander, ordered the retreat back to Albany.

To salvage something from the venture Captain John Schuyler led a raid against La Prairie from which Frontenac had just withdrawn his troops. The twenty-nine whites and one hundred and twenty Indians fell upon the farmers in the fields killing many and taking a number of prisoners including women and children. After burning all the barns and houses he slaughtered the cattle and withdrew.

Frontenac caught the first hint of the seaborne invasion in early October. He sailed back to Quebec to face the expected threat from Phips. Phips, in the meantime, had taken a leisurely pace in his approach

to Quebec. Finally, on the 16th of October, he dropped anchor within sight of his goal.

At ten o'clock in the morning activity could be seen aboard the flagship, *Six Friends*. A boat bearing a flag of truce shove off only to be met half way by a canoe from Quebec and the young officer was forced to dawn a blindfold for the trip. It was not so much to stop him from seeing the defences as to hide the famine that was beginning to grip the city. Soldiers were marched to and fro to lend an air of a mighty army defending the city.

Then he stood in the great hall where his blindfold was removed. When his eyes had adjusted a most extraordinary scene unfolded. There stood Frontenac in all his splendour backed by the venerated figure of Bishop Laval, the intendant and those that would defend the city. There was Claude de Ramesay, not from France, but from the Highlands of Scotland. There were the Le Moyne brothers, Jacques Ste Hélène and Charles Longueuil as well as the Sieur de Subercase. Amidst such a company we can forgive the young officer for stumbling on his words as he presented Phips demand for a surrender. Frontenac was angry beyond measure and finished a long harangue with,

"A man like me is not summoned after this fashion. Let him do his best: I will do mine."

Walley immediately landed at the Beauport Shoals with thirteen hundred men and after wading through freezing water sometimes waist deep gained a foothold on the shore. The Canadians finally realized they were there and poured musket fire into their ranks. Despite the inexperience of the troops they charged and by nightfall had secured a position on the St.

Charles. The next morning Phips moved the "Six Friends" within pistol shot and opened fire on the town. The nuns at the Ursuline convent, being practical as well as spiritual, collected the cannonballs that fell in the convent courtyard and sent them up to the batteries to be returned to the British. The cannon fire from the citadel was so heavy that Phips was forced to cut the "Six Friends" cable so that it could drift out of range. Walley's attack bogged down as well. Phips suddenly discovered that he was down to powder for only two rounds per gun.

Phips saw the hopelessness of the situation and with smallpox raging in the ranks he ordered Walley to embark his troops. However, while Walley was seeing his commander a battle broke out in which both sides lost. For the English a final note that the siege was over; for the Canadians, the second Le Moyne brother, Jacques Ste. Helene, was wounded in the thigh. He died two weeks later. After a council of war Phips weighed anchor and sailed for home. Canada survived to fight another day.

CHAPTER TWENTY-THREE

Madeleine de Verchères: A Canadian legend is born

"'What are you doing with that match,' I asked? He answered, 'Light the powder and blow us all up.' 'You are a miserable coward,' said I, 'go out of this place.' I spoke so resolutely that he obeyed."-Madeleine de Verchères

When a humbled Phips sailed back to Boston he left a Canada on the verge of starvation. If he had arrived a week earlier or stayed a week longer Quebec would surely have fallen for lack of provisions. A long, bitter winter lay ahead. No war parties ventured forth to attack the English colonies; no food or blankets could be spared for such an expedition.

Spring came at last bringing a promise of new life and the Iroquois. They gathered from their winter hunting grounds at the mouth of the Ottawa and despatched war parties to disrupt the planting. A large band attacked Pointe aux Trembles, below Montréal, and burned thirty houses and killed those who could not escape. The farmers remained within their stockades while the fields lay untended. It was time for action.

Contempt for their enemies and the ability to raid into Canada with impunity made the Iroquois uncharacteristically careless. Forty warriors held up in a house near the fort at Repentigny and were spotted by Canadian scouts in the early evening. Some of the Iroquois were in the house with the remainder sleeping in the yard. The Canadians crept in on them killing all in the yard with a volley of musketry. Those inside began firing through the windows and loop holes killing seven men in the French party. Young François de Bienville, one of Charles le Moyne's sons rushed up to a window and yelled his name, firing into the house. He was shot dead. The house was set on fire and the desperate warriors rushed out to be met by a volley. Only one made it through the line. Some were shot, others knocked down and captured, and some rushed back into the flames to perish there. The prisoners were given to the inhabitants, who, in their fury, burned them alive.

The colony above Trois Rivières was in a constant state of siege with empty farm houses attesting to the power of the Iroquois. Sowing and reaping became a communal affair with neighbours banding together to work on one field under the watchful eye of a squad of regulars from the various garrisons. When a period of relative peace would descend on a district the people would begin to spend the nights at their farmsteads with sometimes disastrous results. The people of La

Chesnaye, burned out in 1689, returned to their homes in 1692. The Iroquois struck killing many and burning the settlement once again.

The year 1692 produced, for Canada, a heroine of enduring memory. Thirty-three kilometres down the St. Lawrence from Montréal, on the south shore, was the Verchères Seigneury. In October Verchères, who had been an officer in the Carignan Regiment, was on duty in Quebec City. His wife was in Montréal seeing to provisions for the winter. Their three children remained at home, a girl of fourteen named Madeleine and two sons twelve and ten. On the morning of October 22 the farmers were busy in the fields and the fort was manned by two soldiers, an eighty year old man and the two boys. Madeleine was at the landing place not far from the fort with a hired hand named Laviolette. There was the rattle of muskets from the direction of the fields and Laviolette yelled, "Run, Mademoiselle, run! here come the Iroquois." Fifty warriors swung into view about a pistol shot away. What happened next can best be told by Madeleine herself:

"I ran for the fort, commending myself to the Holy Virgin. The Iroquois who chased after me, seeing that they could not catch me alive before I reached the gate, stopped and fired at me. The bullets whistled about my ears, and made the time seem very long. As soon as I was near enough to be heard, I cried out, 'To arms! to arms!' hoping that somebody would come out and help me; but it was of no use. The two soldiers in the fort were so scared that they had hidden in the blockhouse. At the gate, I found two women crying for their husbands, who had just been killed. I made them go in, and then shut the gate. I next thought what I could do to save myself and the few people with me. I went to inspect the fort, and found that several palisades had fallen down, and left openings by which the enemy could easily get in. I ordered them to be set up again, and helped to carry them myself. When the breaches were stopped, I went to the blockhouse where the ammunition is kept, and here I

Madeleine Makes a dash for the stockade

found the two soldiers, one hiding in a corner, and the other with a lighted match in his hand. 'What are you going to do with that match?' I asked. He answered, 'Light the powder, and blow us all up.' 'You are a miserable coward,' said I, 'go out of this place.' I spoke so resolutely that he obeyed. . . . and after putting on a hat and taking a gun, I said to my two brothers: 'Let us fight to the death. We are fighting for our country and our religion. Remember that our father has taught you that gentlemen are born to shed their blood for the service of God and the King."

Madeleine ordered the little garrison to fire at the enemy from the various loopholes and the Iroquois, reluctant to attack a fortified place occupied themselves by running down and killing those still in the fields. A canoe suddenly rounded the bend and headed for the landing place. It was a farmer named Fontaine attempting to reach the fort with his family. Madeleine feared that they would be killed if something was not done. The two soldiers would not leave the fort, so leaving Laviolette to watch the gate, she boldly marched down to the landing place. She explained later,

"I thought that the savages would suppose it to be a ruse to draw them towards the fort, in order to make a sortie upon them. They did suppose so, and thus I was able to save the Fontaine family."

After sunset a violent storm with snow and hail

68

blew in and Madeleine feared that the Iroquois might slip in under cover of darkness. She ordered Fontaine and the two soldiers to the blockhouse with the women and children. She told them to never surrender even if she were taken and burned before their very eyes. She placed herself, her two brothers and the eighty year old each on one of the four bastions. All night in the wind and snow the cries from the fort to the blockhouse and back was "all's well" was heard by the Iroquois mustered in the woods. It must have sounded like the fort was full of soldiers.

For a week they held out, this desperate little band. Late one night noise was heard by the river and Madeleine described it this way,

"The sentinel told me that he heard a voice from the river. I went up at once to the bastion to see whether it was Indians or Frenchmen. I asked, 'Who are you?' One of them answered, 'We are Frenchmen: it is La Monnerie, who comes to bring you help.' I caused the Gate to be opened, placed a sentinel there, and went down to the river to meet them."

The ordeal was over. A band of Indian allies followed the retreating Iroquois catching up to them on Lake Champlain recovering some twenty French prisoners. The legend of Marie-Madeleine Jarret de Verchères was born.

CHAPTER TWENTY-FOUR
Iberville and the Battle for Hudson Bay
"They carried no tents; only a blanket per man strapped to his back was allowed.
The only provisions were those that could be carried in the blanket."

Despite the constant threat to the settlements along the St. Lawrence, Denonville, with the blessings of the King, looked north to Hudson Bay. The drain of beaver pelts through the bay seriously impacted the viability of Canada. In 1686 Denonville ordered Pierre le Moyne d'Iberville to prepare an expedition to raid the English forts on the Bay.

In March 1686 Iberville, along with his brother Ste. Helene, set out with one hundred men on a march that most would have avoided even in summer. Iberville's goal was to be in place to float down river with the spring thaw to Moose Factory some six hundred and fifty kilometres north. They carried no tents; only a blanket per man strapped to his back was allowed. The only provisions were those that could be carried in the blanket. They followed the frozen Ottawa River passed the Rideau River and the Chaudière Falls; passed the Mattawa River, which led off to the French River route to Michilimackinac. By May they reached Lake Abitibi where a stockade was built and three men left to guard it. Here too they paused to build canoes to take them on their final run to the bay.

If the march had been difficult, the ride down the unknown river was terrifying. Long stretches of rapids smashed canoes against shelves of ice. Downed trees laying across the water would suddenly come into view causing many a near miss. Iberville's canoe was upset sweeping two voyageurs to their deaths. Two others were saved by Iberville himself. Finally they reached James Bay and prepared to complete their mission. Their first target was Moose Factory.

Iberville and his brother boldly walked out in the twilight that served as the Arctic night on the 18th of June. Moose Factory was defended by fourteen cannon in four stone bastions. In the court yard stood the storehouse and residence of the chief factor. The sentry had bolted the main gate and wrapped himself in his blanket to sleep beside the cannon he was meant to guard. Satisfied the two returned to the woods and Iberville gathered his troops to allocate their place in the battle to come. Iberville did not need to tell them that the choice was succeed or die. They had no provisions for the return trip to Montréal and as an added incentive he remained them of the large cache of furs

stored in the fort. The Frenchmen formed up before the gate and the Indians took either flank to fire through the loopholes into the sleeping fort.

Iberville and his brother leaped over the rear palisade, crossed the court yard and dispatched the sentry. With a yell the rest the party fell on the fort. The only other death was a Canadian killed in the cross fire of his own men. Buildings were searched, but little loot was found. Still they had sixteen prisoners and twelve portable cannon to show for their efforts.

There were two other English posts within reach on the bay. One at Rupert River and another at Fort Albany. Iberville chose Rupert as the next target, although the richer stash of furs were at Albany. On the 27th of June they set out by sea. By the 1st of July the bastions of the fort were in sight through the trees. The Hudson Bay Company schooner was in the anchorage with the company flag at the fore indicating that Governor Bridgar was aboard. The ship and governor were quickly captured and Iberville turned his attentions to the fort from which a brisk fire now came forth. The bastions doubled as the barracks for the garrison and Iberville, improvising a ladder, made it to the roof where he broke through the thatch and threw hand grenades down driving the defenders into the main house. The fort quickly fell.

The last objective and the richest was Fort Albany. Forewarned, the English were ready when Iberville's party arrived. Iberville dragged his cannon ashore and waited. The old governor, Sargeant, refused to surrender although he was low on powder and food. After two days of exchanging bullets and shot the fort surrendered.

Rescue parties arrived from Nelson in two ships, the "Hampshire" and the "North-West Fox", but they became trapped in ice. When the crews came ashore to challenge Iberville he simply went out and captured one of the ships, the English burned the other. When the ice cleared Iberville sailed for Quebec with a rich cargo of furs.

In 1693 the English recaptured Fort Albany and the battle for the bay continued with Iberville capturing Nelson in 1694. In 1696 the English were once more supreme in the bay. This was no longer a guerrilla

Iberville pauses at the mouth of the Mattawa River

war between fur traders in the wilderness. This was a battle for supremacy of a continent.

In July of 1697 Iberville sailed from Newfoundland with five warships entering Hudson Strait on the 25th. Iberville commanded the "Pelican" with his brother Bienville on board; his brother Serigny commanded "Le Palmier". Sailing into the straits the ships became trapped in ice and fog. For a month the "Pelican" was lifted and crushed between the ice floes. Finally on the 25th of August the fog lifted and open water appeared. "Le Palmier" had been driven back and of two others there was no sign, but "Le Profound" was in front of him still trapped in ice. Iberville could not believe his eyes. Closing in on "Le Profound" were three English ships, the "Hampshire", the "Dering", and the "Hudson's Bay". Iberville did not wait to ascertain "Le Profound's" fate, he sailed for Nelson to await the rest of his scattered force.

On the 3rd of September three masts appeared over the horizon and Iberville sailed out to greet his reinforcements. Signal flags flew a greeting but there was no reply. Horrified, Iberville realized his mistake. This was the "Hampshire", "Dering" and "Hudson's Bay" come to challenge him. Between them they mounted 112 guns with 175 men. "Pelican" carried fifty guns and 150 men. Outgunned and outmanned Iberville did the only thing the le Moynes knew how to do; he sailed to meet the challenge. Iberville set

course for the flagship, "Hampshire", whose first cannonade stripped the "Pelican of her masts. The other two closed in. For four hours the three cornered battle raged. The English attempted time and again to close with the "Pelican" to board her but the Canadians fought them off. The guns of the "Pelican" poured a continuous barrage of shot at her enemies. Finally they closed the range. they rushed to one side of their respective ships for that mad leap into hand to hand combat, no quarter asked and none given. A sudden shout and all went silent except for the cried of the wounded and dying. The guns of the "Hampshire" had fallen silent. She refused to answer the wheel and as all looked on, still in full sail, she settled and sank like a stone with all hands.

Iberville next turned his attention to the "Hudson's Bay" which quickly struck her colours. The "Dering" made a dash for shelter at Fort Nelson.

In the fury of the fight no one noticed the approaching storm. It struck battering the mortally wounded "Pelican" with pan ice and heavy seas. The wounded were towed ashore tied to the fallen spars. Many never made it. The next day Iberville's fleet arrived and Fort Nelson surrendered.

With the onset of winter only Fort Albany remained in English hands. The legend of the le Moynes grew with each passing exploit.

CHAPTER TWENTY-FIVE

Frontenac: Old Warrior to the End

"If suitable deputation should be sent to Quebec I still would listen, but if they came back with more such proposals as they have just made, they should be roasted alive."-Frontenac to the Iroquois, 1696

With the success of Iberville in Hudson Bay came renewed prosperity and prestige to the French. Frontenac turned again to the thorny problem of the Iroquois. The Iroquois themselves were in a sad state of affairs. With no furs to trade, they were short of European goods, powder and ball. There constant war with the Canadians had cost them their best warriors and, although they encouraged them to raid the St. Lawrence Valley, the English did little to help them. In the meantime the arrive of French regulars at Quebec greatly discouraged the council.

Frontenac was in the process of planning a raid that would humble the Five Nations once and for all when one of their chiefs, Tareha, arrived at Quebec with peace overtures. Frontenac received Tareha with kindness saying,

"my Iroquois children have been drunk; but I will give them an opportunity to repent. Let each of your five nations send me two deputies, and I will listen to what they have to say."

Tareha took back the offer to Onondaga.

In typical Iroquois fashion the council refused, instead inviting Frontenac to a council at Albany to meet with them and their friends the English. Of course he hotly rejected such a proposal. Another delegation was sent, partly to Quebec and partly to the Christian Iroquois in the vicinity of Montréal to come to a council at Onondaga. Frontenac, adopting the Indian style of negotiation, kicked away their wampum belts, scolded them for tampering with the Christian Indians and calling them rebels, accused them of being bribed by the English. He added,

"if a suitable deputation should be sent to Quebec to treat squarely of peace, I still would listen, but if they came back with any more such proposals as they had just made, they should be roasted alive."

In a few weeks the delegation appeared, two chiefs from each nation headed by their best orator, Decanisora. The council was held in the great hall at Quebec with all the dignitaries in their regal splendour. Priests, officers and Christian Indians faced a rather bedraggled group of Iroquois. Only Decanisora was decked out for the occasion, a scarlet coat laced with gold given him by the governor of New York. He stood proudly before Frontenac. One French observer noted that he was "tall and well formed with a face not unlike the busts of Cicero."

He spoke,

"let us bury the hatchet, cover the blood that has been spilled, open the roads, and clear the clouds from the sun."

He offered peace, but he demanded that the English be included. Frontenac replied,

"My children are right to come submissive and repentant. I am ready to forgive the past, and hang up the hatchet; but peace must include all my other children, far and near. Shut your ears to English poison. The war with the English has nothing to do with you, and only the great kings across the sea have power to stop it. You must give up all your prisoners, both French and Indian, without one exception. I will then return mine, and make peace with you, but not before."

After an elaborate feast the delegates departed promising to return with their prisoners before the end of the season. Two delegates remained at Quebec as hostages.

Meanwhile the English tried to prevent the Five Nations from making peace. A council was called at Albany where Fletcher, the governor, told them that they should not hold council with the French except at Albany in the presence of the English. The Iroquois asserted their rights as an independent nation and their speaker told Fletcher,

"Corlaer (Iroquois name for the governor of New York) has held councils with our enemies, and why should we not hold councils with his?

The death of Frontenac November 28, 1698

Besides, we cannot fight the French alone; you leave us to bear all the burden of the war."

Fletcher was in no position to help so he reluctantly consented to the Iroquois peace.

The Iroquois wanted peace, but not a lasting peace. They wanted a little breathing space to gather their strength for the next war. There were those among the tribes, especially the Mohawks, Onondagas and the Oneidas, who wished to spurn the French proposals and they refused to give up their prisoners. The Cayugas and Senecas agreed to a partial compliance and buried the hatchet at Montréal assuring Frontenac that the others would soon follow. The old governor was not deceived. He would accept nothing but the complete fulfillment of his conditions and refused the peace offering. He told his Indian allies to wage war "to the knife" and ordered a dog feast and war dance. The battles began again.

Frontenac made war on the Iroquois Confederacy and held sway over the vacillating western tribes. In 1696 he led an expedition against Onondaga, but the town was a smoking ruin when they arrived. Two murdered French prisoners were all that remained. Like Denonville's, this raid was a failure, however, it had its desired effect and several chiefs went to Quebec to sue for peace, but only with the French. Fron-

tenac held out for the inclusion of the western tribes and negotiations broke down. In the meantime peace in Europe brought the official war between the colonies to and end, but wrangling continued over the status of the Iroquois, the English insisting that they were British subjects and Frontenac countering that they were rebellious children of France. Of course the Iroquois equally asserted their independence. North America was on the brink of its own war. Frontenac postured and rattled his sabre; the English did likewise.

With all this the the old governor, tired and worn out from years of turmoil, was nearing the end. In November, 1698, after the last ship had slipped down the St. Lawrence, sealing Canada from the world for six months, the fatal illness struck the dauntless warrior. On the 22nd he dictated his will seated in an easy-chair in his room at the chateau. Champigny, the intendant, with whom he fought continually, visited him often giving what comfort he could. In the end a complete reconciliation was made between them. Father Oliver Goyer, a Recollet, administered the last rites and on the afternoon of November 28, 1698 the man who arguably was Canada's greatest champion died. He was buried, not in the cathedral, but in the simple church of the Recollets as was his request. He was in his 78th year.

CHAPTER TWENTY-SIX
Peace renewed with the Iroquois
"We assure you by these four belts of wampum that we will stand fast in our obedience."-Iroquois August 4, 1701

With the death of Frontenac, Bonnevue Callières assumed the role of interim governor, a position to which he was confirmed by the king in due course. Although well suited to the job he was no Frontenac and the Iroquois tested the metal of this new Onontio early and often. The English tried to keep the Five Nations in a state of war with Canada telling them that their best warriors were being poisoned by the French. The French in turn pointed out that the English refused to sell them powder and shot and planned to destroy them when they were helpless. The English also tried to assert their authority over the Iroquois. When Bellomont, the New York governor, required them to turn their French prisoners over to him, they replied,

"We are the masters; our prisoners are our own. We will keep them or give them to the French, if we choose."

The treaty of Ryswick gave the Iroquois further pause for reflection. One of the clauses stated that the English and French colonies would combined if necessary to keep the Iroquois in line. Peace was the only solution for them, however, they planned to drive as hard a bargain as they could and test the new governor at the same time. Six delegates arrived at Quebec with no prisoners and singing songs of lamentation for the French killed in the wars. They asked Callières to send a delegation to Onondaga to pick up the French prisoners to which he readily agreed. Frontenac would have never sent a delegation to the Five Nations. The Iroquois had won a small victory. Fr. Bruyas, a Jesuit, Paul la Moyne, Sieur de Maricourt, and Chabert Joncaire were sent to retrieve the prisoners. Joncaire had an interesting history with the Iroquois. He had been captured in a raid along with a number of others. His companions were all tortured and burned to death and he was scheduled to meet the same fate. One old chief decided, as a prelude to the stake, to burn one of his fingers in the bowl of his pipe. Joncaire knocked the chief over rather than submit. Impressed with his courage, the warriors adopted him into the tribe giving him an Iroquois wife. He lived among them for many years.

On their arrival at Onondaga an unforeseen problem arose. Many of the prisoners, especially those who had lived among them for a long period of time, refused to be repatriated having families within the tribe. Many hid themselves in the woods to avoid the would-be rescuers. In the end a ragged bunch of thirteen, most recently captured, many suffering from the ill treatment, straggled into Montréal to be greeted by their love ones who had lost all hope of seeing them again. With them came nineteen Iroquois to conclude the long sought after peace accord.

Callières and representatives of the Indian allies sat in council with the Five Nations delegates. Callières addressed the gathering,

"I bury the hatchet in a deep hole, and over the hole I place a great rock, and over the rock I turn a river, that the hatchet may never be dug up again."

The famous Huron chief, Kondiaronk or the Rat exchanged sharp words with his old enemies, but in the end he, along with the Ottawas and Abenakis present laid their hatchets at the feet of Callières and the peace was signed. The following August was set for ratification with all the tribes from as far away as the Lake Superior present to exchange prisoners as promised.

With the prospects of peace came the thorny problem of convincing those not at the council to bring in their Iroquois captives. The Jesuit, Fr. Engelran was sent to Michilimackinac where he was successful in persuading the Illinois and their allies to come to Montréal. Lieutenant Courtemanche made the long and difficult journey among the western tribes where, due to his great influence, he was equally successful.

In early July a huge flotilla of canoes, led by Courtemanche, filled with chiefs, warriors and Iroquois prisoners came paddling down the lakes to Montréal. Meanwhile a contingent led by Joncaire was trying to arrange for the release of the prisoners held by the Five Nations with little success. Whether French or Indian, the Iroquois insisted that they had been adopted into families and they were reluctant to give

Prisoners of the Iroquois return to Quebec

them up without gifts of compensation. Joncaire at least was able to bring a large delegation of chiefs to Montréal for the council. No sooner had they arrived than Courtemanche and his flotilla came streaming in. Guns fired in salute and a great feast held in preparation for the grand council.

Before the council could begin many questions had to be settled, old jealousies soothed, and grievances addressed. The foremost orator among the western tribes, Kondiaronk, the Rat, spoke for them. Addressing Callières he said,

"My father, you told us last autumn to bring you all the Iroquois prisoners in our hands. We· have obeyed, and brought them. Now let us see if the Iroquois have also obeyed, and brought you our people whom they captured during the war. If they have done so, they are sincere; if not, they are false. But I know they have not brought them. I told you last year that it was better that they should bring their prisoners first. You will see how it is, and how they have deceived us."

The Iroquois were asked to explain themselves and they haughtily promised to return them soon, but of-

fered no hostages to show good faith. The Rat, who was instrumental in persuading the other tribes to bring in their prisoners was mortified. He came to the last meeting ill with fever and so weakened that he was carried in on an armchair. He harangued the gathering for two hours interrupted only by exclamations of approval from his followers. At the end of it he was exhausted and at midnight he died. The French arranged his funeral and even his enemies, the Iroquois, paid their respects to a gallant foe. This tribute soothed the anger of the western tribes and at a great council on the 4th of August, 1701 the Iroquois prisoners were handed over. When all was done the spokesman for the Five Nations rose and said,

"Onontio, we are pleased with all you have done, and we have listened to all you have said. We assure you by these four belts of wampum that we will stand fast in our obedience. As for the prisoners whom we have not brought you, we place them at your disposal, and you will send and fetch them."

Thus the long struggle of Frontenac's to bring peace to Canada was realized. The Iroquois never again became the formidable threat they once were.

CHAPTER TWENTY-SEVEN

The Struggle to subdue a Continent

"The key to stability in the west was the exclusion of the English traders and the Iroquois raiding parties."-Cadillac

While the issue of the Iroquois peace was being played out at Montréal, Albany and Onondaga, the business of intrigue and trading went on in the east in Newfoundland with the fisheries and with the fur trade in the west. Newfoundland was occupied by both France and Britain. The English held the east coast with strong points at St. Johns and Bonavista with the French holding sway at Placentia Bay on the west coast. The French were determined to drive the English from the Island and mounted a number of attempts to capture St. Johns, but only managed to destroy the unprotected fishing villages that dotted the coast. One successful raid took place at Bonavista Bay where Jean Leger de la Grange sailed into the bay and attacked the shipping anchored there. He captured or destroyed a number of English vessels that were landing their catches for drying. The people of Newfoundland were in a constant state of alarm as these intermittent raids usually resulted in destitution for them.

At Michilimackinac the constant wavering of the tribes kept the Canadian traders on edge. With each victory or defeat the pendulum swung from loyalty to the French to peace with the Iroquois and by extension the English. Michilimackinac was an important post for the French and Frontenac had always sent his best man there as commandant. In 1694 he appointed Antoine de la Mothe-Cadillac to the post. The post was nominally under the control of the Jesuits, but, because of the concentration of Coureurs de Bois, it had fallen into a true den of iniquity. Brandy and Indian women were plentiful much to the despair of the missionaries. Like Frontenac, Cadillac had no love for the Jesuits and that fact kept tensions high, the brandy trade being the most thorny problem.

It became apparent to Cadillac that the key to stability in the west was the exclusion of the English traders and the Iroquois raiding parties. The lock into which the key would best fit was at the strait that separated Lake Erie from Lake Huron. If the French controlled it the English and the Five Nations would be effectively barred from the trade. If the English seized it the French trade would be ruined. The French had occupied the site briefly under Denonville when Greysolon du Lhut built a small stockade there in 1686. Cadillac was determined to establish a post there as soon as possible. Of course, opposition was heavy. The merchants of Montréal considered any new up-country posts as a challenge to their dominance of the trade. Other posts would see trade diverted from them especially at Michilimackinac.

In 1699 he laid his plans before the Comte de Maurepas. He proposed to gather all the tribes at Détroit, civilize them and teach them French,

"insomuch that from pagans they would become children of the Church, and therefore good subjects of the King." He continued, "They will form a considerable settlement strong enough to bring the English and Iroquois to reason, or, with help from Montréal, to destroy them both."

He insisted that Détroit should be the chief post thus regulating the trade and preventing the glut of beaver pelts, which brought down prices, spoiling the market.

As expected, opposition was rampant. At a meeting at Quebec in 1699 Cadillac pitched his plan to the governor, Callières, the intendant, Champigny and the leading citizens of Quebec. The fur trade was hotly debated. The intendant finally opposed the project on the grounds that to teach the Indians French would only corrupt them further. Like the Jesuits, he preferred that the Indians remain away from the settlements and kept to their own ways. The "so called" civilization of the Indians invariably led to the worst of European vices taking root in their society.

Cadillac, dissatisfied with the outcome sailed for France to make his case before the king's ministers. He had an interview with the colonial secretary, Ponchartrain and the chief clerk of the Department of Marine and Colonies, La Touche. He gave them the military and political motives for such a move promising that the plan would insure the safety of Canada and prove the ruin of the English colonies. To accomplish this he asked for fifty soldiers and fifty Canadians to begin the work, to be followed the next year by thirty families and two hundred tradesmen. He also re-

The Battle of Bonavista Bay

quested priests from several different communities and nuns to teach the Indian girls and care for the sick. He ended his pitch by saying,

"I cannot tell you the efforts my enemies have made to deprive me of the honour of executing my project; but so soon as M. de Ponchartrain decides in its favour, the whole country will applaud it."

Ponchartrain accepted the plan and, armed with his commission, he returned to Quebec to begin to put the scheme in motion. In early June, 1701 he left Lachine with a hundred men in twenty-five canoes loaded with supplies. With him went Alphonse de Tonty, brother of Henri, the companion of La Salle, and by two half pay lieutenants, Dugue and Chacornacle, together with a Jesuit and a Recollet priest. They reached their destination by following the Ottawa-French River route to Lake Huron arriving at Détroit on July 24th. They immediately built a stockade fifty-five metres square, which he named Fort Ponchartrain. The seed of a great city was planted. While Cadillac establish the post at Détroit other changes in the way the colony did business began to emerge. The fur trade was put into the hands of a company that all Canadians could buy shares in, but, the risks were great and only one hundred and fifty shareholders could be mustered. Everyone else was shut out of the trade to the ruin of many. All trade in furs was restricted to Détroit and Fort Frontenac, both of which were granted to the company. The Indians slowly abandoned Michilimackinac for Détroit and a new era in Canadian history began.

CHAPTER TWENTY-EIGHT

The Deerfield Raid
"In the autumn of 1703 Vaudreuil planned a raid that would be the first overt military operation of the war."

The Treaty of Ryswick had the potential to bring a lasting peace to Europe and by extension to North America, although It was not to the French king's liking. He was forced to recognize William III as the rightful king of England and Anne, a protestant, over the son of James II as his successor. However, wars had all but bankrupted the European powers and as the tutor to the children of Louis XIV had pointed out, "The country is a vast hospital." Neither William of England or Louis had any stomach for another war any time soon. Events, however, conspired against the peace. Charles II of Spain was ill and without an heir. The Spanish Empire had fallen into a mere shell of its former glory. Louis saw an opportunity to control Spain and its vast colonial holdings by engineering the naming of Philip, the young Duc d'Anjou, as Charles' heir to the throne of Spain.

At first nothing happened and it appeared that Louis had pulled off the coup, however, he made a fatal error in judgment. When James, the deposed King of England, died in exile, Louis, in a grand gesture, recognized James' son, the Chevalier de St. George, as James III, King of England. This only served to unite a divided England and the War of the Spanish Succession was on. William III was killed in a fall from his horse and Anne became Queen. In North America the war was known as Queen Anne's War.

In Canada, Governor Callières was dead, replaced by Philippe de Rigaud, Marquis de Vaudreuil. Vaudreuil was no Frontenac nor was he like Callières, but he was a man of action. While the peace lasted he contented himself with keeping the Abenaki stirred up against the English colonies. The Abenaki needed little encouragement as the northern push of the English, with their fences and hostile actions, gave them cause for grievance. With the opening of Queen Anne's War the battles along the frontier heated up once again.

Vaudreuil directed his efforts on the settlements in Maine. To attack New York might upset the delicate peace with the Iroquois. Bands of Abenaki, accompanied by a few French Canadians began raiding the small isolated communities near the border with Acadia. August 10, 1703 saw the village of Wells pillaged with the death of thirty-nine, mostly women and children. In quick succession Purpooduck Point, Casco, Spurwink and Scarborough suffered in their turn. It is estimated that one hundred and sixty men, women and children died and countless others were dragged off into captivity in that period.

As the year 1704 opened Vaudreuil made a policy change that was to spell the beginning of the end of the French presence in North America. Although it encouraged and participated in the border raids of 1703, officially the government in Canada could put it off to some hot heads on the frontier or to the Indians acting alone. In the autumn of 1703 Vaudreuil planned a raid that would be the first overt military operation undertaken by the French in the war. The Target: Deerfield, a small village on the northwest frontier of the colony of Massachusetts.

To lead this expedition he chose Hertel de Rouville, the son of François Hertel, who had led the successful raid on Salmon River some years before. Rouville took with him his four brothers and fifty Canadians with two hundred Indians, Abenakis from the Maritimes and Mohawks from Caughnawaga. They began their trek in the dead of winter from Montréal and traveled 300 miles through one of the bitterest winters on record. Snowshoes were needed most of the way and the heavy sledges had to be hauled over and through the snow drifts. They arrived on the outskirts of their objective late on the afternoon of February 28th. Rouville halted his column on Petty's Plain, three kilometres from Deerfield. He deemed it too late to attack that day so the cold, hungry column settled into the woods to face a bitter night of waiting. No fires were lit for fear of giving the alarm.

Deerfield stood above the river and most of the forty-one houses were along the road to Hatfield a few kilometres further on. There was a small garrison of twenty soldiers with a small palisade enclosing the houses of some of the prominent citizens of the village. The people of Deerfield had been lulled into a false sense of security because of their distance from the border and the years of relative peace in the area. On the night of February 28th the soldiers, who should have been on watch, went to sleep with the rest of the

Preparing to attack Deerfield, February 28, 1704

village rather than stare out at the winter emptiness that greeted them each night. The seeds of a great tragedy were sown.

Two hours before sunrise Rouville roused his men and they moved toward the village. From the edge of the woods they watched for any sign of vigilance and at a signal from their captain they moved across the meadow toward the unsuspecting citizens of Deerfield. The crust of the snow was strong enough to hold their weight so the attackers abandoned their snowshoes. The snow had drifted against the northwest wall to the height of the palisade and the raiders easily jumped over and were among the houses without raising the alarm. The first the inhabitants knew of their presence was the hammering of the axes against their doors.

The village minister was wakened by the crashing in of his door and he snatched a pistol, which misfired in the face of a Caughnawaga chief. He was taken prisoner, but two of his children were killed. The house of Benoni Stebbins was fortified and he was able to mount a defence before his door was attacked. The battle raged around this house, but the raiders could not take it. Others were not so lucky. The wife of John Shelden was killed by a bullet as she sat on the edge of her bed. The stout defence of the Stebbins house probably saved the houses on the south side, one being the fortified house of Militia Captain Jonathan Wells.

The raiders quickly gathered up their prisoners and began the long retreat. The prisoners numbered one hundred and eleven and they left forty-seven bodies in the ruins of Deerfield. On the long trek any that could not keep up were tomahawked, an act of kindness considering the slow death by cold and starvation that was the alterative. It took eight weeks for the party to reach Montréal.

The Deerfield Raid marked a new era in the warfare that raged along the frontier.

The Deerfield Raid and a number of smaller incursions the following summer finally galvanized the New England colonies into action. Joseph Dudley, Governor of Massachusetts, urged the capture of Quebec in 1704 saying,

"In the last two years the Assembly of Massachusetts has spent about £50,000 in defending the province, whereas three or four of the Queen's ships and fifteen hundred New England men would rid us of the French and make further outlay needless."

An attempt was made to negotiate a truce, but the two sides could not agree on terms.

The Province of Acadia, which covered all of present day Nova Scotia and New Brunswick as well as parts of northern Maine, was a government separate from Canada, but subordinate to it. When Jacques François de Brouillan landed at Chibucto, the present site of Halifax, in 1702 to take command, he wrote to the King's minister,

"It seems to me that these people live like true republicans, acknowledging neither royal authority nor courts of law."

When he reached Port Royal he found it in a bad state of disrepair and the settlement in a poor way. New England privateers kept their fishing boats from the sea and all attempts to drive them off failed. The New Englanders swung between plundering the Acadians and carrying on an illicit trade with them.

When war broke out the only strong point in Acadia was Port Royal. The fort was a sodded earthwork, which had been brought into a tolerable state of repair by the efforts of the garrison and the local inhabitants. The garrison was small, consisting of eight officers and one hundred and eighty-five men.

Brouillan died in the autumn of 1705 and the new governor was the same Subercase who had vainly tried to rescue the victims of the Lachine Massacre. He complained to the King's minister that two of the garrison officers had lost their wits, a third was lazy and a fourth eccentric in the extreme. He wrote,

"You see, Monseigneur, that I am as much in need of a mad house as of barracks; and what is worse, I am afraid that the "mauvais esprit" of this country will drive me crazy too."

The eyes of New England fell on Port Royal. In June, 1707 an expedition, consisting of the British frigate "Deptford," a provincial galley and several impressed vessels with 1,000 soldiers, all colonial volunteers, set sail for Port Royal under the command of Colonel John March. All the officers were inexperienced colonials except the British engineer Rednap.

The ships sailed into Annapolis Basin and landed three hundred and fifty men on the north shore, three kilometres below the fort. As they marched up to the mouth of the Annapolis River they were ambushed by a small party of Acadians who quickly withdrew to the fort. Colonel March, in the meantime, landed seven hundred and fifty men on the south shore and marched on the Allen River, crossing it in battle array. Subercase ambushed them with two hundred Acadians as they waded the stream and then he also withdrew to the fort. March advanced his men to within cannon shot of the fort on the hill known as the Lion's Rampart and entrenched his force for the siege.

Soon confusion reigned in the New England camp. The officers quarreled and Rednap refused to soil his reputation on such a motley expedition. The ships' captains backed Rednap in his refusal to bring up the cannon and the expedition decamped and set sail for home. They were intercepted by emissaries of Dudley and turned back. They found Port Royal reinforced, but they landed fighting a sharp skirmish with the crew of a French privateer of Martinique, part of the reinforcements. For seven days they fought small engagements until, ill and discouraged, they set sail for Boston. March was taunted by the children in the streets of Boston, "wooden sword, wooden sword."

A grand scheme was hatched in 1709 by Captain Samuel Vetch, a Scot, to drive the French from North America. It was the Phips' plan resurrected, but better

planned and with better leadership.

Colonel Francis Nicholson moved up the Lake Champlain route to Wood Creek where he was to await word of the naval attack on Quebec before moving on Montréal. Vaudreuil sent Ramesay to destroy Nicholson's force, but he got lost in the forest. The British were forewarned and Ramesay withdrew to Chambly.

Nicholson waited in vain for the signal of a British fleet that was not coming. They had been diverted to the West Indies. He disbanded his army and returned to Albany.

In the meantime the New Englanders were determined to salvage something from this, another plan misfired. They sailed to England and won approval for another attempt on Port Royal. On September 24, 1710 the expedition sailed into Annapolis Basin where one of the ships, caught on the rushing tide, went on the rocks drowning twenty-six men. An ominous beginning, however, the rest made it in safely and the next day the troops began to land. Four hundred British Marines and fifteen hundred colonials divided into four battalions landed to face Subercase's two hundred defenders. Half the colonials were commanded by the competent Colonel Nicholson of New York and the other by Captain Vetch. Subercase could not expect a repeat of the 1707 fiasco and the result was never in doubt. He put up such a stubborn fight, however, that no attempt was made to storm the fort. Finally, on October 2, 1710, the Fleur de Lys came down from the flagstaff at Port Royal for the last time and the Red Ensign flew in its place. Subercase and his troops was allowed to march out with all the honours of war and were returned to France in British ships.

Samuel Vetch was made governor of Acadia changing the name of Port Royal to Annapolis Royal and, in honour of his beloved homeland, renamed the province Nova Scotia.

81

With the fall of Acadia the survival of New France was put in serious doubt. England had at last offered real military aid to its colonies to conquer Canada. The French commandant at Placentia in Newfoundland, Costebelle, had received intelligence from two Irish deserters from the English station at St. Johns about the imperial and provincial preparations for the campaign. At the same time the French court was planning to attack Boston by land and sea. The proposal called for the complete destruction of the city, its industry and its shipping. The rationale was that the other colonies would soon sue for peace to escape Boston's fate.

While the French court thus consigned Boston to the ash heap, the plans for the attack against Canada went forward. The magnitude of the invasion force alone would guaranteed success. Seven veteran regiments, five of them from Flanders, were ordered to embark. Great care was taken to hide the destination of the fleet. Not even the Lords of the Admiralty knew of its mission. Never in its history had Canada faced such a grave threat.

Fortunately for Vaudreuil and his Canadians the choice of commanders for the expedition was left to politics. A confidant of Queen Anne was one Mrs. Masham who had a brother John Hill who somehow had reached the rank of Brigadier General without the benefit of ever having served in a military campaign. To him fell the honour of commanding the troops earmarked for the invasion. The overall commander was Admiral Sir Hovenden Walker, a man whose incompetence was soon to be the talk of the empire.

The plan was again the resurrected scheme of Phips. Nicholson was to repeat his maneuver of the last attempt and move against Montréal via Lake Champlain. At a meeting of the governors of all the colonies, at New London, Connecticut, supplies were pledged and troops arranged. When Governor Dudley arrived back at Boston Nantasket Roads was crowded with sixty transports, nine warships and two bomb ketches. The pastures of Noddle's Island was a sea of tents. The admiral told Dudley,

"by the blessing of God a favourable and ex-

traordinary passage, being but seven weeks and two days between Plymouth and Nantasket."

In the meantime Vaudreuil was not idle. Early in August word came from Costebelle regarding the planned attack and he made plans to vigorously defend the colony. The militia was called out and Indian allies gathered. The regulars were on full alert and defences strengthened. A religious revival of sorts gripped the colony as the danger approached. Mother Juchereau de Saint-Denis described in her journal how Canadians prayed to God and the Holy Virgin for help;

"since their glory was involved, seeing that the true religion would quickly perish if the English should prevail."

All was ready. The seven British regiments, with artillery train, numbered fifty-five hundred men. In addition there was six hundred marines and fifteen hundred provincials. Vetch was recalled from Nova Scotia to command the colonial contingent. The one difficulty was the lack of pilots with knowledge of the St. Lawrence. Every pilot in New England was pressed into service, but all declared their inability to take the fleet to Quebec.

Despite the lack of a pilot the fleet sailed from Nantasket on July 30th on its grand adventure. One of Walker's ships cruising in the Gulf of St. Lawrence captured a vessel commanded by a Frenchman named Paradis, an experienced sailor who knew the river well. He accepted a bribe of 500 pistoles, about $2,000, to act as pilot. The British might have fared better had he declined the money. Whether from patriotism or merely the thought of saving his own skin, he did everything he could to discourage Admiral Walker. He painted a dismal picture of Canadian winters; Walker wrote in his journal,

"That which now chiefly took up my thoughts, was contriving how to secure the ships if we got up to Quebec; for the ice in the river freezing to the bottom would have utterly destroyed and

Planning the defence of Quebec, 1711

bilged them as much as if they had been squeezed between rocks."

All went well until the 18th of August when a strong head-wind drove the fleet into the Bay de Gaspé. In two day the wind shifted and the fleet set sail again. On the evening of the 22nd they found themselves above Anticosti Island where the river is over 100 kilometres wide and no land had been sighted since the day before. There was a strong east wind with fog and Walker thought that they were near the south shore when, in fact, he was eighty kilometres from it and about half that distance north of his true position. At half past ten in the evening the captain of his flagship reported that land had been sighted. Walker assumed it to be the south shore and ordered the ships to wear and head northward, a fatal error. The ships soon found themselves among breakers and Walker was barely able to beat clear. Paradis told the astonished admiral that they were off the north shore. The nine warships were able to get clear, but eight transports, one store-ship and one sutler's sloop were wrecked on the rocks of Isle aux Oeufs with the loss of seven hundred and five officers and

soldiers plus thirty-five women accompanying the regiments. The total does not include the sailors that were drowned.

Walker, already nervous about the enterprise, called a council of war, which decided to retreat back to Boston rather than risk ascending the St. Lawrence. Considering the number of troops left, for indeed the loss incurred in the wrecks represented the losses expected in the first battle, there was no reason to not press on to Quebec. However, the order was given and the fleet headed for home.

The "Sapphire" Frigate raced to Boston to bring the news and a despatch was sent to Nicholson camped at Wood Creek. Nicholson was so enraged at being thwarted yet again that he tore off his wig, threw it on the ground and stomped on it crying "Roguery! Treachery!" When he was done he burned his fort and withdrew to Albany.

At Quebec the report of two large ships approaching the city raised the alarm. Alarm turned to joy as the ships were recognized as French.
Canada had been saved once again from the jaws of certain defeat. But, the struggle for a continent was just beginning in earnest.

CHAPTER THIRTY-ONE

The Treaty of Utrecht
"It is so important to prevent the breaking off of the negotiations
that the King will give up Acadia and Cape Breton."-Louis XIV, 1712

With the disgrace of Walker after the aborted attempt to take Quebec Vaudreuil began to plan the recapture of Acadia. However, time and the circumstances in Europe conspired against him. The great European war was winding down. The combatants had fought themselves to a standstill not to mention the brink of bankruptcy. The peace conference convened in Utrecht in the Netherlands in 1712 and the long, difficult negotiations began. Those negotiations were to have far reaching effects on Canada.

Louis XIV, the Sun King, now old and in decline, wished to recover Acadia. He wrote to his negotiators,

"It is so important to prevent the breaking off of the negotiations that the King will give up both Acadia and Cape Breton, if necessary for peace; but the plenipotentiaries will yield this point only in the last extremity, for by this double cession Canada will become useless, the access to it will be closed, the fisheries will come to an end, and the French marine be utterly destroyed."

He added that if the English would concede Acadia, he would give them the islands of St. Christopher, St. Martin and St. Bartholomew in the Caribbean.

They replied to the King that the offer was refused and the best the French delegates could do was retain Cape Breton as their doorway to Canada. The King upped the ante by offering the fortifications at Placentia in Newfoundland and the exclusion of the French from the Newfoundland fisheries, a concession of great magnitude as the French had fished the Grand Banks for two centuries and this was considered the nursery for sailors to man the naval vessels that were the life line of French power throughout the world. Even these would not prompt England to give up Acadia.

The Treaty of Utrecht was signed on April 11, 1713. In it France made some important concessions that was to spell the beginning of the end of her North American possessions. First they acknowledged that the Iroquois were British subjects, a declaration, with all it implied, that successive governors of New France had refused to do. France also conceded Hudson Bay, Newfoundland and Acadia, "according to its ancient limits." This last phrase was to cause unceasing problems in the thirty years leading up to the Seven Years War. Only Cape Breton was left and they renamed her Île Royale.

The questions that would have fostered a lasting peace were left unanswered or so vague as to inevitably cause disputes. What were the "ancient limits of Acadia?" Did it give England control of a vast country or a strip of coastline? What of the Valley of the Mississippi and the Great Lakes, which would give the holder control of the vast unexplored continent to the west?

What about the Acadians? This pragmatic people who had survived by their wits for one hundred and fifty odd years again showed their resilience in times of trouble. The terms of the treaty allowed the Acadians to stay or go as they wished. Queen Anne had even made a generous offer to those who would leave, they were free to sell their land. Of Course, there were no buyers, however, Queen Anne had no way of knowing that her offer was an empty one. The English were of two minds; the new governor, Richard Phillips, reported that these troublesome citizens were

"growne so insolent as to say that they will neither sweare allegiance nor leave the country."

The outgoing governor, Vetch, on the other hand, argued,

"One hundred French natives of America, familiar with the woods, able to march on snowshoes and accustomed to the use of birch canoes, are of more value and service than five times their number of raw men newly come from Europe. They will no doubt gladly remain upon their plantations (some of which are considerable) provided they may be protected and encouraged by the Crown, and as no country is of value without Inhabitants, so the removal of

Signing the Treaty of Utrecht, April 11, 1713

them and their cattle to Cape Brittoun (sic) would be a great addition to the new colony, so it would wholly ruine Nova Scotia unless supplied with a British Colony, which could not be done in several years."

So the Acadians stayed. Treading softly where the English were concerned while keeping their patriotism alive. They were French, but unwilling to risk all for a government 5,000 kilometres away.

The stage was now set for the next act in Canada's story; the settling of Île Royale and the founding of Louisbourg.

CHAPTER THIRTY-TWO

The Maritimes & the Building of Louisbourg

" After much discussion the harbour called Port à l'Anglois was chosen and its name changed to Louisbourg, in honour of the King."

The Treaty of Utrecht left Canada in a precarious position. At least there was still a toe hold on the Atlantic to keep the door to Quebec open. On the surface Île Royale was ideal for it controlled the entrance to the Gulf of St. Lawrence, however, it was a virtual wilderness, no settlements stood ready to sustain a French presence on the Atlantic seaboard. Despite the obstacles, a plan was put in motion to occupy it for military and political purposes. One of its harbours, garrisoned and fortified, could guard the approaches to Canada and furnish a base for the recovery of Acadia and for raiding New England when the next war began.

After much discussion the harbour called Port à l'Anglois was chosen and its name changed to Louisbourg, in honour of the King. It is situated near the southeastern tip of the island with an entrance to a deep and sheltered basin, where many ships could find good anchorage. The fortress was to be built on the spit of land that lies between the basin and the sea. From a military and fisheries prospective this was an excellent choice, however, the barren, spruce studded hills showed little promise for the farmer.

Great things were expected from this enterprise. Raudot declared confidently to the Marine Council that a strong fortress on Cape Breton would soon make the King master of all North America. The details were settled and the work began. The King was to built the fortifications and send out eight companies of soldiers, besides all the usual government bureaucrats. A well endowed hospital, staffed by nuns as at Quebec, Jesuits and Recollets as chaplains and Filles de la Congrégation to teach girls were also part of the plan. Families were to be recruited with support for two years as well as good young women to marry the soldiers. All seemed ready. The initial settlers were to come from the lost possessions of Newfoundland and Acadia. Some of the Micmacs and Abenakis were also included in the move. In the Autumn of 1713 the commandant at Placentia or Plaisance received the following orders from the King:

"Monsieur de Costebelle - I have caused my orders to be given you to evacuate the town and forts of Plaisance and the other places of your government of Newfoundland, ceded to my dear sister the Queen of Great Britain. I have given my orders for the equipment of the vessels necessary to make the evacuation and transport you, with the officers, garrison, and inhabitants of Plaisance and other places of Newfoundland to my Isle Royale, vulgarly called Cape Breton; but as the season is so far advanced that this cannot be done without exposing my troops and my subjects to perishing from cold and misery, and placing my vessels in evident peril of wreck, I have judged it proper to defer the transportation till the next spring."

Many of the thirty poor families at Placentia would gladly have become British subjects and stayed, but no choice was given them. They and their fishing boats were duly transported to Louisbourg. The big hope for the new colony were the Acadian French. They were too numerous to be handled like the those from Newfoundland and so they needed to be persuaded to move.

Ponchartrain himself wrote the missionaries to use their influence to achieve the desired result. Although the English had allowed the Acadians their religion under certain conditions, the priests insisted their souls were in jeopardy. The Acadians, however, refused to leave their rich farms for the poor soil of Île Royale.

Only the inhabitants around Annapolis Royal were open to emigrating to Louisbourg. They were disillusion by the treatment they received at the hands of the English. Nicholson had replaced Vetch as governor and he began by alienating everyone from his own officers to the local inhabitants. A few set sail in the ship "Marie-Joseph" in 1713 and the rest were promised ships would come the following year. Despite the letter from the Queen that the Acadians were free to go and to sell their property, the governor refused his permission. When ships did not arrive as scheduled they decided to build their own with rigging supplied from Louisbourg. Nicholson turned the shipment back on its arrival.

The building of Louisbourg

Nicholson did everything in his power to hold them in Acadia, but some escaped and settled at Port Toulouse on Île Royale. Aside from these few the rest of the Acadians chose to remain in British territory. The British, for their part, ignored their new province and the Acadians were left to live their lives and practice their religion.

The construction at Louisbourg moved forward steadily and, to the chagrin of the governor, slowly. The stone masons worked their trade and soon bastions and redoubts sprang up to protect France's last doorway to Canada.

While France struggled to strengthen its precarious hold on the mouth of the St. Lawrence by building the fortress of Louisbourg and attempted to entice Acadians to emigrate to Île Royale, another French possession lay fallow in the Gulf of St. Lawrence. Ile St. Jean, the future Prince Edward Island, was a jewel awaiting discovery by those who could prosper on its fertile land.

The island was first visited by Jacques Cartier in 1534, but no attempt was made to settle there. Fishermen landed there to dry their catch before sailing for home, however, this was a seasonal occupation and the Indians were left in peace during the long Canadian winters. The island first appeared in any substantial form in 1634 on Champlain's map on which he called it Isle St. Jean.

The first man to receive title to the island was Nicholas Denys who obtained a concession to it, Île Royale and parts of Acadia in 1654. He noted that the island was crescent shaped with an abundance of caribou and other game. He obtained his grant on condition that he bring out eighty families within six years. Denys, however, was only interested in the fur trade and the fishery so he made no attempt to bring in settlers. In 1663 the concession was revoked and given to the Captain François Doublet of the French Navy.

Acadians arriving at Ile St. Jean, 1720

He died two years later and nothing came of his venture. In 1686 Gabriel Gauthier was granted a sealing concession in the Magdalen Islands, which included the right to establish a fishery on Île St. Jean. Attempts were made in 1686 and 1688 to ship pelts to France, but only one of three ships made it through and the enterprise failed.

With the fall of Port Royal in 1710 and the confirmation of Acadia as a British Colony in 1713, Île St. Jean's day was at hand. A few Acadians crossed the Northumberland Strait in 1710 only to discover that a grant had been given to the Sieur de Louvigny and their request for land grants was turned down and they became tenant farmers. In May of 1716 his concession was revoked and the island returned to Royal Domain, but it came too late as the Acadians began leaving the island for Acadia. Governor Caufield of Annapolis reported to the Lords of Trade,

"the island of St. John is completely abandoned by the people of Annapolis who went to settle there."

In August of 1719 a proprietary grant of Île St. Jean, Miscou and adjacent islands was given to Le Comte de St. Pierre with terms as follows:

"The administration of justice is reserved by the Crown; and of economic rights, the crown also reserves the products of mines which are to be used for the good of the colonists, such lands as might be necessary from time to time for the erection of public buildings or fortifications, and woods suitable for ship-building, although the count is free to build vessels on the islands and to erect sawmills for the manufacture of lumber. The grantee is required to retain or indemnify any inhabitants who might be already settled, to locate 100 settlers the first year and fifty each succeeding year until the islands are populated and supplied with necessary livestock, and to construct such roads as are necessary for the public service."

On April 15, 1720 three small ships bearing three hundred passengers sailed from Rochefort for the new colony. The new governor was Sieur de Gotteville de Bellisle. At Louisbourg he was joined by la Ronde and together they selected the site of Port La Joie (Charlottetown) as their headquarters. The settlers landed and prepared to start their new lives in the new world.

Once the housing requirements were met Bellisle attended to business. La Ronde was sent to Baie Verte and Beaubassin to hire Acadian carpenters to work in the winter shipbuilding program. Three ships were built that first winter. The largest, of 100 tons, was earmarked to take cod to Europe, the second, of 60 tons, was to be used in the West Indian trade while the third of 25 tons was intended for the seal and walrus hunt around the Magdalens.

The affairs of the Comte de St. Pierre soon began to unravel and he made no contribution to the colony after 1722. His partners attempted to hold on, but on November 27, 1724 De Mezy, Commissaire at Île Royale, reported to the Minister in Paris:

"that all the settlers of Île St. Jean had been obliged to abandon the colony and had come to Ile Royale, and that he had embarked all those who would have been at the charge of the King and sent them with their families back to France; that the effects of the company were seized and taken to Louisbourg, where they were sold at auction (including their ship, La Chimene), and the proceeds were divided among the creditors in proportion to their claims. M. Aubert, financial director of the company, returned to France and this marked the last incident in the affairs of the Company of Saint Pierre."

Île St. Jean returned to the Royal Domain November 14, 1724 and in 1725 an ensign and thirty men were sent to establish French interest against any encroachment by the English. In July of 1726 Pensens was named commandant of the island and he found the remnants of St. Pierre's colonists scattered and fighting among themselves. The buildings at Port La Joie were in disrepair and a discouraged Pensens returned to Louisbourg.

Although Acadians continued to trickle into the island no rush of settlers came even though the French authorities now encouraged migration from Nova Scotia. In 1728 a census of the island reported seventy-six men, fifty-one women, one hundred and fifty-six children and fourteen domestics for a total of two hundred and ninety-seven. In that year a further one hundred settlers arrived from Acadia, but the crop was devastated by a plague of field mice. The crop was ploughed under and the population was forced to subsist on the fishery. The following year they sowed again with wheat seed supplied from Louisbourg.

The island then entered a period of prosperity A good crop in 1730 along with an excellent fishery drew another sixty Acadian families to the island. The future looked bright for Île St. Jean.

CHAPTER THIRTY-THREE

The Search for the Western Sea

"He spared nothing,which might bring success; he bought and prepared the needed goods; he
inspired me and my brothers with his own enthusiasm."-François la Vérendrye on his father, 1749.

In the last years of the reign of Louis XIV, France gave little thought to the New World. However, under the regency of the Duc d'Orléans interest in the affairs of North America was renewed. Plans for reaching the great western sea were brought before the regent in 1716. With the failure to find a Northwest Passage, an expedition across the continent was put forward. It was proposed to set up base camps by establishing three posts, one on the north shore of Lake Superior, at the mouth of the Kaministiguia River, another at Lac des Christineau (Lake of the woods), and the third at Lake Winnipeg. The last was to be the jumping off point for the expedition. The posts would cost the crown nothing, as those who built and maintained them would be compensated by a monopoly in the fur trade. The actual exploration, however, was to be charged to the government, and would require fifty good men, at three hundred francs a year each, besides equipment and supplies. The total cost of reaching the Pacific Ocean would be in the neighbourhood of 50,000 francs.

The project was approved and in that same year Lieutenant La Noue, of the colonial troops, built a stockade at the mouth of the Kaministiguia, but nothing further was done until 1720. The Duc d'Orléans ordered the Jesuit, Charlevoix, to go to Canada and get all the information he could concerning the western sea.

Charlevoix went to the Upper Lakes and questioned as many missionaries, officers, voyageurs, and Indians as he could. The missionaries and officers could tell him nothing; the voyageurs and Indians knew little more, but invented stories to hide their ignorance. Charlevois kept notes and reported to the Comte de Toulouse that the western sea probably formed the western boundary of the country of the Sioux. Some Indians told him that they had seen its shores and found white men there that were different from the French.

Charlevoix believed that there was some truth to the stories and he advanced two plans as likely to lead to the discovery of the western sea. One involved ascending the Missouri River,

"the source of which is certainly not far from the sea, as all the Indians I have met have unanimously assured me."

The other plan was to establish a mission among the Sioux from whom, after learning the language, the missionaries could gain the necessary information. The hostility of the Sioux, however, prevented the mission from being established for several years.

Before continuing the search for the western sea it is imperative that we go back some fifty years to pick up the story of the family that was to energetically push the project. In 1667 René Gaultier de Varennes, a Lieutenant in the Regiment de Carignan, married Marie, the daughter of Pierre Bouchard, the governor of Trois Rivière. Upon the death of his father-in-law, Varennes succeeded him as governor. With his salary of twelve hundred francs per year, plus the profits from a forty acre farm along with a little illicit trading in furs, Varennes managed to live quite well on the banks of the St. Lawrence. Marie gave birth to many children among them a son, Pierre, born in 1685. Pierre participated in the Deerfield Raid and campaigned in Newfoundland.

During the War of the Spanish Succession, young Pierre crossed the sea, obtained a commission as lieutenant, and was nearly killed at the Battle of Malplaquet. He was shot through the body, received six sabre cuts, and was left for dead on the field. He recovered and returned to Canada with the name, La Vérendrye added to his own. His full name was now Pierre Gaultier de Varennes de la Vérendrye.

Pierre married Marie Anne Dandonneau and settled down to run a small trading post on the upper St. Maurice River called La Gabelle. In a dozen years he learned the Indian languages and gained a reputation in fur trading circles. He listened intently to the tales of mighty rivers, vast lakes and strange peoples to the west of the known world. Pierre tried to sift fact from fancy, and became intrigued by the possibilities. Events worked in his favour and when a post on Lake Nipigon became vacant, the Marquis de Beauharnois, the new governor, appointed him to take over there. With his new post came the rather impressive title of

Trading furs, circa 1730

"Commandant of the Northwest."

La Vérendrye spent two years at Nipigon where the stories of the west grew in detail and emphasis. Tales of vast lakes beyond Superior and of a river that flowed into the western sea were spun around the temporary lodges of the Indians who came to trade. The spur that finally drove La Vérendrye to action was a conversation with a chief from the Kaministiquia who gave a personal account of following a river until he came in sight of waters that ebbed and flowed. He said that he was so frightened by the sight that he hurried back the way he came. Stories were told of cities and forts to the west with people with white skin who rode horses and were dressed in metal.

La Vérendrye told a friend,

"These people are great liars, but now and then they will tell the truth."

La Vérendrye dreamed the dreams of Champlain, La Salle and Frontenac, but with a difference. Pour-ing over his diary he became convinced that the route lay, not to the south, but, due west across the continent through the territory of the Christineau and Assiniboin tribes. A new era in the exploration of Canada was about to begin.

Pierre Gaultier de Varennes de la Vérendrye was now determined to find the western sea. He petitioned the King for one hundred men, canoes, arms, and provisions to undertake the expedition. Although the governor, Le Marquis de Beauharnois, lobbied for the schemes approval, all help was refused. He was authorized to find a way to the western sea at his own expense in consideration of a monopoly on the fur trade in the regions north and west of Lake Superior. At first glance this might seem like a generous proposal, however, the lands involved were held by tribes who were not necessarily favourably disposed to the French, and were perpetual enemies of each other. The risks of the trade were as great as its potential profits, and before they could be tapped, an initial outlay of funds was necessary. Forts had to be built,

La Vérendrye leaving Montréal, June 8, 1731

manned, and stocked with goods brought through 3,300 kilometres of dangerous wilderness.

There was also another danger, more insidious than those physical ones met on the trail. The merchants of Montréal would surely be jealous of his monopoly and would attempt to discredit him in his absence. Should his patron, Beauharnois, be recalled, his successor might cancel his privileges and his forts would be transferred to his rivals, as had happened to La Salle on the recall of Frontenac. On the other hand, the country was known to have the finest furs on the continent and they were presently going to the English on Hudson Bay. The proposed forts/trading posts of La Vérendrye would secure much of this trade for Canadians.

Undaunted, Pierre took on a number of partners, and raised enough money to finance the first expedition. All was ready for the beginning of the great adventure.

It was unusually hot for the 8th of June in Montréal in 1731. The sweat ran down the faces of the young adventurers as they prepared to depart for the west. With La Vérendrye went three of his sons, Jean Baptiste, eighteen; Pierre, who was seventeen; and François, known as Le Chevalier, who was sixteen. Only

Louis Joseph, fourteen, was considered too young to accompany them. As second in command La Vérendrye appointed his nephew, Christophe Dufros de la Jemeraye, a young twenty-three year old ensign in the marines, with considerable experience on the frontier. Not all were hardened fighting men. A sprinkling of blacksmiths, carpenters, and the like were along to help build the forts. They would soon be as tough as the voyageurs once the journey began. The citizens of Montréal came out to see the adventurers on their way, some of the merchants probably regretting their participation in the venture already.

The expedition fought the currents up the Ottawa, portaging around the many rapids. It took them a month to reach Lake Nipissing and then on to the French River to Georgian Bay and Lake Huron. they lingered briefly at Michilimackinac before pushing on to the Fort at Kaministiquia that La Noue had built years before. Seventy eight bone weary days had passed since the cheers of Montréal had faded from their ears.

La Vérendrye decided to push on from Kaministiquia and, after covering seventy kilometres, arrived at the mouth of the Pigeon River. This was his doorway to the west.

The men, driven to near exhaustion, began to complain. Winter was coming and the Pigeon River turned out to be a bad choice. A few kilometres from its mouth the river broke into turbulent rapids with long portages, the voyageurs had had enough, they refused to go any further. No amount of pleading could move them. Finally, La Vérendrye agreed to return to winter at Kaministiquia, sending some volunteers forward to establish the first post further west. Four heavily laden canoes under the command of Jemeraye proceeded up the Pigeon into the unknown. With Jemeraye went La Vérendrye's eldest son Jean Baptiste. The decision to send just volunteers ahead was a fortunate one, for, there were forty back breaking portages before clearing the Pigeon River into Rainy Lake. The main party would surely have mutinied had the whole force push on. From Rainy Lake all rivers flowed west.

Here the advance party stopped and built their first post, for winter was fast approaching and shelter against the elements was required for survival. Half fort and half trading post, it enclosed log cabins that would adequately protect them through the coming cold weather. They named it Fort St. Pierre in honour of the elder La Vérendrye. Soon Indians came with

their furs to trade, glad that they were spared the long trip to the English at Hudson Bay.

The party at Fort St. Pierre passed the winter in relative comfort, while La Vérendrye tried to stir up some enthusiasm among the malcontents at Kaministiquia. Months were wasted and it was not until June 1732 that he could get them moving again toward the great portage on the Pigeon River.

He finally arrived at Fort St. Pierre on July 14th to a tumultuous welcome. The Cree were greatly impressed, not only by the gifts given, but by the possibility of help from the French in their perennial wars with the more warlike Sioux. To show their goodwill they gathered fifty canoes filled with warriors and offered to lead the expedition westward.

The party reached the Lake of the Woods in August and La Vérendrye viewed his diminishing supplies with some misgivings. It was bad enough with his own men, but the additional Cree made the situation desperate. Everything hinged on the twenty year old Jean Baptiste, who was hurrying from Michilimackinac with the much needed resources. Would he make it before winter set in? They skirted the American shore of the Lake of the Woods and camped 6.5 kilometres up the Northwest Angle Inlet, west of

American Point and Bucket Island. Here they constructed the second in their string of forts and prepared for their second winter in the wilderness. They named it Fort St. Charles after the governor, the Marquis de Beauharnois, whose Christian name was Charles.

The fort was completed and there was nothing to do but wait and watch for Jean Baptiste and the supply train that promised survival. An early freeze and snow storm threatened the existence of the search for the western sea.

La Vérendrye watched anxiously for his son Jean and the critical supplies he was bringing. Snow fell heavily and he knew that in all probability the canoes would be halted by ice far from the fort. If so, the men wintering with him at Fort St. Charles would be hard pressed to survive until spring. He worked at his rude table bringing his accounts, such as they were, up to date. A sudden shout brought him to his feet and he rushed out to see what new disaster threatened his enterprise. To his great relief, trudging through the early winter snowdrifts, Jean La Vérendrye came out of the woods, followed by his snowshoed men. Each man was bent over with the heavy bundles of supplies that would sustain them in the long, cold months to come. The greetings over, the story of the trek to the fort was told. The canoes lay locked in ice some eighty kilometres away. The men had donned their snowshoes, hoisted the supplies on their backs, and fought their way through sleet and snow to reach their comrades.

Little time was spent contemplating their good fortune. La Vérendrye knew in his heart that the Montréal merchants were loosing interest in the expedition. Another year and they might abandoned the project altogether. He decided to send his nephew Jemeraye to Montréal to rekindle the enthusiasm among his backers. With him went the Jesuit missionary Messager to add weight to his arguments. La Vérendrye's heart had been right. Jemeraye found the merchants had lost the stomach for the risk and the faith that it could be brought to a successful conclusion. The fact that they had received two cargoes of furs made no impression. This was a modest return and they had been expecting a fortune. The best they would offer was to advance supplies in proportion to returns. The fact that this could mean starvation for the fifty men in the wilderness meant little to these practical business men of early Canada.

While Jemeraye was facing the reluctant merchants in Montréal, young Jean and Pierre de la Vérendrye were making their way up the long reaches of the Winnipeg River to Lake Winnipeg. Here they built the third fort in the chain of posts that was to sustain the drive to the western sea. They called it Fort Maurepas after the King's minister in Paris who had done little to warrant the honour.

With the return of Jemeraye it was obvious that the expedition was in grave difficulty. La Vérendrye decided to go to Quebec and plead his case directly to the governor. Leaving Jean and Pierre at Fort Maurepas and Jemeraye in over all command at Fort St. Charles, La Vérendrye set out in a light canoe with a few voyageurs for Quebec.

It was the summer of 1734 and the journey of 3,500 kilometres was a long and arduous one. Today a comfortable drive of a few days would bring us to our destination; but for La Vérendrye, making all haste, the journey took months. Further weeks of planning and discussions left him stuck in Quebec until spring.

The governor wrote to the King's minister on La Vérendrye's behalf, pointing out the long term benefits of a route to the western sea. He wrote:

"He is facing so many difficulties alone. He has failed to secure any associate who, like himself, prefers the glory of success to gain in money."

Maurepas was unmoved by this plea. Instead of offering help, he made thing more difficult. La Vérendrye was ordered to forgo the fur trade and concentrate on finding a route to the western sea.

The Montréal backers had other ideas, as you might imagine. La Vérendrye finally lost his patience and confronted his partners. He made it clear that they could lose their entire investment or continue their involvement in the hope of profits to come. They reluctantly agreed to continue, however, La Vérendrye was to be responsible for any losses. He had little choice but to accept the terms.

Spring finally arrived and La Vérendrye was anxious to get back. This time his youngest son, Louis Joseph, now eighteen, joined the expedition. A young chaplain also accompanied them, a Jesuit, Pierre Aulneau. They set out in early June and as had happened on their initial departure three years before, it was extremely hot. In the early stages of their journey forest fires were everywhere, blanketing the route with thick

Deadly encounter, Lake of the
Woods, June 1736

layers of smoke. It was September before they reached the Lake of the Woods. The supply canoes could not keep up with La Vérendrye's torrid pace and they anxiously awaited their arrival.

In anticipation of a problem with the supplies, La Vérendrye split up his party with Jemeraye taking half the men to Fort Maurepas and the balance remaining at Fort St. Charles thus expanding the hunting and fishing area, which increased the chances of seeing the spring.

La Vérendrye waited in vain for the supply canoes to arrive. Before they passed into Lake Superior the frost arrived closing the rivers and isolating the two forts. When hunting and fishing was poor they were reduced to eating roots and moccasin leather. Eventually their hunting dogs were sacrificed to ward off the angel of death.

With the coming of spring, hope was renewed and plans moved forward. Young Father Aulneau wrote a friend of his experiences. He headed his letter,

"Fort St. Charles among the Kiristineaux." He observed that the fort was "merely an enclosure made with four rows of posts of 12 to 15 feet in height in the form of an oblong square. Within

are a few rough cabins, constructed of logs and clay and covered with bark. Several streams put it in communication with other lakes, all of which empty into another which the savages say is larger. . . . They call it Ouinipignon. This is all the information I am able to give you at present concerning this wretched country."

One face was missing among those that gathered at Fort St. Charles that spring. Young Christophe de la Jemeraye was not with them. Hearing of the plight of those at Fort St. Charles, he had gathered up the furs and what supplies they could spare to go to their relief. However, he died on the way of some mysterious illness. La Vérendrye had lost a nephew and staunch supporter who would be impossible to replace.

June 1736

The lost of his nephew Jemeraye weighed heavily on the mind of La Vérendrye, but there was little time for mourning. There was scarcely enough powder for a month and the Cree were beginning to arrive to trade the winter catch of furs. The possibility of aid in their wars with the Sioux was one of the incentives that the Cree had to trade at Fort St. Charles. Should they discover the weakness of the post they might seize every-

95

thing and go on to Hudson Bay.

La Vérendrye decided to send three fast canoes with twenty men to Michilimackinac to trade their winter cache of furs for food and ammunition. With Jemeraye gone the command of the supply party fell to Jean, La Vérendrye's eldest son. With him went the young Jesuit, Father Aulneau. Of all the members of the expedition, the winter was hardest on him. He had not yet been hardened to life in the wilderness. He needed rest and the spiritual nourishment of a retreat. It was hoped that he would return refreshed both in body and spirit. The young priest felt confident that this was all he needed, but fate was to step in and a little sport led to tragedy.

A small group of Cree warriors, lately in possession of some new muskets, decided to try their luck on some Sioux that happened to be in the neighbourhood. The Cree were far from sharpshooters and no harm was done save to the dignity of the Sioux warriors. They demanded to know who had fired on them. Realizing that the joke had misfired the Cree told the Sioux that some Frenchmen were responsible. The incident seemed to end there.

On June 8th Jean de la Vérendrye, with his party of twenty men in four canoes, set out for Michilimackinac. It was as intended to be a fast convoy. They made thirty-three kilometres that first day and set up camp on one of the many islands on the Lake of the Woods. They lit their fire and settled in for the night. It was probably the fire that led the Sioux, still fuming over being shot at by the Cree, to their camp. The first arrow caught the young Jesuit in the back of the head as he prayed. The rest, taken by surprise, were quickly overcome. Two weeks later a party of voyageurs and Indians found the camp and the reason why they had failed to appear at Michilimackinac.

Father Aulneau was still on his knees, his right hand stretched out in a gesture of invocation. Jean de la Vérendrye was face down, his back badly mutilated and his headless body gaily decorated with coloured porcupine quills. The rest lay scattered across the campsite. All had been scalped.

The bodies were brought to Fort St. Charles for burial by the little Chapel that served the spiritual needs of the community. Eight hundred Cree gathered for the funeral. They anticipated that this would mean war between the Canadians and the Sioux. Surely La Vérendrye would destroy the enemy that had killed his son. The Cree demanded that the murders be avenged.

They were ready to follow La Vérendrye into the land of the Sioux to wipe them from the face of the earth. But when La Vérendrye spoke it was with the voice of peace. Despite his grief and the temptation to avenge his first born, he knew that a war would set the entire region ablaze. The search for the western sea would come to a bloody end and the fur trade could be disrupted for years.

On July 17th young Louis Joseph de la Vérendrye arrived from Michilimackinac with the needed supplies. They now made plans to set out on the expedition to find the western sea. Despite the urgency he felt, La Vérendrye was not able to start out from Fort St. Charles for Fort Maurepas until February 8, 1737. The merchants of Montréal had to be considered. Furs needed to be shipped to them to insure supplies, without which all would be lost. When the day came it promised only hardship and misery. The wind, gusting from the north, drove the temperature to 40 degrees below zero. All along the borderlands of what is now Minnesota the snow lay in four metre drifts throughout the forest. Ordinarily, the trip took twenty-one days by canoe; but, La Vérendrye pushed his men and on the seventeenth day Pierre de la Vérendrye, scouting ahead, saw the fort nestled on the shores of Lake Winnipeg.

On his arrival La Vérendrye began by assuring the Indians that he came in peace and then he warned them not to deal with the English for they were bearers of the smallpox that they so dreaded. He next listened to the reports of his two sons who told him of the Indian stories of a meeting of rivers where game was plentiful. The stories also hinted at a river that flowed westward and he sent his sons to reconnoitre the unknown lands to the west. Then he wearily turn eastward for the long journey to Montréal and his timid backers. This was his third trip since the expedition first set out and he knew that the battle for further supplies would be a hard one. As well, he would be bringing the news of the death of their son to his wife and the grieving would begin again.

It was good that La Vérendrye brought fourteen heavily ladened canoes with him. This was proof of the viability of the project and it was needed. Even the governor seemed concerned and demanded new guarantees of immediate progress.

The merchants were even more dubious. Never mind that he had lost his son and his other sons were risking all for them, they demanded more. To watch

La Vérendrye and the Mandans, 1738

over their investment, they decided to send one of their number back with La Vérendrye to help spur him on. The overseer was to be the Sieur de la Marque, a heavy investor in the project.

In early spring, 1738 he set out with his party from Montréal. He was at Michilimackinac by July, and there gathered twenty-two men and six canoes to continue the journey. He passed Forts St. Charles and Maurepas with but a brief stop and caught up to his sons at the confluence of the Red and Assiniboine Rivers, where the City of Winnipeg now stands.

Plans were immediately put in motion to continue the push west. They were about to tread where no European had gone before.

September 1738

Before pushing on La Vérendrye established Fort Rouge at the confluence of the Red and Assiniboine Rivers. The expedition started up the westward flowing Assiniboine River. There was great hopes that the Assiniboine would continue to flow west to the Pacific, however, it soon became too shallow for the heavily ladened canoes. Here La Vérendrye split his party in two parts. The fighting men marched overland while the rest pushed on by water with the bulk of the supplies. A week after leaving Fort Rouge they reached what was to become known as the Portage la Prairie. Here the Canoes caught up and another post

was built on the site of today's Portage La Prairie, Manitoba. They named the post Fort La Reine.

No sooner was the post completed then the Sieur de la Marque, the Montréal merchant, caught up to the main party. With him was his brother Nolant and eight followers. It was late in the season and prudence suggested remaining at Fort La Reine for the winter, but with the demands of the governor and the merchants ever in his mind, Le Vérendrye decided to continue west.

Information was scarce on the object of their search. The Assiniboin and Christineaux knew nothing of the great Western Sea, but declared that there was a tribe on the Missouri called Mantannes (Mandans), who knew the way and would guide them there.

On October 16th La Vérendrye announced that he would push on to the country of the Mandans in hopes of getting information on the western sea. The Mandans occupied much of present day Minnesota and the Dakotas.

It was impossible to take the whole party with him, so, leaving the bulk of the expedition at Fort La Reine, he headed out with two of his sons, Pierre and Le Chevalier, La Marque and his brother with their entourage and the best fighting men in the party, twenty in all. With an equal number of Assiniboin to act as guides La Vérendrye marched into the unknown.

After ascending the Assiniboine and the Souris Rivers they struck cross country toward their objective. For once food was not a problem. The Assiniboin hunted the vast herds of buffalo along the way and the party killed and cured enough meat to sustain them. It was well that they did, for by the time they reached the territory of the Mandans their party totaled six hundred as more and more Assiniboin and Cree joined the trek.

In late November they reached the outskirts of Mandan territory. La Vérendrye got his first lesson on the exaggerations of his Indian guides. From the talk of the Assiniboin he expected to meet men much like himself in both appearance and manners. But this first delegation of Mandans came with sparse gifts of corn and tobacco and were described by La Vérendrye this way:

"just like the Assiniboin; they are naked; a buffalo robe may be thrown carelessly about them but they have not even breechcloth." His disappointment was also reflected in his journal, "From that moment," he wrote, "I resolved that we must discount all that we had heard."

Small troubles dogged their first contact with the Mandans. An Assiniboin youth made off with La Vérendrye's personal effects and in the excitement of the Mandan welcome another absconded with the gifts destined for their hosts. Ammunition was given instead. One of La Vérendrye's sons spoke the Cree language and their was a young Cree who spoke Assiniboin. The Mandans understood some of the Assiniboin tongue and by this rather roundabout way communications were maintained. However, the young Cree fell in love with the daughter of an Assiniboin chief and when he decided to leave for home, the young Cree was in hot pursuit. Thus La Vérendrye and the Mandans could only sit and stare at one another.

Little could be gained from prolonging their visit, so Le Vérendrye left two men, one his personal servant and the other, one of La Marque's men who showed a knack for picking up Indian languages, to learn the Mandan dialect. It was hoped that they could illicit the information regarding the Western Sea for follow up in the spring.

January 8, 1739 was set as the day they would start back to Fort La Reine, but La Vérendrye was too ill to travel. By the thirteenth he was somewhat better and it was decided to set out. The open prairie was a daunting place in the middle of winter. An endless world of white stretched before them with the lee of the great snowdrifts the only shelter to be found.

La Vérendrye recorded his suffering in his journal,

"I was very ill, but hoped to get better on the way. It would be impossible to suffer more than I did. It seemed that nothing but death could release me from such misery."

For a month they plodded through the most bitter weather imaginable and by some miracle they reached Fort La Reine. After two weeks La Verendrye reported himself "a little restored."

Feeling better, La Vérendrye's thoughts turned back to the prospects of a westerly flowing river. He first established a post to the north of Fort La Reine on Lake Manitoba, which he named Fort Dauphin. On April 16, 1739 he sent his son, Le Chevalier, up Lake Winnipeg to search for the way to the Pacific. Near the northern fringe of the lake it appeared that he might have made the discovery at last. Concealed in the swamps was the mouth of a great river and Le Chevalier excitedly paddled upstream in search of its source. To his disappointment it flowed east and he turned back where the river broke into two parts near present day La Paz, Manitoba. These were the two rivers that came together to form the mighty Saskatchewan.

Of all his discoveries this was probably his most important, although he didn't realize it at the time. Le Chevalier heard from the Cree in the area of vast mountains many leagues away, and beyond them the water that came and went and was unfit for men to drink. Not long after a post was built there where the Pasquia River joined the Saskatchewan. They called it Fort Bourbon and it was to become a thorn in the side of the English at Hudson Bay, for why should the Cree travel seventeen hundred kilometres when Fort Bourbon was right there?

In September the two men who had spent the winter with the Mandans arrived at Fort La Reine with stories of men who rode horses, whose skin was white and who lived in forts made of stone. The dream was at last within reach. But, before La Vérendrye could pursue the dream of the western sea, another trip to Montréal was in order to ensure the steady flow of the

A smoke signal at last ,
September, 1742

essential supplies to the west.

January 1741

While La Vérendrye lobbied for the continued support of the Montréal merchants for his expedition, plans for the coming season were being formulated at Fort La Reine. The two men who had spent the winter among the Mandans told of several Indian tribes arriving at the Mandan village in the spring to trade embroidered buffalo robes for beans and corn. They rode horses and their camp across the Missouri consisted of two hundred lodges. One tribe came from the far west and told of white men who lived in stone houses.

The two men had spent some time in their camp and with their newly acquired knowledge of the Mandan tongue were able to converse with the visitors. The white men had beards and prayed to the Master of Life in large buildings, holding books, singing together Jésus Marie. These Indians had met the Spanish of California. The chief of these traders offered to take the two Canadians with him to this strange country.

On his return La Vérendrye sent his son Pierre to follow up on the discovery of the two men. He attempted to hire Mandan guides, but none were willing to undertake the journey. Pierre returned to Fort La Reine empty handed.

April 1742

Undaunted by this failure La Vérendrye sent his son Le Chevalier, the most aggressive of the brothers and the youngest, Louis Joseph, with the two men who had wintered with the Mandans to try again to reach the Pacific. It was a familiar route and after three weeks of paddling the four arrived at the Mandan village and here they waited for the Indian traders to appear; none came. Finally on July 23rd they hired two Mandan guides and set out across the prairie. Loaded down with provisions and gifts, the going was slow. The Black Hills lay on their left and the upper reaches of the Missouri on their right. Weeks went by with no sign of any other human beings, but game was plentiful, with deer springing up from the lush river bottoms and buffalo streaming by in endless columns. They came at last to the place the Mandans called the Mountain of the Horse People where the weary travelers decided to stop and rest. They built a signal fire in the hope of making contact with the illusive people for which the spot was named.

At last on September 14th an answering column of smoke was seen on the horizon. They immediately moved off to investigate and they found a camp of Indians that Le Chevalier called Les Beaux Hommes in his journal. They were greeted with curiosity rather than hostility, however, the two Mandan guides quietly slipped away as these were their enemies.

The brothers spent twenty-one days with Les Beaux Hommes who then guided them to the Horse

People who, true to their name, had horses aplenty. They were, however, in great distress and their village was full of wailing and weeping. Their enemies, the Snake or Shoshone Indians, had decimated their tribe. The previous year they had destroyed seventeen villages, killing the warriors and carrying off the women and children as slaves.

The Horse People knew nothing of the western sea, but, despite their situation, they did provide mounts and guides to get the Canadians on to the next phase of their journey. They next reached the lands of the Gens de l'arc, or Bow Indians (more than likely a branch of the western Sioux) and were received with great courtesy. Le Chevalier wrote in his Journal,

"Thus far we had been well received in all the villages we had passed; but this was nothing compared with the courteous manners of the great chief of the Bow Indians, who, unlike the others, was not self interested in the least, and who took excellent care of everything belonging to us."

The first questions asked were of the Pacific, but these Indians knew nothing of it except what they had heard from Snake prisoners taken in war. The Canadians were surprised at the extent of the camp and the chief explained that they had gathered bands from far and wide to mount a raid on their common enemy. He invited the brothers to join them as they were moving to the west and they might see the great waters they sought.

Soon the camp broke up and the westward journey began across the endless prairie, now brown with the withering touch of autumn. Le Chevalier described the march thus:

"We continued our march sometimes south-southwest, and now and then northwest; our numbers constantly increasing by villages of different tribes which joined us."

At last, on January 1, 1743 they reached the Big Horn Range of the Rocky Mountains where they set up camp, and, leaving the women and children, advanced toward the Snake's winter camp, hoping to surprise them, striking a significant blow to their power in the region.

Leaving Louis Joseph to watch over the baggage, Le Chevalier joined the war party as it moved into attack. As they approached the foothills scouts came back to the main party with word that the Snakes had decamped. Only one thought raced through the minds of the Indians; the Snakes had been forewarned of their coming and were now making a wide sweep to take the unprotected women and children in their own camp. The anxious warriors' retreat was made worse by the snow that now fell, leaving four foot drifts that had to be circumvented or ploughed through. On reaching the camp they found that all was well and a second attack was planned.

The brothers did not wait for a second attempt and struck out on their own. In March they reached a tribe called the Little Cherry Indians where they remained a short time before starting on their return journey to Fort La Reine having failed to find the Pacific. They reached the fort on July 2, 1743, much to the relief of their father who had heard nothing of them for over a year.

La Vérendrye and his sons had opened up a vast territory with unlimited potential for commerce and profit. The highest honours should have been their due, but such was not the case. On their return to Montréal La Vérendrye found himself replaced and forced to pay his backers 3,000 livres a year out of the fortune he had realized in the west, a fortune that existed only in the mind of Maurepas. All appeals failed, however, Maurepas was deposed and his replacement reversed all his decisions and gave La Vérendrye permission for one last expedition to the west.

The earliest date for departure on this new adventure was May of 1750. Le Chevalier wrote in his journal,

"He spared nothing, which might bring success; he bought and prepared the needed goods; he inspired me and my brothers with his own enthusiasm."

The last great adventure of Pierre de Varennes, Sieur de la Vérendrye was not to be. On December 6, 1749 he reached the end of his life, his dream unfinished. He was laid to rest in the chapel of Ste. Anne in the Church of Notre Dame.

CHAPTER THIRTY-FOUR
The Race to Win a Continent
"I have charged M. de Saint-Pierre with this business. He knows these countries better than any officer in all the colony."-La Jonquière to the minister in France, 1750.

The death of La Verendrye in no way impeded the French sense of their destiny. The North American continent was theirs by exploration and right. Canadians, with their thirst for adventure and furs, were willing to take hardship and risk, all to achieve the dream of reaching the Western Sea. United under a strong government controlled from Versailles, the voyageurs pushed ever westward.

The English, on the other hand, were divided into thirteen independent colonies, each jealous of its rights and rarely agreeing to act together. Their vision stopped at the Allegheny Mountains.

Regretting their concessions in the Treaty of Utrecht, the French government began formulating plans, not only to recover Acadia, but to claim the entire eastern seaboard from Newfoundland to Florida. As early as 1720 Father Bode of the Congregation of Missions drew up a paper laying out the claims. The demands included the return of Port Royal, at which time a commission was to be set up to administer the territory as far as Cape Cod, which would include Boston.

Father Bode thought that England was bound by honour to return all territories ceded, and France would agree to a boundary drawn from the mouth of the Kennebec, passing midway between Lake Champlain and Schenectady and along the ridge of the Alleghenies to the River Jordan (probably the Savannah River of South Carolina). The country between the line and the sea belonged to England; the rest of the continent was to be the domain of France.

Father Bode advised his government to build forts on the Niagara, the Ohio, the Tennessee and the Alabama Rivers, as well as other commanding points, to shut the English out of the west.

Of all the posts the one at Niagara was the most important as it closed off access to the upper lakes and prevented the western tribes from going to Albany to trade furs. The Iroquois Confederacy and the governor of New York were alarmed at the prospects of the French scheme, but the other colonies could not be roused to action.

To gain the consent of the Senecas for the building of a fort at Niagara Vaudreuil had Joncaire, who had married a Seneca woman and considered a member of the tribe, try to persuade them. Yet the Iroquois were so concerned about a French fort at Niagara that they sent three chiefs to see what they were doing. The French were in the process of building a stockade on the heights overlooking the Lower Landing (Lewiston, N.Y.) and the chiefs insisted that it be torn down. The French refused. After many negotiations the Senecas finally gave permission for a house, not a fort, to be built at the mouth of the Niagara River. The French accepted the proposal and agreed to build a house of peace there.

This house of peace turned out to be a loopholed castle capable of holding off any attack that the Iroquois could hope to mount on it. This castle can be seen at Old Fort Niagara today.

The English countered with a fort of their own at Oswego on Lake Ontario. It soon became the favourite post for the western tribes who preferred English goods and English prices.

Quebec drew up plans to destroy the fort, but the court at Versailles wanted to avoid another war and no action was taken against it. Instead a post was established at Toronto with two armed ships at Fort Frontenac to control navigation on the lake.

To strengthen their position to the south of Montréal the governor built a stone fort at Chambly. In 1731 the French built Fort Frédéric at Crown Point where Lake Champlain narrows to the width of a river. The English were outraged, but could not muster a consensus among the various colonies to do anything about it.

While baiting the lion in his den, the French did not neglect the west. Forts at Niagara, Détroit and Michilimackinac closed the upper lakes to English traders. Other forts at the head of Green Bay and at the Maumee River prevented English access to the Mississippi. The French stranglehold on the continent west of the Alleghenies was growing ever tighter.

In the meantime the sons of La Verendrye were desperately trying to retrieve the fortune of their dead father. They were on the verge of succeeding when disaster struck. La Galissionière, the gover-

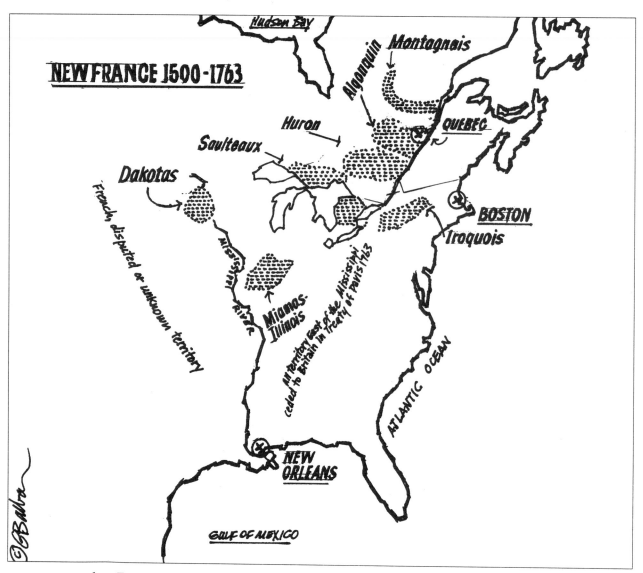

NEW FRANCE 1500-1763

Hudson Bay

Montagnais

Algonquin

Huron

Saulteaux

QUEBEC

Dakotas

BOSTON

Iroquois

French disputed or unknown territory

Mississippi River

Miamas-Illinois

All territory east of the Mississippi ceded to Britain in Treaty of Paris 1763

ATLANTIC OCEAN

NEW ORLEANS

GULF OF MEXICO

nor, returned to France and the Marquis de la Jonquière succeeded him with the notorious François Bigot as intendant. The sons were overlooked and La Jonquière wrote the minister,

"I have charged M. de Saint-Pierre with this business. He knows these countries better than any officer in all the colony."

Saint-Pierre had never seen them.

The brothers begged to return to save their property, but they were refused. They had risked their lives and spent their youth building the posts and laying in stores to reap the bounty due them. They were shamefully robbed.

Saint-Pierre set out for Manitoba in June of 1750. Although he had lived in the woods for thirty-six years, nothing could have prepared him for the trek he had undertaken.

"I was told," he wrote, "that the way would grow harder and more dangerous as we advanced, and I found, in fact, that one must risk life and property every moment."

His men were starving. He sent a party under Ensign Niverville to the Saskatchewan, but they failed to reach it and almost starved to death. Saint-Pierre wrote,

"I was more fortunate. Food was so scarce that I sent some of my people into the woods among the Indians, which did not save me from a fast so rigorous that it deranged my

102

health and put it out of my power to do anything toward accomplishing my mission. Even if I had strength enough, the war that broke out among the Indians would have made it impossible to proceed."

Niverville attempted to salvage something from the expedition and in May 1751 headed for the Saskatchewan again with orders to build a fort. On reaching the river he sent ten men in two canoes up river to a place they called Rock Mountain where they built a small stockade, which they named Fort La Jonquière.

Saint-Pierre set out to follow Niverville, but was met by two of his men who informed him that a band of Assiniboin had slaughtered their Indian guides. Saint-Pierre returned to Fort La Reine to spend the winter of 1751-52.

Toward the end of February 1752 the stockade was suddenly full of armed Assinboins who broke into the guardhouse and began to steal the guns there. A massacre would have surely followed had not Saint-Pierre seized a torch and threatened to blow himself and the attackers up. At this the Indians bolted for the gate and Saint-Pierre quickly locked it behind them.

Further exploration was pointless and he left Fort La Reine in charge of some friendly Assinboins, who promised to keep it safe, and headed for home. Four days after he left they burned the fort to the ground. Saint-Pierre and his party reached Quebec empty handed in the autumn of 1753.

La Verendrye must have smiled from his resting-place in the little chapel of Sainte Anne.

As the year 1744 dawned Louisbourg continued to grow both in substance and its role as a symbol of the French presence in the New World. To the French it was the great gesture, the guardian of the gateway to Canada. To the English it was threat to their trade with the American colonies. To the English colonists of New England it represented a constant threat to their livelihood and the seagoing commerce on which it depended. It also threatened the fishery, which was a major part of the trade carried on with England.

The Treaty of Utrecht left unsettled the question of the boundaries between the colonies in North America. As much as Vaudreuil and then his successor, Beauharnois, were willing to precipitate a quarrel over these issues and their American counterparts in New England were more than ready to oblige, London and Versailles still hesitated to apply the sword to the problem. As usual, it was not a colonial, but a European match that lit the fires again. Frederick II ascended the throne of Prussia with some grandiose ideas. He saw Prussia's star rising at the expense of his neighbour, Austria. On the death of Charles VI of Austria Frederick laid claim to the province of Silesia and precipitated the War of the Austrian Succession. Spain sided with Prussia, and France, Spain's ally, followed suit. England was at war with Spain and felt it could not very well be at peace with France under the circumstances. War was declared.

News from Europe usually was very slow to reach the New World. However, in this instance, Versailles informed Governor Duquesnel at Louisbourg some weeks before the news reached Boston. Duquesnel was not one of France's shining lights. We have a first hand account from Louisbourg, which gives us some insight into the man,

"Poor man, we owe him little, he was whimsical, changeable, given to drink, and when in his cups knowing no restraint or decency. He had affronted nearly all the officers of Louisbourg and destroyed their authority with the soldiers. It was because his affairs were in disorder and he was ruined that he had been given the government of Cape Breton."

Whatever his shortcomings Duquesnel moved with speed and resolve upon receiving the news. The small fishing settlement of Canseau stood on the southern end of the Strait of Canseau about eighty kilometres from Louisbourg. Here the governor saw an opportunity to strike a blow for the honour of France and the retrieval of his own fortune. Captain Duvivier was put in command of six hundred men, who set sail in May in a motley fleet of which only two vessels were armed. Canseau was a scattering of houses with a wooden redoubt for protection. There were about eighty defenders capable of manning the walls.

The fishermen of Canseau were unaware of the turn of events in Europe and the first notice came from Captain Duvivier as he sailed into the harbour demanding the surrender of the garrison. There was little the English could do under the circumstances, so they negotiated terms and surrendered. The terms of the capitulation were that they were to be sent to either Annapolis or Boston. There was one small qualification, they must first spend a year as prisoners at Louisbourg. Canseau was burned to the ground and the small fleet returned to Louisbourg with their prisoners and some much needed supplies.

The transport of the prisoners to Louisbourg was a blunder that far outweighed the victory at Canseau. It became obvious that the fortress was incapable of supporting the extra mouths represented by the English prisoners. They had to be returned to New England immediately and they went armed with the knowledge of conditions at Louisbourg. The impregnable fortress was far from impregnable. Leadership was lacking, the pay of the Swiss mercenaries who made up a large portion of the garrison was in arrears, and there was a chronic shortage of provisions and munitions. The English colonists saw an opportunity to rid itself of this perennial thorn in their side.

Oblivious to the folly of his actions in returning the English prisoners, Duquesnel now pushed forward a plan to seize Annapolis, the Port Royal of old, and recover Acadia for Louis XV. Duvivier

Louisbourg, circa 1744

was again given command. His heart was in the fight for he was a descendant of la Tour, feudal claimant to all of Acadia in the previous century. He set sail with a modest force of Four officers and ninety regular soldiers. They picked up three hundred Micmac warriors on the way and all was set. On the surface it appeared to be an easy task. Like Canseau, the defences were minimal having fallen into disrepair over the proceeding years. It was said that the cows of Annapolis routinely strolled over the ramparts at their leisure. Annapolis was commanded by Major Paul Mascarene, a French Protestant, whose family had been driven into exile. He had one hundred men to defend his post. Things did not look good for the garrison. Governor Shirley of Massachusetts had sent a small reinforcement of State militia, but they had arrived without arms and Mascarene had none to spare. The siege began.

Three weeks of attacks failed to make an impres-

sion on the town. Duvivier failed to enlist the active participation of the Acadians other than to get them to construct one hundred and fifty scaling ladders for the final assault for which the canny Acadians insisted on being paid.

The attack on Annapolis just petered out. Duvivier sent word to Mascarene that two ships were enroute from Louisbourg with reinforcements, which would make his position untenable. He demanded that he surrender. Mascarene replied that he would make up his mind when the ships arrived. He was spared having to make the decision. Governor Duquesnel quarreled with the two captains and they sailed off, but not to Annapolis. When two ships did arrive they were from Boston with fifty rangers sent to bolster the garrison. All heart went out of the besiegers and the army melted away. The expedition was a failure. With this failure was planted the seed of the destruction of French power in the New World.

CHAPTER THIRTY-SIX

The Siege of Louisbourg

"May it please your honour to be informed that by the grace of God and the courage of 13 men,
I entered the Royal Battery about 9 o'clock."-William Vaughan to William Pepperrell

With the failure of Duvivier's expedition against Annapolis, the people of New England looked to settle the question of the French presence on the Atlantic seaboard. Louisbourg was a standing menace to British interests in North America. It was the only French naval base on the continent and was the haunt of privateers that preyed on English shipping. It threatened New England's participation in the fisheries, which was nearly as vital to them as the fur trade was to the Canadians. William Vaughan advised Governor William Shirley of Massachusetts to capture Louisbourg and end the menace once and for all.

Plans were put in motion and on the 9th of January 1745 Shirley went before the General Court of Massachusetts and, after swearing this august body of city merchants to secrecy, put forward the plan to reduce Louisbourg. We can only imagine their reaction to this scheme. Louisbourg, the most powerful fortress in North America, to be captured by a colonial expedition; madness, absolute madness. They listened, however, to the governor's logic and appointed a committee to consider the proposal. After several days of deliberation the committee rejected the scheme and the court followed suit. In the meantime, despite the oath, the secret got out and was soon the talk of the colony.

After this defeat Shirley returned home where he received a visit from James Gibson, a Boston Merchant, who wished that the assembly would reconsider its position. Gibson agreed to circulate a petition to reopen the debate. Traveling to Marblehead and Salem, he solicited the aid of the merchants there. It was not hard to get their signatures, for Louisbourg was the arch-enemy of English commerce in the New World.

The petition was presented, and the question came before the assembly. Shirley argued passionately for his cause. Had not the returning prisoners from Canseau brought news of shortages and mutiny at the fortress? His opponents countered that the harbour would have to be blockaded to prevent supplies reaching the town from France. For that the help of England would be needed. Shirley argued that to delay would be to let the golden opportunity slip away. Here Vaughan, the author of the scheme, put all his energies into the fray and the proposal passed by a single vote.

To command the force Shirley chose a merchant of Kittery, William Pepperrell, a popular figure among the colonists that he would lead. He had no military experience, but it was more important, for the purposes of recruitment, that he be popular. All was ready.

On March 24, 1745 the expedition was ready to sail from Nantasket Roads. The ninety transports were escorted by a motley assortment of armed sloops and other brigs that made up the navies of the New England colonies. There was obviously no guns large enough to act as siege artillery with the expedition. The commander's answer was that the French would supply these. It was known that a detached battery at Louisbourg called the Grand, or Royal Battery mounted thirty heavy guns. It was proposed that these be captured and turned on the town. One contemporary observer remarked that it was "like selling the bear's skin before catching him."

The ships sailed only to be greeted by a storm, which was described by Seth Pomeroy, a gunsmith of Northhampton and a Major in one of the Massachusetts regiments,

> "A terrible northeast storm" had fallen upon them and, he says, "we lay rolling in the seas, with sails furled, among prodigious waves. Sick, day and night, so bad that I have no words to set it forth."

The fleet was scattered, a ominous beginning to the enterprise.

On Friday, April 5th Pomeroy's vessel sailed into Canseau, Eighty kilometres from Louisbourg and sixty-eight of the transports followed quickly. Others staggered in over the next few days. All were damaged to one degree or another, but all arrived safely. Sloops of the fleet were sent to cruise off Louisbourg and report. They arrived back with six French prizes taken with supplies for the fortress, but also with some unsettling news. Louisbourg and the adjacent bay were still clogged with ice and landings would be im-

Opposing the Louisbourg landings, April, 1745

possible. This put the expedition in serious jeopardy. Any day reinforcements from France could appear making the doubtful mission worse. Indeed ships had already begun to appear. On Thursday the 18th heavy cannon were heard far out to sea. It was the colonial cruisers attacking the French frigate "Renommée" of 36 guns. She escaped after a chase of thirty hours.

On Monday the 22nd a large ship wearing British colours sailed into the harbour. She proved to be the "Eltham" Frigate escorting the first convoy of the season to the New England ports. She had received orders from the British Squadron at Antigua to sail to Canseau. She brought the happy news that a British squadron was coming to their aid. They duly arrived the following day, the 60 gun "Superbe" accompanied by the "Launceston" and the "Mermaid" of 40 guns each. On the 29th of April the expedition left Canseau

arriving off Louisbourg the following day.

Louisbourg stands on a tongue of land, which lies between its harbour and the sea. The land was prolonged seaward by a series of shoals and reefs that partly blocked the entrance to the harbour leaving a navigable passage of only one kilometre wide. This passage was defended by the powerful "Island Battery" at the west side of the channel and the "Royal Battery" on the shore of the harbour itself. A fleet trying to force an entrance would suffer flank fire from the former and head on fire from the latter. The garrison consisted of Five hundred and sixty regulars and thirteen hundred militia. The regulars were in bad condition and the officers distrusted them. The governor, Chevalier Duchambon, was not a man of decisive action and he did nothing to prepare for the attack that they knew was coming.

Duchambon sent the privateer, Morpain with one hundred and twenty men to oppose the landing. Pepperrell's landing went surprisingly well considering the raw troops employed. The rocks and surf were more dangerous than the enemy. Several boats heading for Flat Point were ordered back. Morpain thought that his appearance had frightened the force off, but instead they joined with other boats and headed for a landing at Anse de la Cormorandière three kilometres farther up Gabarus Bay. Morpain rushed to meet them, however, the boats won the race and as soon as they got ashore the New Englanders rush the French defenders firing as they came and fought a sharp engagement amid the rocks and trees of the shoreline. Six of the defenders were killed and as many more captured, including an officer named Boularderie, the rest of the force withdrew to await reinforcements. A further challenge to the landings was impossible and by nightfall two thousand men were ashore and had consolidated the beachhead. The fate of the Fortress of Louisbourg was in the balance.

With the landing at Anse de la Cormorandière the English began to exploit their success. Governor Shirley had worked out the invasion plan carefully. He realized that the most important feature next to the fortress itself was the Royal Battery. Its capture would be crucial to the operation. Colonel William Vaughan was given command of four hundred men to accomplish this vital task.

On the 2nd of May Vaughan led his party to the hills in the rear of the fortress. Behind the Royal Battery were a number of buildings housing naval stores of tar, sails and cables. These Vaughan torched and the resultant smoke and flames convinced the defenders that a full scale attack was imminent.

A young reporter for the Louisbourg Journals recorded the incident and its aftermath:

"They were much blamed for destroying so much. I can't suppose they had any prospects of doing any good thereby." But good did result for the English. Our reporter observed, "From that moment the talk was of abandoning this splendid battery, which would have been our chief defence had we known how to make use of it . . . Not a single musket had been fired against this battery . . . Unless it was from a panic fear which never left us again during the siege, it would be difficult to give any reason

for such extraordinary action."

In Louisbourg the council met and, on the advice of Captain Thierry, the commander of the battery, decided to abandon the Royal Battery without firing a shot. Thirty guns were spiked and the garrison moved into the fortress.

As the English party moved back toward their own lines after completing the destruction of the French stores, William Vaughan noticed that no flag flew from the flagstaff of the battery. No Smoke curled from the barracks chimney. An Indian with his party was given a bottle of brandy and, pretending to be drunk, staggered toward the battery for a closer look. He noisily mounted the parapet and slipped through an embrasure. To his amazement the battery was empty. Vaughan took possession and ran a redcoat up the pole in lieu of a flag. He immediately sent a note to Pepperrell:

"May it please your honour to be informed that
by the grace of God and the courage of 13 men,
I entered the Royal Battery about 9 o'clock, and
am waiting for a reinforcement and a flag."

Unaware that the English had taken the battery, Duchambon sent four boats to complete the destruction of the battery. The boats came under fire from the English forces and, despite covering fire from the town, were unable to affect a landing after Lieutenant Colonel John Bradstreet of Massachusetts arrived with a relief force. Soon boats with more reinforcements for the English garrison arrived under the fire of the fortress, but they completed their mission ending any chance of recapturing the battery. The enemy fell into the possession of twenty-eight 42 pounder guns and two eighteen pounders along with a quantity of cannon cartridges and other ordinance stores. Several of these were drilled out and were ready to open fire on the town the next morning. The young Louisbourg reporter recorded,

"The enemy saluted us with our own cannon,
and made a terrible fire, smashing everything
within range."

The capture of the Royal Battery was the turning point in the siege. Once entrenched a few hundred colonials could hold off an army of thousands. The

The British enter Louisbourg, June 17, 1745

defenders watched in dismay as, under the cover of darkness and fog the English dragged their siege artillery over the marshy ground on sledges of timber. Some of these were taken from the Royal Battery. Batteries were planted at strategic points around the town, one within two hundred and fifty yards of the main gate. All this took place without interference from the garrison. Duchambon feared that many of the troops would desert if a sortie was attempted, thus, the English set their siege train in place and prepared to bombard the town in earnest.

Despite a constant bombardment the fortress showed little sign of damage. It would take the guns of the English fleet to make an impression on the great walls. But, as long as the Island Battery commanded the harbour entrance the fleet had to stand out to sea.

The impatient Pepperrell made his one disastrous decision of the campaign. He ordered the capture of the Island Battery.

At midnight on the 26th of May three hundred men left the Royal Battery and were joined by a further one hundred and fifty from Lighthouse Point. They used paddles instead of oars for the heavy boats to cut down on the noise. Captain d'Aillebout, commanding the battery, was unaware of the danger as the first boats landed. He might have remained in ignorance until too late had the English colonial officers followed their instructions, but the undisciplined troops let out three cheers and the vigilant battery came alive with cannon and musket fire. The landing party and the boats inshore came under a withering fire from the garrison. Come morning one hundred and nineteen surrendered. Of the attacking force nearly half were killed, wounded or captured.

Louisbourg rejoiced at this great victory. Faint hearts took courage from the exploits of the battery garrison. The enthusiasm was short lived. A few days later the French man-o-war "Vigilant" of sixty-four guns was lured into the midst of the English fleet. Sixty of her crew were killed and the ship captured.

The English next turned their attention to the Island Battery and what could not be taken by storm was systematically pounded to pieces by artillery brought up for the purpose. In the meantime the bombardment on the town continued. The citizens found security in artificial caves and bomb shelters. They were made with long pieces of timber and an observer in Louisbourg left us this account:

"Deadening the force of the bombs and turning them aside that their momentum had no effect. It was underneath this that we buried them (women and children). We feared at every moment that the enemy, waking from their blindness, would press forward and carry the place by assault. I am able to affirm that we had not enough powder left for three charges."

Soon eleven ships of war arrived from England and the fate of Louisbourg was sealed. Governor Duchambon asked for terms of surrender. After protracted negotiations terms were agreed on. The terms were generous indeed. The French would be allowed to march out with flags flying, drums beating and with their arms, which would be surrendered later. The French troops would be returned to France and bound not to fight against England for one year. Canadians were allowed to return to their homes and all private property was to be respected. One unusual clause was added and it read:

"If there be any person in the town or garrison, which you shall desire may not be seen by us, they shall be permitted to go off mask'd."

This clause has never been explained.

At the prescribed hour the gates were opened and the English marched into the great fortress where the surrender was accomplished. The gateway to Canada was closed.

The battle for Louisbourg was over and the New

Englanders had achieved their goal of ending the threat to the fisheries and to their seafaring trade. Commodore Warren, commanding the British ships of war visited the Grand Battery and gave the regiment stationed there a hogshead of rum to drink his health. In his speech he promised them that they would,

"soon keep a good house together, and give the ladys of Louisbourg a Gallant Ball."

Whether the ball ever took place has not been recorded, however Pepperrell celebrated the victory with a dinner for the commodore and all the officers of the forces employed. The general's chaplain, the Rev. Samuel Moody, celebrated by desecrating the church. He took an axe to the altar and smashed the statues in violation of the surrender terms.

Despite the apparent success, all was not well in the camp of the conqueror. The meager pay of the militiamen was to be supplemented by the booty that the sacking of Louisbourg had promised. The terms of the surrender put an end to that dream. All property was to be respected. One of the soldiers in Pepperrell's army wrote in his journal,

"Sabbath Day, ye 16th June. They came to termes for us to enter ye sitty to morrow, and poore Termes they bee too. . . .by which means the poor soldiers lost all their hopes and just demerit (desert) of plunder promised them."

They had also expected, after the wet and dreary camp to be housed in the comfort of quarters in the town. To their disgust the inhabitants still occupied their homes. To make matters worse, they were forced to guard these homes against looting.

"A great Noys and hubbub a mongst ye solders a bout ye plunder; som Cursing, som a Swarein," wrote one of the disillusioned victors.

Order was not maintained for long. When, in accordance with the terms of capitulation, the French troops and citizens were put on board ship for France, the troops began looting the town. Fortunately their was little left to steal.

With only the Canadians left in the town the victors had all the shelter they needed. Poor shelter it

Burying the dead, Louisbourg, winter, 1746

turned out to be. Their own bombardment during the siege now came back to haunt them. The town was in a filthy state. Make shift repairs needed constant attention to keep out the worst of the weather.

The troops clamoured for discharge, having enlisted only to serve until the fortress was captured. Pepperrell, much to the chagrin of Commodore Warren sent seven.hundred men home. Warren and Pepperrell jointly governed Louisbourg under martial law and spent half their time conducting courts-martial; for the militia was in a constant state of near mutiny. Under these conditions the expected Canadian attempt to retake the fortress would be accomplished by default. Pepperrell begged Shirley to come to Louisbourg and bring the militia back to duty. Shirley accordingly boarded a man-o-war and sailed for Louisbourg along with his wife and the wife of the Commodore. The militiamen fell in to receive the visiting party and Shirley immediately offered them a raise in pay from 25 shillings to 40 shillings a month. After providing a keg of rum to toast the King's health, the militiamen were pacified and some even promised to stay until the following June. The promise of troops from Gibraltar and the raising of two colonial regiments in New England seemed to end the crisis.

Winter set in and the troubles of the English garrison mounted. A pestilence set in and Dr. Douglas, the army surgeon wrote in his journal,

> "After we got into the town a sordid indolence or sloth, for want of discipline, induced putrid fevers contagious, and the people died like rotten sheep."

Fourteen to twenty-seven were buried daily in the cemetery behind the fortress, outside the Maurepas Gate. Slowly the fever ran its course and soon the burial parties were only carrying out three or four a day. The end of January found five hundred and sixty-one men dead from disease, eleven hundred on the sick list, leaving about one thousand fit for duty. The promised Gibraltar regiments had failed to come and had Quebec sent a modest force against Louisbourg, it would surely have changed hands again.
The Gibraltar regiments had wintered in Virginia and finally arrived in April armed with a commission for Commodore Warren as governor of Louisbourg. The New England contingent finally sailed for home. The threat was now more tangible than ever. Warren and Shirley began to plan the conquest of Canada.

111

France had two gateways to their New World colonies. The ancient route down the St. Lawrence, now threatened by the fall of Louisbourg, was the most direct access to Canada and, secondly, the link between Louisiana and Canada through the maze of rivers and lakes dominated by the mighty Mississippi, the Ohio and the Illinois. The recovery of Louisbourg was essential to the survival of Canada and the link to Louisiana was important in maintaining Canadian dominance of the fur trade. The maintenance of the Louisiana link necessitated the control of the entire continent west of the Allegheny Mountains. For one hundred and fifty years this control was exercised indirectly by Canadian traders. They knew the Indians and their ways and were able to control English access to the region by encouraging Indian resistance to the encroachment of American settlements. The French officials at Quebec could plead innocence of any knowledge of the resultant raids while quietly cultivating the friendship of the offending tribes. The English could fume and fuss, but with no proof of Canadian involvement, they could take no offensive action without appearing to start a war; a war that neither England nor France wanted.

Despite the lose of Louisbourg, or perhaps because of it, France pressed its claim to the bulk of North America. To establish that claim she proceeded on a program of building forts along trade routes to keep out English traders and keep the Indians within the sphere of French influence. As early as 1726 the French attempted to build a post opposite Crown Point on Lake Champlain, but were thwarted by the vigorous opposition of Massachusetts. However Crown Point was claimed by both Massachusetts and New Hampshire and the two colonies fell into a dispute over its ownership. As one writer of the day observed,

"While they were quarrelling for the bone, the French ran away with it."

In 1731 the French took advantage of the turmoil and established a fortified post on the opposite side of the lake from Crown Point on land nominally claimed by New York. New York was embroiled in a dispute with New Jersey at the time and her governor was at war with the assembly, so no action was taken to stop the French intrusion. Sainte Luc de la Corne, Lieutenant du Roi at Montréal, urged Versailles to seize control of Lake Champlain and subsequently the governor was ordered to build a fort at Crown Point. The Sieur de la Fresnière was sent with troops and workmen to build Fort Frédéric. It contained a massive stone tower mounted with cannon to command the lake, which was but a musket shot wide at this point. New York and New England protested, but could not agree to unite to drive the French from their new stronghold.

If the American colonies were unwilling or unable to act, England had no such problem. The government in London realized that France was at once its chief enemy and its greatest rival in trade. The North American continent was the future and the expansion of the English colonies the key to becoming the predominant trading nation in the world. It became obvious to all that only one of the two powers could emerge as masters of the continent. Canada was the linchpin in the survival of France in North America, and uninterrupted communications with Louisiana was necessary for Canada to survive. New France could not flourish without Canada and Canada could not prosper without the other French colonies. The ministers of the British Crown laid plans to cripple the French Navy, plans that eventually led to the Seven Years War.

To ensure the security of the vital routes that linked the colonies of New France, a string of forts were planned to keep English traders out of the Ohio Valley in particular and the west in general. Fort Niagara closed access to the Lakes Ontario and Erie and the post at Détroit guarded the fur trade route into Lakes Huron, Michigan and Superior. Détroit soon became the major trading post of the fur trade surpassing Michilimackinac in that role. Fur traders still passed through Michilimackinac on their way to Montréal via the northern route through the French and Ottawa Rivers while those coming through Détroit used Lakes Erie and Ontario to reach Montréal. Fort Presqu'Ile was also built on the south shore of Lake Erie opposite Long Point. To further guard the west,

Building forts in the west

posts were built on the Maumee to guard the carrying place between it and the Wabash. A fort at St. Joseph guarded La Salle's old route by way of Kankakee and the Illinois, and, should the English get past all these obstacles, they faced the cannon of Fort Chartres on the Mississippi. Fort La Baye kept watch on Marquette's route via the Fox and Wisconsin Rivers.

To defray the high cost of these posts, each one was also a fur trading post. Some were run be agents of the Crown who kept the lion's share of the profits for themselves others were leased to independent traders at a fix price. At others the commanding officer was allowed to participate in the trade on condition that he maintained the post, pay the soldiers, and maintained a missionary.

France eventually occupied and asserted its claim to the valley of the Mississippi. The stage was set for the momentous conflict to come.

CHAPTER THIRTY-EIGHT

Planning the Destruction of Canada
"If all these stories are true, all the English on this continent must be in arms."-Canadian journalist, 1745

With the fall of Louisbourg the pulse of British America quickened. Governor Shirley of Massachusetts had visions of this victory being but the first in the scheme to drive France from the North American continent. Scarcely had the New England militia sailed for Louisbourg, when he wrote the Duke of Newcastle in April of 1745 that, should the expedition succeed, all New England would be on fire to attack Canada, and the other colonies would do their share if so ordered by the mother country.

The plan was a familiar one. A two prong invasion, one over the much used Lake Champlain route against Montréal. Volunteers from the western and southern colonies were to be the mainstay of this expedition along with a large number of Indians. The other attack would ascend the St. Lawrence with Quebec as its objective. This prong was to be manned by New Englanders, supported by the British fleet and eight battalions of regulars promised by the Duke of Newcastle, now head of the British government.

In Canada the alarm bells rang. Louisbourg was lost and reports of the pending invasion were coming in daily to Quebec. Preparations were made to meet the crisis. Despite the overwhelming odds that the enemy promised to bring against them there was a quiet confidence throughout the colony. Had they not prevailed before? At the darkest moments had not the English menace melted away? As we shall see; far from taking a defensive attitude in the crisis, the Canadians looked to the offense to relieve the pressure on their homes.

For once, in the English camp, all parties seemed to be in agreement on a plan of action. Newcastle directed Shirley to consult with Admiral Warren as to the proposed attack on Canada. At the same time he sent a letter to the governors of the provinces from New England to the Carolinas, directing them to call upon the assemblies for as many men as they could muster to aid the proposed expedition. Warren endorsed Shirley's plan and the levies made accordingly. Massachusetts voted to raise thirty-five hundred men, offering a bounty of £4 sterling to each volunteer, besides a blanket for every one and a bed for every two. New Hampshire contributed five hundred men, Rhode

Island three hundred, Connecticut one thousand, New York sixteen hundred, New Jersey five hundred, Maryland three hundred, and Virginia one hundred. The Pennsylvania Assembly, controlled by Quakers, would give no soldiers; but, four hundred volunteers came forward to serve without the help of the assembly.

All was ready. The promised regulars and the fleet were all that was needed to complete the contingent. The eight battalions of regulars under Lieutenant-General Saint Clair, along with the fleet, were to meet the New England force at Louisbourg and all were to sail for Quebec together. Days turned into weeks as the colonials watched the horizon from the battlements of the fortress in vain.

In Canada things looked glum indeed. Letters written by English prisoners being held at Quebec showed them to be expecting a quick delivery from their bonds. In July, reports reached Quebec that forty to fifty thousand men were poised to invade Canada. A prisoner taken at Saratoga declared that there were thirty-two ships of war at Boston ready to sail against Quebec, and that thirteen thousand men were to march from Albany against Montréal.

"If all these stories are true," wrote a Canadian journalist at Quebec, "all the English on this continent must be in arms."

Feverish preparations were made. Fireships were made ready at Quebec, and fire rafts at Isle aux Coudres for use against the English fleet. Provisions were gathered and ammunition distributed. Reconnaissance patrols were sent to watch the gulf, the river, and the approaches to Montréal. Canadians and Indians that had been sent to Acadia were ordered back to defend Quebec.

Thanks to the Duke of Newcastle, all the preparations were needless. The Fleet and troops never came. Shirley wrote him in August that it would be impossible to reach Quebec before October, which would be too late. The eight battalions had been sent to Portsmouth for embarkation, ordered on board the transports, then ordered ashore again, and finally sent on a

Boston braces for invasion, 1746

sortie against the coast of France. Shirley was ordered to make no further attempt at conquest.

History repeated itself on the Montréal front and the Lake Champlain force simply melted away. This was to have an unforeseen affect on the future of the region. The Indians saw, in this latest English fiasco, proof that the French were invulnerable on the frontier. Even the Iroquois, the ancient enemies of Canada, began to turn from their English allies.

In the autumn of 1746 Shirley developed a less ambitious plan to capture Crown Point, the kick off point for the raids into New York and Massachusetts. For once Governor Clinton of New York agreed to a joint expedition and by the middle of October thirteen hundred Massachusetts militiamen were on their way to join their New York compatriots in the reduction of that most obnoxious post.

Even this modest enterprise was doomed. As the troops marched to their rendezvous astonishing news

fell upon New England like a thunderclap. It was reported that a great French fleet and army were on their way to recapture Louisbourg, reconquer Acadia, burn Boston, and lay waste the other seacoast towns. The Massachusetts contingent was recalled and every able-bodied man called to arms. In a few days the narrow, crooked streets of the Puritan capital were crowded with more than eight thousand armed men from the farms and villages of Massachusetts. Connecticut promised a further six thousand the minute the fleet was sighted.

Canada rejoiced at the news although their joy was somewhat tempered when the fleet failed to appear. At length in September a ship slipped into port with news that she had met the fleet in mid ocean, and that they had counted one hundred and fifty sail. France was about to attempt what the English had failed to do, conquer a continent.

115

CHAPTER THIRTY-NINE

The French Armada

"The waves ran as high as the masts; and such was their violence that a transport, dashing against the ship"Amazone", immediately went down, with all on board."-A Captain of the Regiment de Ponthieu

The great fleet assembled at Brest under the Duc d'Anville in the spring of 1746. It was a formidable force. Sixty-six vessels consisting of eleven ships of the line, twenty frigates and fire ships, and thirty-four transports. The transports carried munitions, provisions, and thirty-one hundred and fifty veteran soldiers charged with the task of recovering Louisbourg and Acadia and ensuring the supremacy of France in the New World.

From Brest Anville sailed for some reason to Rochelle on the Bay of Biscay, where the ships were kept in harbour by head winds until the 20th of June when they were finally able to put to sea. From the beginning the omens were sinister. The Bay of Biscay was stormy and spars, sails and bowsprits were carried away. Some of the ships were slow sailers and lagged behind forcing the rest to shorten sail and wait for them. In the longitude of the Azores the entire fleet was becalmed and it drifted aimlessly for several days. Then came a squall, with lightning. Several ships were struck. On one six men were killed, and on the seventy gun ship of the line, "Mars" a box of musket and cannon cartridges exploded, killing ten men and wounding twenty others. A transport began to sink and was abandoned and burned. To add to the Anville's troubles the fleet was swept by a pestilence, and in many ships their were more sick than healthy sailors.

The fleet finally neared the coast of Nova Scotia on the 14th of September and they were in dread of the infamous shoals of Sable Island, the position of which they were unsure. They groped their way in dense fog until a gale descended on them. A captain in the Regiment de Ponthieu, on board the "Prince d'Orange," left us a description of the plight of the expedition.

"The waves ran as high as the masts; and such was their violence that a transport, dashing against the ship "Amazone," immediately went down, with all on board. The crew of the "Prince d'Orange," half blinded by wind and spray, saw the great ship "Caribou," without bowsprit or main topmast, driving towards them before the gale, and held their breath in expectation of the shock as she swept close alongside and vanished in the storm."

The tempest raged all night and the fleet became so scattered that the threat of further collisions disappeared.

In the morning our journalist could only see five sail, but as the day wore on more gathered until, by three o'clock, he counted thirty-one. Wreckage floating on the waves told a tale of disaster for some of the ships of the fleet. The "Argonaut" was rolling helplessly without masts or rudder; the "Caribou" had thrown all her starboard guns overboard; and the vice admiral's ship, the "Trident," was in a poor way as well.

On the 23rd they were again wrapped in thick fog and fired guns, rang bells and beat drums to avoid collisions. When the weather cleared they searched in vain for Anville's ship, the "Northumberland." She was not lost, however, but was well ahead of the fleet with two other ships near Chibucto Bay. Without a local pilot Anville was uncertain as to its location, but luck, for once, was with him and he captured a small English vessel. He offered one of the men his freedom and one hundred louis if he would pilot the ship in. He agreed, but when he rejoined his fellow prisoners they accused him of being a traitor and he refused to guide the ships. Captain Duperrier of the "Northumberland" threatened to throw him into the sea with a cannon ball tied to his feet if he didn't keep his promise and by nightfall they were safely anchored in the bay. Anville hoped to find the four ships of Conflans from the West Indies waiting for him, but there was only a solitary transport from his own fleet their to greet him. Conflans had waited three weeks and then sailed for France.

Anville was devastated by the turn a events. The ships that had accompanied him into the bay were full of sick sailors. He had no reason to doubt that those others of his fleet, spared by the storm, would be in no better condition. At two o'clock in the morning, on the 27th of September he died in his cabin of apoplexy. Rumours persisted among the crew that he had

Battling the sea, September, 1746

in fact committed suicide by poison.

At six o'clock in the afternoon of the same day Vice Admiral d'Estournel, with the ships he had been able to gather, sailed into the harbour. To his dismay he was now in command over an expedition doomed to failure. The long voyage had consumed all the provisions, and in some ships the crews were starving. The pestilence grew worse and men died by the score every day. On the twenty-eighth Anville was buried without ceremony on a small island in the harbour. The officers met in council and examined the late admiral's papers. Among them was a letter from the King urging him to make the recovery of Louisbourg his first priority. This, of course, was impossible under the circumstances. Many of the officers urged an attack on Port Royal, now called Annapolis by the English, but Estournel opposed the project as hopeless, arguing instead for an immediate return to France. The council prevailed, however, and the vice admiral was seen entering his cabin in a state of distress and agitation. An unusual sound was heard emanating from the cabin followed by groans. The door was bolted from the inside. The door was burst open and the unfortunate commander was found lying in a pool of blood. Enraged and mortified by his failure, he had thrown himself on his sword. The surgeon pulled out the blade, but it was only on the urging of two Jesuits that he allowed the wound to be dressed. The dying commander called his captains to his side and said,

"Gentlemen, I beg pardon of God and the King for what I have done, and protest to the King that my only object was to prevent my enemies from saying that I had not executed his orders."

He named M. de la Jonquière to command in his place. Jonquière was later to become governor of Canada.

Jonquière remained at Chibucto until late in October. Messengers were sent to the Acadian communities in search of provisions, which were desperately needed. Because payment was to be in good metal and not the paper money normally used in the colonies, the Acadians responded with considerable supplies.

The men were encamped on shore but still the pestilence continued to ravage the crews. Two English prisoners were told that between twenty-three and twenty-four hundred men had been buried at sea or on land since the fleet left France. The survivors used the clothes of the dead as gifts to the neighbouring Indians, who subsequently were ravaged as well. Three quarters of the band at Cape Sable died of the fever. Jonquière still clung to the hope of a successful attack on Port Royal. The troops were re-embarked; five hospital ships were allocated for the sick and the "Parfait," a fifty gun ship was burned, as were several other smaller vessels, and the fleet sailed for Annapolis Basin. Ill luck was not done with the French fleet yet. Off Cape Sable a storm scattered the ships, two of which made their way to Annapolis Basin hoping to find some of their company there. Instead they found the fifty guns "Chester" frigate and the Massachusetts frigate "Shirley" anchored under the guns of the fort. The two wisely withdrew and sailed for home. The great fleet was no more.

CHAPTER FORTY
The Struggle for Acadian Loyalty
"If a thousand French troops should land in Nova Scotia all the
people would rise to join them."-Gov. Shirley of Massachusetts

Undaunted by the disastrous failure of the Anville expedition, the French court assembled another fleet to attempt to recapture Louisbourg and Acadia. Although not as powerful as the one commanded by Anville, it was still formidable. It was placed under the command of the Marquis de la Jonquière and sailed on the 10th of May 1747. On May 14, off Cape Finisterre, the fleet fell in with a numerically superior English fleet under Admiral George Anson. Despite the odds la Jonquière turned his six ships of the line to fight the seventeen British warships to give the transports time to slip away. After a five hour battle the six French ships were captured, but the transports made good their escape.

Despite these setbacks France was determined to recover Acadia. At the time of the Anville expedition a large force of Canadians under Claude de Ramsay marched to Acadia to assist in the reduction of the English and American forces there. The greater portion was recalled to counter the threat to Quebec, but Ramsay advanced with part of his command to support the projected attack on Port Royal (Annapolis) and camped a few miles from the fort. On hearing the news of the disasters that had visited the Anville fleet, he fell back to Chignecto, on the neck of the Acadian Peninsula, where he made his headquarters. His force, including Micmac, Malicite, and Penobscot Indians, numbered about sixteen hundred.

If France was bent on recovering Acadia, the American colonies were just as determined to hold on to it. Governor Shirley of Massachusetts urged the Duke of Newcastle to protect it. But Newcastle did not seem to know where Acadia was, much less care what happened to it. The defence was left to the Americans. Shirley wrote to Newcastle,

"If a thousand French troops should land in Nova Scotia all the people would rise to join them, besides all the Indians."

The government at Quebec was of the same opinion. Governor Beauharnois wrote to the minister in France,

"The inhabitants, with few exceptions, wish to return under French dominion, and will not hesitate to take up arms as soon as they see themselves free to do so; that is, as soon as we become masters of Port Royal, or they have powder and other munitions of war, and are backed by troops for their protection against the resentment of the English."

Although the Acadians felt an affinity for France, they were not always prepared to make sacrifices for her. They refused to supply Ramsay's army with provisions in exchange for promissory notes, but insisted on hard currency, something he did not have. At the same time they were supplying fuel to Louisbourg and helping to repair the ramparts at Annapolis in exchange for the same.

Major Masarcene, commanding at Annapolis, being a Frenchmen himself, tended to go easy on the Acadians. He wrote to Shirley,

"The French inhabitants are certainly in a very perilous situation, those who pretend to be their friends and old masters having let loose a parcel of banditti to plunder them; whilst, on the other hand, they see themselves threatened with ruin if they fail in their allegiance to the British Government."

The Acadians were caught between two empires trying to eliminate one another. France claimed them as their own and demanded loyalty. The British, on the other hand, insisted on their allegiance. Neither side paid any attention to the welfare of the people they sought to bring under their sphere of influence. The banditti that Masarcene referred to were Micmacs whom the French used to force the Acadians to renounce their oath of allegiance to King George I, which they had given under the terms of the Treaty of Utrecht. Technically they were British subjects, but since their oath was accompanied by a promise that they would not be required to take up arms against Frenchmen or Indians, they were referred to as "Neutral French." Matters were made worse by the

Governor Shirley presents his invasion plan

fact that they were, for the most part, Illiterate. Living in isolation, they had little knowledge of affairs outside their immediate country. They were far behind Canadians in the realm of business and were looked down on by them as inferior.

When Ramsay built a fort at Baie Verte on the neck of the peninsula English control of that area came to an end. The Acadians there broke off all contact with Annapolis, even detaining the officers sent to gather intelligence.

France pinned its hopes on the recovery of Acadia on the rising of the Acadians against English rule. This threat hung over the British administration of the province like a hatchet. Early in 1745 a violent and cruel solution to the problem was put forward. William Shirreff, provincial secretary, suggested that the Acadians should be removed, being a standing menace to the colony. In December Shirley gathered his officers in a council of war to discuss their options. He informed Newcastle that the French will get possession of Acadia unless the most dangerous inhabitants

were removed, and English settlers put in their place. He further offered that he only had two hundred and twenty soldiers at Annapolis to defend against the Acadians and Indians, and unless the expedition against Canada should end in the conquest of that country, the removal of some Acadians would be necessary.

Commodore Knowles, the governor of Louisbourg, called for the wholesale expulsion of the Acadian population. He opined that the Acadians had broken their neutrality and should be expelled at once. Shirley felt that the expulsion of whole communities was cruel and unjust. He preferred a more selective process believing that the bulk of the Acadians could become good British subjects. To facilitate this process he suggested a fortified town where Ramsay had built his fort to pacify the Acadians and to give them a ready market for their produce. He reasoned that prosperity bred loyalty. This plan of action was to result in the great tragedy of 1755.

120

CHAPTER FORTY-ONE

Attack on Grand Pré

"Noble was assured that Grand Pré could not be reached from Chignecto in the dead of winter."

1747

The thorny problem of Acadia continued to occupy the minds of the British Americans that occupied Nova Scotia. Shirley felt that the conversion of the Acadians to Protestantism was a political measure of the first priority. Various schemes were proposed including the setting up of schools and the offering of rewards to Acadians who would renounce their faith, but, Newcastle merely directed Shirley to tell the Acadians that as long as they were peaceable subjects, they should be protected in property and religion.

In the meantime Ramsay and his Canadians at Chignecto were openly campaigning to have the Acadians join the French colours for another attempt on Port Royal. To strengthen his hold he advanced to the Mines Basin on the Bay of Fundy. Shirley thought it necessary to check this threat and at least drive Ramsay back to the isthmus, but as Newcastle would give no soldiers he was forced to draw them from New England. Massachusetts gave five hundred men and Rhode Island and New Hampshire added as many between them and in November, 1746 they set sail. Less than half reached Acadia. The Rhode Island vessels were wrecked near Martha's Vineyard and a New Hampshire sloop was intercepted by a French man of war and was forced back to Portsmouth. Four hundred and seventy men from Massachusetts under Colonel Arthur Noble were all that reached Annapolis. They immediately sailed for Mines. On December 4th they were forced to go ashore at French Cross and march overland to their destination.

Ramsay, outnumbered and fearful that this force was bent on destroying the Acadian settlements, tried to convince the Acadians to defend their home, however, the Acadians trusted Shirley's promise of protection and refused to join the fight. Ramsay and his Canadians were forced to withdraw. Noble occupied Grand Pré, the principal settlement of the Mines region without incident.

Grand Pré was a village consisting of small wooden houses scattered over two and a half kilometres making defence a problem. The English had brought the frame of a blockhouse with them, but, the ground being frozen solid, it was decided to leave its erection until the spring. The ships with all the supplies including five small cannon, snowshoes, ammunition and stores finally arrived, however, they were left on board as the troops were billeted with Acadian families.

Noble's position was critical, but he was assured that Grand Pré could not be reached from Chignecto in the dead of winter and so he and his men settled down to await the coming of spring.

At the head of the Bay of Fundy an isthmus separates the Bay of Chignecto and the Mines Basin. Ramsay quartered his men at Beaubassin at the head of the Bay. On the 8th of January 1747 an Acadian arrived at Beaubassin with the news that there were two hundred and twenty English at Grand Pré, and more were expected. Ramsay immediately formed a daring plan for a rapid march and a night attack to surprise the garrison. His party of Canadians had been greatly depleted by disease and he sent word for the Indians at Miramichi to join him along with those at Shubenacadie and Cobequid. Meanwhile the Canadians made snowshoes and dog sledges in preparation for what was sure to be an arduous march.

Ramsay could not command the expedition himself as an accident had injured one of his knees. Fortunately he had the flower of the Canadian nobility as his officers and the command was given to Coulon de Villiers.

On the 21st of January they crossed the isthmus to Baie Verte where they were joined by the Indians and some Acadians from Beaubassin and Île St. Jean (Prince Edward Island). They began their march on the 23rd covering four kilometres that first day. They began their second day's march in a snow storm driven by gusty winds. The men bent their bodies into the wind that froze their feet and their faces. The blowing snow finally forced them to stop at noon and seek shelter in the pine forest. While there, two Acadians arrived with news of the English. There were more than originally reported, but to compensate the party was joined by some Acadians from the surrounding settlements. On the 27th they reached Tatmagouche where their numbers were augmented with more Acadians.

The march to Grand Pré, January 1747

The storm continued and their march was further complicated by drifting ice on the Shubenacadie River, which forced a wide detour. To prevent word from reaching Grand Pré, Boishébèrt with ten Canadians crossed by canoe to block the road to the settlement. It took a further ten days of dragging sledges over fallen trees and drifting snow to put them within ten kilometres of their objective. On the 10th of February, in driving snow, they split into ten groups in order to attack as many houses simultaneously as possible. They reached the Gaspereau River near Grand Pré and settled down in the cold to await nightfall. When darkness fell they moved forward and took possession of some houses to warm themselves and to dry their guns in preparation for the assault. By a stroke of luck the house that Villiers and his party chose was in the midst of a wedding feast with most of the in-

habitants of Grand Pré present. They gave the Canadians intelligence as to the location of the garrison. They were scattered in twenty-four houses and as the attackers were too few to hit them all at once, knowledge of the houses billeting the officers was invaluable.

All was ready and the parties assigned their targets. The main party was to assault the stonehouse in the middle of the village containing the guard, while others secured the other important buildings. The Acadian guide lost his way in the snow and Villiers assaulted a small wooden house instead. He was severely wounded as he charged the door. Soon all resistance ceased with twenty-one of the twenty-four Englishmen killed. Meanwhile forty Canadians under La Corne attacked the house occupied by Colonel Noble and his brother. Smashing the door with axes, they

122

burst in wounding Noble with two musket balls to the body. Noble fired his pistols and was struck in the forehead by a musket ball, which killed him instantly.

With Villiers wounded command now fell to La Corne who gathered his forces as daylight broke. The English not captured had retreated to the stone house and La Corne had managed to blockade them there. La Corne made his headquarters in the house where Noble had been killed. This was within easy musket shot of the stone house in which the English garrison was holed up. The two parties exchanged fire with little result until the English made an attempt to recapture the house occupied by La Corne. Two companies sallied forth, but they only had eighteen pairs of snowshoes among them and most of the assaulting party floundered in the snowdrifts while the Canadians poured an unmerciful fire into their ranks. They fell back in disarray. About three o'clock Captain Howe, who had been wounded in the initial attack, requested that the English surgeon come and dress his wound lest he bleed to death. Since the French surgeon was back at the Gaspereau, the Canadians agreed and a Canadian officer, Morin, approached the stone with a flag of truce. The surgeon came and tended his wounds. The truce was to last until 9 o'clock the next morning.

When the truce expired Goldthwait, the English commander asked for terms of capitulation. It was agreed that within forty-eight hours the English were to march for Annapolis with the honours of war; prisoners taken were to remain in Canadian hands; that the Indians, who had been the only plunderers, could keep the booty they had taken; that the English sick and wounded should be left, until their recovery, at the neighbouring settlement of Rivière aux Canard, protected by a Canadian guard; and that the English engaged at Grand Pré not bear arms in the district about the head of the Bay of Fundy for six months.

Thus ended one of the great exploits in Canadian history.

CHAPTER FORTY-TWO
Acadia in turmoil
"The fluctuating state of the inhabitants of Acadia seems, my lord, naturally to arise from their finding a want of due protection from His Majesty's Government."-Governor Shirley to the Duke of Newcastle, April, 1747

Although the Canadians had been successful in their expedition against Grand Pré, food was scarce in the area and there was some doubt as to the ability of the expedition to maintain itself. La Corne called a council of war and it was resolved to return to Beaubassin. Many of his troops were ill and it was decided to leave them and the wounded at Grand Pré to recover.

Ramesay took advantage of their success and sent a circular letter to the Acadians assuring them that their country had been reconquered by the arms of the King of France. He further commanded them to be faithful subjects, breaking off all dealings with the English under any circumstances, on pain of severe punishment. He concluded his letter by saying,

"If we have withdrawn our soldiers from among you, it is for reasons known to us alone, and with a view to your advantage."

Unfortunately, Shirley, on hearing of the capture of Grand Pré, immediately sent a detachment of Massachusetts militia to reoccupy the place. This they accomplished in early April. The Acadians, as usual, were between the proverbial rock and a hard place. Unable to determine which way the affair would end, they tried to placate both French and English. They sent a desperate letter to Ramesay, telling him that their loyalties were always French, but begging him to remember that they were a poor people with large families in constant danger of being deported if they offended the English. They wrote at the same time to Mascarene at Annapolis explaining the situation they were in, enclosing a copy of Ramesay's threatening letter. They begged him to consider the danger they were in if they did not answer it. At the same time they renewed their pledge of fidelity to King George. It was obvious that the Acadians could not win.

Ramesay, not satisfied with his first letter, sent another ordering the Acadians to take up arms against the English in the name of the Governor General of New France. He included an abstract from the governor's letter to him. Ramesay wrote:

"These are his words;" "We consider our self as master of Beaubassin and Mines, since we have driven off the English. Therefore there is no difficulty in forcing the Acadians to take arms for us; to which end we declare to them that they are discharged from the oath that they formerly took to the English, by which they are bound no longer, as has been decided by the authorities of Canada and Monseigneur our Bishop."

"In view of the above," continued Ramesay, "we order all the inhabitants of Memeramcook to come to this place (Beaubassin) as soon as they see the signal fires lighted, or discover the approach of the enemy; and this on pain of death, confiscation of all their goods, burning of their houses, and the punishment due to rebels against the King."

The Acadians were in a desperate situation. Death as rebels on one hand or expulsion, should the English prevail, on the other. The Canadians had the means to carry out their threat immediately, whereas the English were prepared to threaten them, but reluctant to commit troops to protect them against their French compatriots. Governor Shirley of Massachusetts was growing impatient with the situation and the lack of action from England to remedy it. He wrote to Lord Newcastle just after the capture of Grand Pré by the Canadians,

"The late secresy (sic) of the inhabitants of Minas with regard to the Enemys Motions, and the very certain Intelligence which the enemy gain'd of the particular quarters of the English Officers, notwithstanding their Supplying the King's Troops with Provisions, and the Curtesy of their Behavior to 'em before this surprize, and their profession of being sorry for it afterwards seems to shew the necessity of his Majesty's Keeping a strong Blockhouse there with a Garrison of 150 men; And the constant ill behaviour of the Inhabitants of Schiegnecto seems to make another Blockhouse with a like garri-

Acadians petition both Ramsay and Mascarene, 1747

son there equally necessary, as I at first pro-pos'd to your Grace from Louisbourg."

No aid was forthcoming and Shirley could only use the meager resource of his own colony to try to sustain British control over Nova Scotia. Of course this was too little to help sway the loyalties of the embattled Acadians. In April of 1747 Shirley wrote to Newcastle,

"The fluctuating state of the inhabitants of Acadia seems, my lord, naturally to arise from their finding a want of due protection from his Majesty's Government."

The governor at Quebec was determined to recover Acadia. He began by declaring the territory held by the Canadians at Beaubassin, French Acadia and he invoked a policy of, first, persuading Acadian to emi-grate to the "French" zone, and then attempting to force them. Some moved to Île St. Jean (Prince Edward Island) in an attempt to get out from under an impossible situation. Between the Canadians and the English the fate of the Acadians was sealed, culminating in the expulsion of 1755.

CHAPTER FORTY-THREE
The Destruction of Saratoga
"You burned your own fort at Scraghtoga and ran away from it, which
is a shame and a scandal to you."-Iroquois to the English, 1747

While the Acadians struggled to keep their distinct identity in the battle between the French and English for their loyalty, the Canadian government was busy on other fronts as well. Canada was blessed with an enemy that was hopelessly divided. Though numerically superior, the colonies were so jealous of their rights and freedoms that they could not agree to joint action against Canada. Where the Canadians were aggressive and daring, the English Americans procrastinated and seemed unable to cope with the raiding parties that devastated the outlying areas.

Nowhere was the differences more pronounced than in New York. Here the attitude of the Five Nations or Iroquois Confederacy was a vital piece of the puzzle. After one hundred and fifty years of warring on the Canadians, the confederacy had slipped into a form of armed neutrality. The Treaty of Utrecht had made them British subjects, a concept of which they had no understanding. The English Americans told them it meant children, while the Canadians told them it meant dogs and slaves. They ignored the rhetoric and jealously guarded their territory against encroachment by either side. The Canadians would have enlisted them against the English if they could, but were content to prevent them from assisting the English. This was accomplished when Shirley's plan to invade Canada in 1745 via Lake Champlain was stillborn. Governor Clinton of New York managed to get the confederacy council to meet him in Albany and with many speeches and presents they were persuaded to take up the hatchet against the French. The Iroquois were disgusted when the invasion was abandoned.

The situation in New York was further compounded by the opposition of the assembly to the royal governor, George Clinton. Two factors contributed to the problem. Many merchants opposed the war because of the lucrative contraband trade carried on with Canada. The other was an unfortunate after dinner quarrel between Clinton and the colonial chief justice, James de Lancey. The chief justice promised to make the governor's seat uncomfortable, which he proceeded to do. The assembly thwarted his every move to strengthen the defences of the colony, not because his proposals were not sound, but, because he

had proposed them.

Clinton had wished to send a body of colonials in the pay of the King, who had been mustered for the ill fated invasion, to protect the northern frontier and capture Crown Point from the Canadians. The assembly, determined to cross him at any price, refused to provide supplies and transport beyond Albany. They effectively defeated the governor's military plans. In vain he told them,

"If you deny me the necessary supplies, all my endeavors must become fruitless; I must wash my hands, and leave at your doors the blood of the innocent people."

He pleaded for forts to be built at two of the portages between the Hudson River and Lakes George and Champlain, thus blocking Canadian war parties from the region. They would do nothing, insisting that neighbouring colonies should pay their share. When the neighbouring colonies agreed to participate the assembly still refused.

Clinton sent a bitter complaint to Newcastle,

"They (the assembly) are selfish, jealous of the power of the crown, and of such leveling principles that they are constantly attacking its prerogative. . . . I find neither dissolutions nor fair means can produce from them such Effects as will tend to a publick good or their own preservation. They will neither act for themselves or their neighbors. . . . Few but hirelings have a seat in the assembly, who protract time for the sake of their wages, at great expence to the province, without contributing anything material for its welfare, credit, or safety."

At Saratoga their was a small Dutch settlement with a fort erected for their protection. This was the farthest outpost in New York and the only defensive position between Canada and Albany. In 1745 it was manned by a sergeant, a corporal and ten men. These testified before a court of inquiry that conditions were so bad that in rainy weather neither they nor their

Canadians burn Saratoga, November 28, 1745

powder could be kept dry. Since neither the assembly nor the merchants were prepared to put up money for repairs, the garrison was withdrawn with the onset of winter.

No sooner was this been accomplished when five hundred Canadians and Indians surprised the settlement on the 28th of November, burned the fort, houses, mills, and stables, killed thirty people and carried off one hundred prisoners. Nothing now prevented a direct attack on Albany. The New York Assembly finally voted £150 in New York currency to rebuild the fort. A feeble stockade was erected, but it soon fell into disrepair like its predecessor. Colonel Peter Schuyler was stationed there with his regiment in 1747, but was forced to withdraw for lack of supplies. Governor Clinton then directed Colonel Roberts, the commander of the Albany garrison, to inspect the fort, and if he found it indefensible, to burn it, which he did. This action astounded a Canadian war party that visited the place soon after and found it in ashes.

The burning of Saratoga, first by the Canadians and then by the English, had a profound effect on the Iroquois. They taunted their English neighbours mercilessly.

> "You burned your own fort at Scraghtoga and ran away from it, which was a shame and a scandal to you."

With no knowledge of partisan politics and jealous infighting, the Iroquois took this as a sign of cowardice.

Unfortunately for the Canadians a man came along that could rival the French influence of Joncaire and the missionaries among the Iroquois. William Johnson was to become a significant force in English relations with the Iroquois Confederacy.

CHAPTER FORTY-FOUR

The Iroquois Take Up the Hatchet

"Should any French priest now dare to come among us, we know no use for them but to roast them."-Iroquois, 1746

The stage was now set for the English to seriously attempt to destroy Canada and drive the French from North America. On the surface, in the middle of the 18th century, it should have been easy. The British-American colonies, from Maine to Georgia had a population of 1,600,000, including two hundred thousand slaves. Of the available European males, there were more than two hundred thousand of military age.

To counter this immense resource, Canada, including Louisiana, muster a total population of eighty thousand of which but nineteen thousand men were of military age. To this number only a garrison of three thousand to thirty-five hundred regulars could be added. The only advantage the Canadians had was in their Indian allies, who were fanatically loyal to them in the early part of the 18th century.

Despite the huge numerical superiority, the English colonies could not muster a consensus on a course of action, each jealously guarding their little empire. Nowhere did this petty rivalry flair up more than in New England. Massachusetts claimed a large tract of land north of her present boundary, which was also claimed by New Hampshire. In the belief that her claim would be upheld, Massachusetts built Fort Dummer, a small fort on the Connecticut River, to protect a new settlement about forty-five miles north of the Massachusetts line. New Hampshire referred the dispute to London and the crown ruled in her favour. Massachusetts immediately withdrew her troops from Fort Dummer, but the New Hampshire Assembly refused to garrison the fort as it was fifty miles from any settlement built by "New Hampshire" people. The settlement, called Number Four, because it was in the fourth township, was left exposed. Unfortunately it was right on the route raiding parties from Canada would take to attack more worthwhile targets. The ten families living there were forced to build their own fort. Number Four was attacked five times in 1746 with the loss of a number of scalps as well as cattle, horses and hogs. Massachusetts finally agreed to garrison their fort only because it prevented the raiders from reaching the province's borders.

Although the influence of the Iroquois Confederacy on the affairs of the conflict between the British American colonies and Canada diminished as the 18th century rolled on, they were still a force to be reckoned with. The success of the Canadians in their raids against targets in the Province of New York, coupled with the work of the Jesuit missionaries and especially the relationship of Chabert Joncaire, who had lived for many years among the Seneca, had at least put the Iroquois in a position of neutrality when it came to the battles fought between the Europeans. But the English soon found a man to rival Joncaire. William Johnson, a nephew to Admiral Warren, was an intelligent young Irishman who managed his uncle's estates on the Mohawk River. He soon showed a keen interest in his Mohawk neighbours and quickly learned their language, and joined in their games and dances. He often borrowed their dress and their paint, whooping and yelling like one of them. The Mohawks adopted him into the tribe and made him a war chief. He sat in their councils and his advise was eagerly sought by the chiefs. Governor Clinton saw the value in Johnson's relationship with the Iroquois and soon disbanded the ineffectual commissioners of Indian affairs, transferring their function to Johnson. Of course anything that Clinton supported, the New York Assembly opposed, thus they refused the customary presents making the job all but impossible. Despite this, however, the Confederacy promised to take up the hatchet against the French. One of their orators stated the position of the Iroquois at a conference in Albany on the 23rd of August 1746:

"Should any French priests now dare to come among us, we know no use for them but to roast them."

Johnson was more troubled by the habits of the Dutch and English traders than by the comings and goings of a few French priests. He begged the assembly to pass an act prohibiting the sale of liquor to the Indians,

"as it is impossible to do anything with them while there is such a plenty to be had all round the neighborhood, being forever drunk."

William Johnson in council with the Iroquois, 1746

Johnson placed the number of Iroquois at nineteen thousand and despite their professions of loyalty, their support was far from certain. The tug of war between Johnson and Joncaire kept an uneasy peace between the Iroquois and Canada.

In the meantime Canadians and their Indian allies were raiding the frontier and burning farmhouses from Maine to New York, some within sight of Albany, in an attempt to keep the English off balance. Johnson managed to garner a few war parties two of which reached the Island of Montréal, but this resulted in only a temporary check to the incursions. The assembly offered a bounty on the scalps of the marauders, but they were slow to pay and raised the ire of the Iroquois. As we shall see, despite the efforts of William Johnson, this indifferent policy of the New York government was to drive many Iroquois into the arms of the Canadians.

CHAPTER FORTY-FIVE

The Attack on Fort Massachusetts
"As they advanced they passed deserted Dutch farms, however, they did not stop to burn anything, but did kill some poultry and hogs to supply themselves with meat."

As the year 1746 dawned, Canadians kept up their guerrilla war against the English colonies. As those colonies pushed their settlements westward, they came within easy striking distance of forces sent from Montréal along the Lake Champlain route. Massachusetts was especially vulnerable and was forced to build forts to protect the settlements, garrisoning them with paid militia. One such post was called Fort Massachusetts located at the present town of Adams, then known as East Hoosac, on the Hoosac River. In the spring the two brothers de Muy moved onto Lake Champlain to protect Fort Frédéric from an expected English attack, however, the approach of Anville's fleet forestalled the English expedition. On the 3rd of August Rigaud de Vaudreuil, the town-major of Trois Rivière, left there with a larger force to join the de Muys to repel any English attack or, if none was forthcoming, to take the offensive.

Rigaud reached Fort Frédéric on the 16th and was joined by the elder de Muy with sixty Canadians and a band of Indians. They had made an incursion in the direction of Albany, but all was quiet leaving the fort in no danger. The problem now was where to strike the English. The Indians held council after council, but could not agree. Rigaud gave them a wampum belt, and told them he had decided to attack Schenectady at which the Indians seemed happy. War songs were sung and preparations were well in hand. By morning they had changed their minds and asked for a council to debate the question. It appeared that the Mohawks of Caughnawaga opposed the plan because some of their relatives from the Finger Lakes district visited the town and might be killed by some of the Abenaki and western Indians in the party. The debate raged on.

It was the Abenakis who finally came up with a solution. They knew the New England frontier well and, drawing a rough map on the council room floor proposed attacking Fort Massachusetts, the western most post of the Massachusetts colony. Cadenaret, one of their chiefs, was killed there the previous spring, and they wished to avenge his death. All agreed and the march to the Hoosac River began. Rigaud stopped at East Bay where a stream joined Wood

Creek and left the younger de Muy with thirty men to guard the canoes. Five hundred French regulars and Canadians, and two hundred Indians were guided by Cadenaret's brother toward their objective.

After a march of four days, they encamped opposite Saratoga on the 26th of August. There was an English garrison stationed there, but they slipped by undetected. Early the next day they reached the Hoosac, well above its mouth; which was still within the colony of New York. Now their march became easier, "for," says Rigaud, "we got out of the woods and followed a large road that led up the river." In fact there were two roads, one on each bank and Rigaud formed his expedition into two brigades, one of which, commanded by Sieur de la Valterie, marched along the right bank, and the other, under the Sieur de Sabrevois, kept to the left. The Indians scouted the advance and acted as flankers as well as covering the rear.

As they advanced they passed deserted Dutch farms, however, they did not stop to burn anything, but did kill some poultry and hogs to supply themselves with meat. Before nightfall they had passed the New York line where they camped near present day Williamstown. They were joined here by Beaubassin and La Force, who had gone ahead with eight Indians to reconnoitre. Aside from a man stationed in the watchtower, there was no sign of alarm. Apparently the fleeing Dutch farmers had not bothered to forewarn the English garrison of the danger, for the relations between these neighbours were strained at the time.

Before breaking camp Rigaud called the chiefs together and said,

> "My children, the time is near when we must get other meat than fresh pork, and we will all eat it together."

"Meat" meant prisoners to the Indians; and as these were valuable for the ransoms paid for them, the Indians suspected that the French would keep them all. This figurative assurance of Rigaud's, that they would get their share pleased them and redoubled their en-

Tamping down ball with ramrod...

Pouring powder into pan from powder horn...

cock, aim, fire...

Typical powder horn

Flintlock musket c1728

Ball shot...

THE FLINTLOCK MUSKET

thusiasm for the project.

The plan was simple. The Abenaki scouts were to halt at the edge of the woods and build scaling ladders and battering rams for a predawn assault; but the sight of the watchtower was too much for them and some young Canadians with them and they rushed forward, firing their muskets. Driven back, they could do nothing but snipe from behind the stumps that dotted the field around the fort.

Fort Massachusetts was normally garrisoned by fifty-one men under Captain Ephraim Williams. However, he had taken some of his men to participate in the proposed invasion of Canada and had not yet returned. The fort was under the command of Sergeant John Hawks with twenty-one men, many of which were suffering from dysentery. There were also three women and five children in the fort. Their supply of ammunition was extremely low, however, they kept up an effective fire killing one Abenaki chief and wounding sixteen Indians and Canadians including Rigaud himself who was hit in the arm by a stray ball. As night fell the situation within the fort was bad. Two men had been wounded leaving only nine effective defenders.

Rigaud spent the night preparing for the decisive assault in the early, predawn hours. His plan was to push trenches forward and, stacking fagots against the wall, burn a breach in the defences. Rain prevented him from his predawn attack and he was forced to wait until morning.

Firing was renewed after first light and one of the men in the watchtower was shot through the head reducing the garrison to eight effectives. Rigaud was about to order the assault when a flag of truce appeared above the watchtower. Rigaud sent the elder de Muy and two others to parley, offering quarter to the garrison if they surrendered, noting that control of the Indians would be difficult should an assault be necessary. After two hours of deliberation, Hawks agreed to the terms and the French officers were admitted to the fort. The Canadians and Indians, who were excluded, removed some of the stone foundation and crawled in. The sight of the blood dripping from the watchtower from the man shot thorough the head that morning sent the Indians into a frenzy and they dragged the body down, scalped it and mutilated the corpse. The prisoners were moved to the French camp and the fort was burned to the ground. After sending raiding parties toward Deerfield, Rigaud prepared to take his prisoners on the long trek back to Canada.

CHAPTER FORTY-SIX

Mercy in a Savage Land
"I trembled, thinking they had murdered some of our people, but was filled with admiration when all our prisoners come up with us, and John Aldrich carried on the back of his Indian master."-Mr. Norton, Ft. Massachusetts Chaplain

With the capitulation of Fort Massachusetts the immediate problem for Rigaud was the disposition of the prisoners. One of the articles of the surrender stated that all prisoners would be held by the French. As we have seen, Rigaud promised the Indians their share of captives. The prisoners were initially held in the French camp, but the Indians were demanding their captives as promised. Rigaud's interpreter begged the English men to agree to have some go with the Indians to avoid an incident which might get out of control. They refused. Nonetheless some prisoners were turned over to them. All the women and children remained with the French.

The first night passed without incident and the following morning Mr. Norton, the chaplain, was allowed to pin a note to one of the charred posts of the fort explaining what had happened. It read:

"August 20, 1746. These are to inform you that yesterday, about 9 of the clock, we were besieged by, as they say, seven hundred French and Indians. They have wounded two men and killed one Knowlton. The General de Vaudreuil desired capitulations, and we were so distressed that we complied with his terms. We are the French's prisoners, and have it under the general's hand that every man, woman, and child shall be exchanged for French prisoners."

The column moved off the way they had come, down the Hoosac Road. The march was slow because of the sick and wounded, two Englishmen among them. Rigaud gave the Indians presents, asking them to treat their prisoners with kindness. De Muy was walking with Norton when the Indians began shouting from the rear. Norton later wrote,

"I trembled, thinking they had murdered some of our people, but was filled with admiration when I saw all our prisoners come up with us, and John Aldrich carried on the back of his Indian master." Aldrich had been shot in the foot, and could not walk. "We set out again, and had gone but a little way before we came up with Josiah Reed."

Reed was very sick and Norton was certain that they would kill him, instead one of the Indians carried him on his back. Reed died from his illness shortly thereafter.

The wife of John Smead, was pregnant and when she went into labour the French made allowances. Norton wrote,

"Some of them made a seat for her to sit upon, and brought her to the camp, where, about ten o'clock, she was graciously delivered of a daughter, and was remarkably well. . . . Friday: this morning I baptized John Smead's child. He called its name Captivity."

Rigaud ordered a litter of poles covered with deer and bear skins to be made to carry the mother and child. Three days later a sudden rain shower soaked the pair, but, they were none the worse for it. On the return along the Hoosac River several horses were found on the abandoned farms and the sick and wounded were allowed to use them, including John Aldrich.

Rigaud recorded the return march in his journal:

"I divide my army between the two sides of the Kaskékouké (Hoosac) and ordered them to do what I had not permitted to be done before we reached Fort Massachusetts. Every house was set on fire, and numbers of domestic animals of all sorts were killed. French and Indians vied with each other in pillage, and I made them enter the little streams that flow into the Kaskékouké and lay waste everything there. . . . Wherever we went we made the same havoc, laid waste both sides of the river, through twelve leagues of fertile country, burned houses, barns, stables, and even a meeting house, in all, above two hundred establishments, killed all the cattle, and ruined all the crops. Such, Monseigneur, was the damage I did our enemies during the eight or nine days I

An act of mercy, Fort Massachusetts, August, 1746

was in their country."

The column left the Hoosac where they had entered it and followed an old Indian trail northward. They finally reached Wood Creek where they had left their canoes and found them safe. Here Rigaud allowed the Indians to leave the expedition to continue raiding the countryside. Now afloat the party made good progress and arrived at Crown Point without incident. Rigaud was relieved to reach a place of refuge as his wounded arm was inflamed and needed medical attention. They remained camped there for some time while the sick and wounded recovered.

In due time the prisoners reached Montréal where they stayed a short time before going on to Quebec. Within a year, those who remained alive were exchanged and returned to their homes. Mrs. Smead and her infant daughter died of fever at Quebec. Ten others also died in captivity leaving ten to return to New England.

For two years after the raid led by Rigaud, French, Canadians and Indians checked the growth of the English colonies with their incessant guerrilla warfare. At length, in July, 1748, news came that France and England had come to an agreement, and in October of that year the Treaty of Aix-la-Chapelle was signed. Peace returned to the Canadian Frontier.

CHAPTER FORTY-SEVEN
The Treaty of Aix-la-Chapelle
"the British ministers gave up the important island of Cape Breton in exchange for a petty factory in the East Indies."

The year 1748 saw both France and England weary of the war. The enormous cost of keeping armies on two continents and the spiraling debt load led to the Treaty of Aix-la-Chapelle, signed in October of 1748. It was agreed to return to the prewar boundaries, each belligerent giving up their conquests. In the case of England this meant restoring Cape Breton and Louisbourg to French control. The British colonies were indignant. Their contention was that they had conquered Cape Breton, and, indeed King George II had initially told Louis XV that it was not his to give as it had been captured by the people of Boston. But his sense of justice was forced to give in to diplomatic necessity. One of the commentators of the day wrote,

"The British ministers gave up the important island of Cape Breton in exchange for a petty factory in the East Indies" (Madras).

Thus the gateway to the St. Lawrence was again in French hands insuring the continued viability of Canada, at least in the near term. This intermission in the dramatic play on the American stage allowed the Canadian authorities to gather their strength for the trials that lay ahead, for they knew that the American colonies would not rest until the threat posed by Canadians was ended forever. The final struggle for North America waited patiently in the wings.

Before continuing our story of the struggle for Canada, let us look at the state of the two main combatants and their relationship to their North American colonies. England, after the peace of Aix-la-Chapelle, was in no shape to wage war. Her army was reduced to eighteen thousand men in Great Britain plus the garrisons of Minorca and Gibraltar. There were seven independent companies in the American colonies as well. Politically England was relatively stable. The King's power had been curbed at the time of the restoration of the monarchy in 1660. The men in power were, for the most part, competent, though almost exclusively from the aristocracy. Taxes were spread throughout the social strata, so noble and common folk alike shared the burden, if not equally, at least the gentry felt the pinch to some extent. The nobility were a thriving part of English life and if they had privileges, they paid for them by service to the state. France, on the other hand, appeared to be at the height of her power. The House of Bourbon ruled in France, Spain, and Naples; and their family compact was the scourge of European diplomacy. She contested England for control of India and claimed all of North America except Mexico and a strip along the seacoast, which she graciously ceded to the English. Her navy was powerful and her armies well equipped, making her the foremost power on the European continent. Her weakness lay in her political structure. All power was held in the hands of the King. Louis XV showed little interest in the affairs of state and often left decisions to his mistress, Madame de Pompadour. She appointed and dismissed generals; made and unmade ministers. Her personal dislikes coloured every policy. The tax burden fell on the poor while the nobility paid little or none. The aristocracy played little or no part in the daily life of the nation, content to spend their time in the circus that was Versailles. The quality of the officer corps was mediocre at best. France's best generals were foreigners, Lowendal from Denmark and Saxe from Saxony among others. Through all this intrigue, the greed for power lay bubbling just under the surface.

All came to a head in 1740 with the death of Emperor Charles VI of Austria. The War of the Austrian Succession rolled over Europe and America until the Treaty of Aix-la-Chapelle brought it all to an end.

With the Peace of Aix-la-Chapelle life returned to a semblance of normality in the American colonies. France pushed forward plans to consolidate their hold on the Ohio and the Mississippi valleys while strengthening their position in Canada. This was no mean feat as the disparity in population between the English colonies and Canada remained. To further exasperate the situation, Canada still depended on France for her manufactured goods and supplies. The fur trade was the beginning and the end for New France in commercial enterprises. France controlled every aspect of life in Canada. For all that, Canada had a vitality all its own. Though France was its mother, the child developed a heartiness and an attitude quite alien to the pomp and circumstance of Versailles. Les habitants lived in poverty, but not abject poverty, like the peasants of France. They were not burdened by heavy taxes as were their old country brethren. The nobility, far from living the decadent life of courtiers, engaged in the pursuit of adventure and war, undeterred by the rude climate or rugged terrain. With their Indian allies the Canadians defended their borders with a competence and ability that nullified the disadvantage of being outnumbered by a wide margin.

The thirteen British colonies were alike in that they all had representative governments based on English law. But, their differences were great. As we have seen they each jealously guarded their prerogatives even to the detriment of the whole. Military weakness and intercolonial squabbling were Canada's greatest ally as the struggle for a continent was ready to begin again.

The Struggle for the Heartland Begins
"In some places, and they were but too frequent, the water was only two or three inches deep." Fr. Beauchamp

When the Treaty of Aix-la-Chapelle was signed, the Marquis de la Galissonière was governor of Canada. Like all the later governors of Canada, he was a naval officer, who, a few years later, won a famous victory over the British Admiral Byng, who was subsequently shot by a firing squad on the deck of his flag ship as the scapegoat for the defeat. La Galissonière suffered from curvature of the spine, but his bold spirit and great intellect more than made up for his physical deformity. He felt that France must hold Canada at all costs, and link her to Louisiana by a chain of forts to hold back the British colonies while flooding the interior valleys with settlers brought from France. He was convinced that, though Canada had always been a burden, to abandon her was to give England mastery of America and its vast potential; increasing her trade and naval power to the detriment of French power in Europe.

Aix-la-Chapelle had done nothing to settle the thorny question of boundaries between the two rivals. It only held off the inevitable conflict for a short time. English traders were crossing the mountains from Pennsylvania and Virginia, ruining the Canadian fur trade and stirring up the Indians against the Canadian traders. Worse still, English land speculators followed in the wake of these traders claiming vast areas for future settlement by Americans. Something had to be done to drive out the usurpers and assert the French claim to the Ohio Valley. To this end Galissonière ordered Céloron de Bienville, a Chevalier de St. Louis and Captain of colonial troops, to the area in 1749.

For this mission he was allocated fourteen officers and cadets, twenty soldiers, one hundred and eighty Canadians, and a band of Indians, all loaded in twenty-three birch-bark canoes. He left Lachine on the 15th of June and pushed up the rapids of the St. Lawrence losing one man and damaging several canoes in the process. In ten days they reached the mouth of the Oswegatchie River, where Ogdensburg, New York now stands. Here they met Abbé Piquet, a Sulpician missionary who was building a mission to evangelize the Iroquois. Two of the Iroquois at the mission accompanied Bienville as guides.

The expedition stopped for a short time at Fort Frontenac, but avoided the English post at Oswego, on the south shore of Lake Ontario. They reached Fort Niagara on the 6th of July where they were received by the commandant of this, one of the most important links in the chain of forts guarding the French line of communication with the west. They moved up the Niagara River to the Lower Landing (Lewiston, N.Y.) where they unloaded their canoes for the portage around the Falls of Niagara. With the aid of the Seneca porters that were employed to carry the supplies over the portage, they made the difficult climb up the escarpment to the Portage Road that followed along the top of the gorge. The climb was so steep on leaving the landing that the Seneca name for it was Duh-jih-heh-oh or "crawl on all fours." They moved on to Lake Erie and landed near present day Portland, New York. They portaged nine miles over steep hills to Chautauqua Lake were they embarked and made good progress entering a stream flowing under the canopy of the great forest. Their luck ran out, however, and, despite the heavy rains that had drenched them, the stream was shallow. Father Bonnechamp, the chaplain of the expedition, wrote in his journal:

> "In some places, and they were but too frequent, the water was only two or three inches deep; and we were reduced to the sad necessity of dragging our canoes over the sharp pebbles, which, with all our care and precaution, stripped off large slivers of the bark. At last, tired and worn, and almost in despair of ever seeing La Belle Rivière, we entered it at noon of the 29th."

The part of the Ohio or La Belle Rivière, which they had reached is now called the Allegheny River.

French America had two heads, one among the snows of Canada and the other in the canebrakes of Louisiana. Canada communicated with the outside world through Gulf of St. Lawrence, the other through the Gulf of Mexico. Communication between these two heads was maintained by a chain of military and trading posts, which snaked 5,000 kilometres through the wilderness. Midway between Canada and Louisi-

Bienville at the Lower Landing on the Niagara, 1749

ana lay the Valley of the Ohio. If the English could seize it they would sever the chain of posts, cutting New France in two. If the French held it, and could strengthen their position, they would shut the English up between the Allegheny Mountains and the Atlantic Ocean. They would also control the western tribes, and turn them, in case of war, against the English borderlands.

The Indian population of the Ohio and its northern tributaries was considerable. The eastern half was occupied by Delaware, Shawnees, Wyandots, and Iroquois who had migrated from New York and were now called Mingoes by the English. A few Abenakis, Nipissings and Ottawas rounded out the mix in that area. Farther west, along the Miami, the Wabash, and other streams, was the territory of the confederacy formed by various bands of Miamis and other affiliated tribes. Still further west, toward the Mississippi were the remnants of the Illinois who had been decimated by the Iroquois in 1680.

France's attempt to solidify its hold on the Ohio Valley and points west was greatly aided by the Canadians who traded with the Indians. Unlike the Eng-

lish, who came just to trade, the Canadians lived among the tribes, learning their language and adopting their customs. Many married Indian women and raised their families in the wilderness. To further stake their claim they built posts at strategic locations. A small fort stood on the Maumee with another at St. Joseph and two more on the Wabash. In Illinois country, on the meadows of the Mississippi, was a larger, more formidable post called Fort Chartres. This was the strongest link in the chain. With its four stone bastions it was impregnable to musket fire and there, in the depths of the wilderness, there was no fear of cannon being brought against it. It was the centre of a fledgling settlement. At Kaskaskia were eighty houses; thirty or forty stood at Cahokia, opposite St. Louis and a few more at the hamlets of St. Philippe and Prairie à la Roche. They thrived on the fur trade and the cultivation of corn for the New Oléans market. Twice a year they made the voyage down the Mississippi in a large galley propelled by twenty oars.

The struggle for this heartland was about to heat up.

While the French tried to solidify their hold on the Ohio, the English traders began crossing the Alleghenies making significant inroads into the fur trading empire of their rival. English goods were cheaper and often of better quality. English woollens were especially sought after by the Indian traders, so much so that the Canadian traders had to purchases English goods to compete. Several tried to pass off European blankets as English, but, the Indian consumer was not fooled; they could tell by the colour of the material, which was English and which was bogus. The French became alarmed as some of these Englishmen were said to have crossed the Mississippi to trade with the Osage Indians. In 1749 it was said that over three hundred came over the mountains.

Céloron de Bienville came to the Ohio to rectify the situation. On reaching the Allegheny River he began to work on the mission given him. The men were formed up and he proclaimed Louis XV, lord of all that region. The arms of France, stamped on a sheet of tin, was nailed to a tree and a lead plate was buried at its foot, which read,

"Year 1749, in the reign of Louis Fifteenth, King of France. We, Céloron, commanding the detachment sent by the Marquis de la Galissonière, commander-general of New France, to restore tranquillity in certain villages of these cantons, have buried this plate at the confluence of the Ohio and the Kanaouagon (Conewango), this 29th July, as a token of the aforesaid River Ohio, of all streams that fall into it, and all lands on both sides to the sources of the aforesaid streams, as the preceding Kings of France have enjoyed it, and which they have upheld by force of arms and by treaties, notably by those of Ryswick, Utrecht, and Aix-la-Chapelle."

The ceremony completed, the expedition moved down stream taking possession of the country as they went. The Indians enroute were inclined to flee into the woods on their approach. To prevent this Bienville sent Chabert de Joncaire, who had great influence among the Five Nations, to act as a messenger of peace. One village that received Céloron was a settlement of Senecas called La Paille Coupée. Here Céloron read them a message from La Galissonière. It said,

"My children, since I was at war with the English, I have learned that they have seduced you; and not content with corrupting your hearts, have taken advantage of my absence to invade lands which are not theirs, but mine; and therefore I have resolved to send you Monsieur de Céloron to tell you my intentions, which are that I will not endure the English on my land, Listen to me, children; mark well the word that I send you; follow my advice, and the sky will always be calm and clear over your villages. I expect from you an answer worthy of true children."

Four leagues below French Creek, by a rock bearing Indian hieroglyphics, they buried another plate. As they continued their march, the villages they passed were all empty. At one deserted Shawnee village they found six English traders, whom they ordered to leave the country, and return at their peril. Bienville gave them a letter addressed to the governor of Pennsylvania, which expressed surprise that the English would trespass on the domain of France. It concluded,

"I know that our Commandant-General would be sorry to be forced to use violence; but his orders are precise, to leave no foreign traders within the limits of his government."

As the expedition proceeded they warned the English traders they met to leave. They passed the site of present day Pittsburgh and some twenty-eight kilometres further on approached the village of Chininqué, called Logstown by the English, where both the French and English flags were flying. The Indians lined the shore and greeted their visitors by firing their muskets into the air. The salute was not entirely welcome as the muskets were charged with ball. Bi-

Burying the plate: on the Allegheny River, 1749

enville had to threaten to open fire on them to get them to stop. The town was crowded with refugees from the villages through which the French had passed and Bienville feared a night attack. Sentries were posted and the men ordered to sleep in their clothes. Joncaire, through some women of his acquaintance, discovered that an attack was planned, but the precautions of the French prevented it. Instead a council was held and Bienville read a message from the governor, which was more conciliatory than the one read to the villages further up river. It read in part,

"Through the love I bear you, my children, I send you Monsieur de Céloron to open your eyes to the designs of the English against your lands. The establishments they mean to make, and of which you are certainly ignorant, tend to your complete ruin. They hide from you their plans, which are to settle here and drive you away, if I let them. As a good father who tenderly loves his children, and though far away from them bears them always in his heart, I must warn you of the danger that threatens you. The English intend to rob you of your country; and that they may succeed, they begin by corrupting your minds. As they mean to seize the Ohio, which belongs to me, I send to warn them to retire."

Having procured the assent of the chiefs, the expedition moved on. They buried a plate near the mouth of Wheeling Creek, another at the mouth of the Muskingum, and another at the Kanawha. Each read the same save the date and place.

Burning the canoes: on the Miami River, September, 1749

On the 22nd of August they approached Scioto, a large Shawnee town. Unsure of his reception, he send Joncaire ahead to talk to the chiefs. The Indians shot holes in his flag of truce and surrounded him. Some wanted to kill him immediately, while others wanted to burn him alive. Only the intervention of some Iroquois that knew him, saved his life.

Bienville had no choice but to proceed to the town as he was short of supplies and his canoes were badly damaged. He wisely camped opposite the town and, after much negotiation, arranged a council where the only satisfactory response they received was for the cup of brandy given the Indians. Several English traders were resident in the town and Bienville ordered them to leave without the means of enforcing his directive. He could only make his repairs and go on his way. The position of French influence in west was on the decline, which was to cause great difficulties for Canada in the years to come.

Céloron de Bienville left the Shawnee towns behind and continued his voyage. On the 30th of August, 1749 he reached the Miami River, which the French called Rivière à la Roche. Here Bienville buried the last of his lead plates. He then left the Ohio, and the chaplain gave us an indication of the troubles the French faced,

"La Belle Rivière, that river so little known to the French, and unfortunately too well known to the English." He spoke of the multitude of Indian villages on its shores, and still more on its tributaries. "Each, great or small, has one or more English traders, and each of these has hired men to carry his furs. Behold, then, the

English well advanced upon our lands, and, what is worse, under protection of a crowd of savages whom they have drawn over to them, and whose number increases daily."

The expedition moved up the Miami battling against shallow water and the tricky currents. It took them thirteen days to reach the village of the Miamis led by the chief the French called La Demoiselle. Their new village stood at the mouth of Loramie Creek. On the approach of Bienville, the English traders prudently withdrew leaving two hired men to guard their gear. Bienville's chief objective was to induce Damoiselle to return to his old villages near the French fort on the Maumee River, where they would be safe from English influence.

A council was called and ample gifts presented to the chiefs at which time Bienville delivered a speech in the name of the governor. Damoiselle accepted the gifts, thanked the French for their advice and promised to follow it at a more convenient time. Bienville insisted that they moved at once. He coaxed and threatened, but to no avail. His attempt to move the Indians failed. Far from abandoning the site, Damoiselle gathered his followers there and in less than two years its population increase eight fold. Pique Town or Pickawillany, as the English called it, became the most important Indian town in the West, the centre of English trade and influence, and the source of the greatest concern to Canada.

Bienville was in a quandary. His canoes were damaged, many beyond repair. He was facing, if not hostile Indians, at least Indians sympathetic to the English cause. Help was not forthcoming from that sector.

He made his decision. He stacked his shattered canoes and burned them before leading his party on the difficult portage to the French post on the Maumee River. He arrived there to find its commander, Raymond, and all of his men, shivering with fever and ague. His party did what they could for them and when they had somewhat recovered, they borrowed wooden canoes for the trip down river.

In early October they reached Lake Erie where they were delayed by a drinking spree by the Indians that were traveling with them. The chaplain called them,

"a species of men made to exercise the patience of those who have the misfortune to travel with them."

It took the expedition another month to reach Fort Frontenac, where they paused briefly to rest. On his way to Montréal, at the request of the governor, he stopped at the mouth of the Oswegatchie River to check on the progress of the Sulpician missionary, Abbé Piquet. Piquet's new fort had been burned by the Indians, promoted, no doubt, by the English at Oswego; but, undaunted, the priest was rebuilding for the greater glory of God and King.

Finally Bienville reached Montréal, and closing his journal wrote:

"Father Bonnechamp, who is a Jesuit and a great mathematician, reckons that we have traveled twelve hundred leagues; I and my officers think we have traveled more. All I can say is, that the nations of these countries are very ill disposed towards the French, and devoted entirely to the English."

While Bienville wrote his reports and conferred with the governor, a new threat to the French presence in the west was forming. An association to settle the Ohio country was formed in Virginia and a grant of 500,000 acres was given by King George on the condition that one hundred families should be established within seven years, a fort built, and a garrison maintained. The Ohio Company counted some of the leading men of Virginia in its number, including a young colonial officer named George Washington and his brother. In 1750 they hired the English trader Christopher Gist to explore the country and select land.

Events were being set in motion that was to have a profound effect on the history of Canada.

CHAPTER FIFTY
The Struggle Continues
"The English had sent it to meet us, well knowing that this was the best way to cause disorder
among my new recruits and make them desert me."-Abbé Piquet, July, 1751

With the organization of the Ohio Company, the English moved with uncharacteristic speed to enlist the aid of the western tribes. Despite this new found energy, rivalry between the colonies persisted. In November, 1751 Gist, the Virginia agent, reached Logstown, where he found what he called a "parcel of reprobate Indian traders.' These "reprobates" were Pennsylvanians, mostly of Scotch-Irish descent, who were in competition with the Virginians. The fact that he bore a message from the King was all that prevented an incident.

At the village of the Wyandots called Muskingum he found another Pennsylvanian, George Croghan, who was sent by the governor of Pennsylvania to renew the chain of friendship with the Indians. They met amicably, and Croghan had with him the interpreter, Andrew Montour, who was to prove a great help to Gist. They traveled together, eventually reaching Pickawillany. Gist was impressed with the land and sent his report to his employers,

"it is fine, rich, level land, well timbered with large walnut, ash, sugar trees, and cherry trees; well watered with a great number of little streams and rivulets; full of beautiful, natural meadows, with wild rice, blue grass, and clover, and abounding with turkeys, deer, elks, and most sorts of game, particularly buffaloes, thirty or forty of which are frequently seen in one meadow."

They crossed the Miami on a raft with their horses swimming after them. They were met on landing by a group of warriors who escorted them to the town where they received a warm welcome from Demoiselle, the Miami chief. Much had changed since Bienville had visited a year and a half before. The town boasted a population of two thousand and the English traders had built a fort of pickets strengthened with logs.

There was a series of councils held and a solemn treaty finalized between the Confederate tribes and the English. In the middle of all this four Ottawas arrived with a French flag and gifts of tobacco and brandy with an invitation for the Miamis to visit the French commandant at Détroit. Damoiselle rose and made a speech,

"Brothers the Ottawas, we let you know, by these four strings of wampum, that we will not hear anything the French say, nor do anything they bid us." Then addressing the French as if they were there: "Fathers, we have made a road to the sun-rising, and have been taken by the hand by our brothers the English, the Six Nations, the Delawares, Shawnee, and Wyandots. We assure you, in that road we will go; and as you threaten us with war in the spring, we tell you that we are ready to receive you." Then turning to the four envoys: "Brothers the Ottawas, you hear what I say. Tell that to your fathers the French, for we speak it from our hearts."

The chiefs then took down the French flag and sent the envoys on there way with their answer.

Despite these serious inroads by the English, the French influence was not totally eradicated. The Miamis were firmly in the English camp and so to were the Shawnee, however the Delawares had not forgotten that it was the English who had driven them from their ancestral homes east of the Alleghanies. The Mingoes, or immigrant Iroquois, like their relatives in New York, felt the influence of Joncaire and other Canadians, who spared no efforts to sway them back to the French. Such was the courage of Joncaire that he made anti-English speeches to the Ohio Indians with English traders present. Because of the regard that the Indians had for him, these traders dared not molest him.

Of course the English quickly fell into the old ways. The Ohio Company built a trading post at Will's Creek, a tributary of the Potomac to which the Indians flocked with their goods. The Pennsylvania traders, out of jealousy, told the Indians that the Virginians meant to steal their lands. This confirmed what the Canadians had been telling them, which helped the French cause immensely.

The Mission at la Présentation, 1751

On Croghan's return from his mission of renewing the friendship with the Indians the assembly rejected his report.

"I was condemned," he wrote, "for bringing expense on the government, and the Indians were neglected."

Despite this, Hamilton, the governor sent him back with gifts for the Delawares and Mingoes. He persuaded them that it was in their best interests for the English to build a fortified trading post at the confluence of the Ohio and the Alleghany Rivers where Pittsburgh now stands. But, in the words of Croghan, the assembly, "rejected the proposal, and condemned me for making such a report."

The Indians next turned to Virginia, but they also refused to build the post. The question of disputed boundaries contributed to the inaction. Each refused to spend money that might eventually profit the other. With no boundaries, no magistrates could be appointed, thus the traders could do as they pleased to the detriment of the English cause.

Clinton, the governor of New York, invited all the colonies to send commissioners to Albany to meet with the tribes, however, only three of the thirteen responded. A frustrated Clinton took out his wrath on his own assembly saying,

"The Assembly of this province has not given one farthing for Indian affairs, nor for a year past have they provided for the subsistence of the garrison at Oswego, which is the key for the commerce between the colonies and the inland nations of Indians."

The French saw this split as the way to Canada's salvation. They hoped to wage war in the guise of peace and to deal with the English colonies piecemeal. They saw what Croghan saw, that is, that the forks of the Ohio together with Niagara, formed the key to the domination in the west. If France could hold these two posts, she might boast that she was mistress of the continent.

The struggle for the North American continent was waged by the French on three fronts; military, trade and religion. Canadians made up the bulk of the first two components, with the missionaries, both Jesuit and Sulpician, rounding out the third. One of those missionaries, a Sulpician named Abbé Piquet, took on the daunting task of taking the faith to the Six Nations of Upstate New York. His mission at La Présentation, visited by Bienville on his return from the west, quickly gathered one hundred converts from the Onondagas alone as well as from the Cayugas and the Senecas. The mission consisted of a chapel, fortifications, and storehouses. As the mission grew, a barn, stable and saw mill were added. Soon fields of corn and beans sprang up to feed the three villages of Iroquois that settled around the post.

The merchants of the post, including two women, were busy carrying on trade with the Indians that found their way there. They also participated in a profitable, but illicit, trade with the Dutch at Albany with the aid of a Jesuit, Father Tournais. The authorities in Quebec turned a blind eye to this at first, but La Jonquière, the governor, finally put an end to this contraband trade in 1751.

In 1751 Abbé Piquet, known as the Apostle of the Iroquois, set out on a missionary journey around Lake Ontario. Six Canadians paddled him up the St. Lawrence, with five of his Iroquois converts following in a second canoe. They kept to the north shore stopping at Fort Frontenac for supplies and a rest. The fort, once the chief trading post on the lake, was devoid of any activity, the English post at Oswego having supplanted it as the destination of choice for the Indians. He found the food bad and complained that "there was not brandy enough in the fort to wash a wound." He crossed to a neighbouring island where he was able to convince the Indians living there to go to the mission at La Présentation.

For eight days the party moved along the north shore of Lake Ontario with Piquet faithfully recording each incident in his journal. He mentions a meeting with "a fine Negro of twenty-two years, a fugitive from Virginia." Slaves were seeking freedom in Canada even in those early days.

On the 26th of June he reached the new fort at Toronto, which offered a contrast to their stop at Fort Frontenac. He wrote,

"The wine here is of the best; there is nothing wanting in this fort; everything is abundant, fine, and good."

The fort at Toronto was completed in 1749 to intercept the northern tribes who were taking their furs to Oswego. It was kept well stocked with goods to entice the warriors to stop and trade. Piquet found a band of Mississaugas there and was on the verge of persuading them to move to La Présentation; but the governor had ordered him to confine his efforts to other tribes. To remove the temptation to disobey the governor, he moved his camp some six leagues to the west.

Two days later he arrived at Fort Niagara and was warmly greeted by the commandant, M. de Becancour; the chaplain, and the storekeeper; the triumvirate of military, religion and trade that marked every French presence in the New World. Piquet was impressed by this fort and its castle that guarded the inland route to the west. He rested there for a day and then set out for the post at the Lower Landing where he found Joncaire encamped with a large band of Senecas. To his disgust they were all drunk and he was forced to wait to try and persuade them to go to La Présentation. The following day, finding them partially sober, he invited them to accompany him. He noted in his journal,

"but as they had still something left in their bottles, I could get no answer till the following day. I pass in silence, an infinity of talks on this occasion. Monsieur de Joncaire forgot nothing that could help me, and behaved like a great servant of God and the King. My recruits increased every moment. I went to say my breviary while my Indians and the Senecas, without loss of time, assembled to hold a council with Monsieur de Joncaire."

**Abbé Piquet at
Fort Niagara, June, 1751**

The result of the council was to beg the missionary to avoid Oswego lest something evil should happen to him. He gave his promise and turned back to Fort Niagara. He recorded the journey in his diary,

"Whenever we passed a camp or a wigwam, the Indians saluted me by firing their guns, which happened so often that I thought all the trees along the way were charged with gunpowder; and when we reached the fort, Monsieur Becancour received us with great ceremony and the firing of cannon, by which my savages were infinitely flattered."

On the 6th of July he embarked for home followed by a swarm of canoes carrying his new converts. On the 12th they stopped at the Genesee River, and went to visit the falls located where the city of Rochester, N.Y. stands today. On his return he found a canoe loaded with kegs of brandy waiting. He wrote,

"The English had sent it to meet us, well knowing that this was the best way to cause disorder among my new recruits and make them desert me. The Indian in charge of the canoe, who had

the look of a great rascal, offered some to me first, and then to my Canadians and Indians. I gave out that it was very probably poisoned, and immediately embarked again."

On the 16th they came in sight of Oswego and Piquet kept his promise and did not land there. However, he did approach in his canoe and made a close observation of the post and its defences.

"It is commanded," he wrote, "on almost every side; two batteries, of three twelve pounders each, would be more than enough to reduce it to ashes."

Piquet enlarged on the evils of allowing Oswego to exist,

"It not only spoils our trade, but puts the English into communication with a vast number of our Indians, far and near. It is true that they like our brandy better than English rum; but they prefer English goods to ours, and can buy for two beaver skins at Oswego a better silver bracelet than we sell at Niagara for ten."

145

He pushed on to Fort Frontenac and then on to La Présentation. He closed his journal with a boast and a complaint,

"that establishment, which I began two years ago, in the midst of opposition; that establishment which may be regarded as a key of the colony; that establishment which officers, interpreters, and traders thought a chimera, that establishment, I say, forms already a mission of Iroquois savages whom I assembled at first to the number of only six, increased last year to eighty-seven, and this year to three hundred and ninety-six, without counting more than a hundred and fifty whom Monsieur Chabert de Joncaire is to bring me this autumn. And I certify that thus far I have received from His Majesty, for all favor, grace, and assistance, no more than a half pound of bacon and two pounds of bread for daily rations; and that he has not yet given a pin to the chapel, which I have maintained out of my own pocket, for the greater glory of my masters, God and the King."

The struggle continues.

CHAPTER FIFTY-ONE
The Battle lines are Drawn
"The situation is charming. A fine river flows at the foot of the fortifications."-Father Bonnechamp

Despite limited resources and manpower, the governor of New France, the Marquis de la Jonquière, was determined to hold the west. He rightly observed that the holding of key links in the chain constituted control of the region. Fort Niagara was the all important sentinel at the mouth of the Niagara River, which protected the portage around the Falls of Niagara. To further secure their hold here, Senecas were employed to carry goods up the escarpment at the Lower Landing for loading onto wagons for the eight kilometre journey to the Upper Landing above the falls thus en-...ring their loya...y. The vast expanse of inland waterways was safe in the hands of France as long as they held Niagara. If Niagara fell to the English, the Great Lakes as well as the Ohio Valley would fall with it.

Détroit was the next most important link, guarding the passage from Lake Erie to Lake Huron. It was no only a military post, but a settlement as well; the only settlement in the west, with the exception of Fort Chartres on the Mississippi. It was true that there was only a few families, however, the prospects for expansion were excellent. Father Bonnechamp stopped there on his return from the Bienville expedition and wrote,

"The situation is charming. A fine river flows at the foot of the fortifications; vast meadows, asking only to be tilled, extend beyond sight. Nothing can be more agreeable than the climate. Winter lasts hardly two months. European grains and fruits grow here far better than in many parts of France. It is the Touraine and Beauce of Canada."

The white flag of the Bourbons floated over the town, with its population of soldiers and traders; and from the blockhouses, which served to protect the community, one saw on either side the houses of the settlers, which ranged along the waterfront. A short distance away stood three Indians villages of Ottawa, Pottawattamie and Wyandot, who traded furs for European goods.

Céloron de Bienville received a royal commission to command at Détroit upon his return from the Ohio, with the mission of making it the centre of French power in the west. To accomplish this families willing to take up land there were given free passage and equipment consisting of a gun; a hoe; an axe, a ploughshare; a scythe; a sickle; two augers, large and small; a sow; six hens; a rooster; six pounds of powder; and twelve pounds of lead. Twelve families took up the offer. The population of Détroit in 1750 was four hundred and eighty-three.

Michilimackinac controlled the straits between Lake Huron and Lake Michigan, while Fort Ste Marie (Sault Ste Marie) watched over the outlet to Lake Superior. The latter was converted from a mission and trading station to a military post in 1750 complete with a garrison.

Closer to Quebec, La Jonquière looked to the problem of Oswego, the perennial thorn in Canada's side. He had special instructions from the colonial minister in France to eliminate the problem. To attack it openly while the two nations were at peace would be indiscreet, however, if the Iroquois could be persuaded that it posed a threat to their liberty, they might destroy it themselves.

"If Abbé Piquet succeeds in his mission," wrote the minister, "we can persuade these savages to destroy Oswego. This is of the utmost importance; but act with great caution."

The following year the minister wrote again:

"The only means that can be used for such an operation in time of peace are those of the Iroquois. If by making these savages regard such an establishment as opposed to their liberty, and, so to speak, a usurpation by which the English mean to get possession of their lands, they could be induced to undertake its destruction, an operation of the sort is not to be neglected; but M. le Marquis de la Jonquière should feel with what circumspection such an affair should be conducted, and he should labour to accomplish it in a manner not to commit himself."

147

Fort Détroit, 1751

La Jonquière aggressively asserted French rights in the Lake Ontario basin. When Clinton, the governor of New York, wrote to protest the establishment of a post at the Lower Landing on the Niagara, nominally the country of the Iroquois, as an invasion of English territory, he did so on the basis of the Treaty of Utrecht, which declared that the Five Nations were British subjects. La Jonquière rejected the argument. He went further by arresting four Englishmen who were trading with the Miamis and offering rewards for the scalps of Croghan and another trader named Lowry.

When news of this reached William Johnson he wrote Clinton an urgent letter stating,

"If the French go on so, there is no man can be safe in his own house; for I can at any time get an Indian to kill any man for a small matter. Their going on in that manner is worse than open war."

The Canadians on their side made counter accusations. The captive traders told La Jonquière that Croghan had incited Indians to kill Canadians. Other traders were guilty of the same charge.

The English were not the governor's only problem. Versailles refused to follow his advice. He asked for new forts near Lake Erie to counter the influence of the English. The minister answered,

"Niagara and Détroit will secure forever our communications with Louisiana. His Majesty thought that expenses would diminish after the peace; but, on the contrary, they have increased. There must be great abuses. You and the intendant must look to it."

Abuses there were. The colony was rife with official corruption; and at the centre of it was François Bigot, the intendant. The minister directed La Jonquière to remedy certain malpractices that had come to his attention. The governor replied,

"I have reached the age of Sixty-six years, and there is not a drop of blood in my veins that does not thrill for the service of my King. I will not conceal from you that the slightest suspicion on your part against me would cut the thread of my days."

La Jonquière was fighting not only the English, but the home government and the corruption in his own administration. His attention was not only on the west, but happenings in the Maritimes also caused him sleepless nights.

CHAPTER FIFTY-TWO

The Founding of Halifax
"The finest, perhaps, in the world."- Cornwallis describing Halifax Harbour, 1749

While the struggle for the west continued, a no less monumental conflict raged on the eastern seaboard. With the restoration of Louisbourg to France, the struggle for the hearts and minds of the Acadians flared anew. Louisbourg quickly became the military and naval base for French activities in the region as well as protection for the communication route to Quebec. To counter this influence, the British had only a small garrison at Annapolis and an even weaker one at Canseau.

Of course the weakest point of English security in Nova Scotia was the predominance of French speaking Acadians in the province. To minimize the impact of this problem the British government was determined to settle English protestants there. Governor Shirley of Massachusetts argued that New England colonists were best suited for settlement as they knew the climate and the vagaries of farming in the New World. Shirley was convinced that within ten years there would be an English population large enough to support self rule.

Paul Mascarene supported Shirley and urged the Lords of Trade to establish a number of English families on the Atlantic coast and erect the necessary fortifications to protect them. Ironically this made Mascarene, a Frenchman, the father of the fortress city of Halifax.

The government in England mulled over their options and chose to ignore the advice of their colonial officials. Settlers would be sent out from the mother country to fill the need. In June of 1749 a fleet of thirteen transports sailed from England for Chebucto Harbour with twenty-five hundred settlers. These ships carried everyone that would be required to build a self sustaining community.

To establish this new enterprise the young, energetic Edward Cornwallis was named governor, replacing Paul Mascarene, who was more than ready to retire quietly to Boston. Wolfe described Cornwallis as

"a man of approved courage and fidelity;"

**The Founding of Halifax
1749**

Horace Walpole, the English statesman, referred to him as

"a brave, sensible young man, of great temper and good nature."

Cornwallis arrived well ahead of his new colonists to reconnoitre the area. He wrote immediately to the Duke of Bedford, the British Secretary of State,

"The country is one continual wood, and no clear spot is to be seen or heard of." This pessimism was somewhat negated by the harbour, which he described as, "The finest, perhaps, in the world."

Mechanics, tradesmen, farmers, labourers, sailors, and soldiers along with their families landed at this magnificent harbour of Chebucto on July 2 to begin a new life for themselves in Nova Scotia.

The harbour and the fledgling settlement was renamed Halifax in honour of the Earl of Halifax, who, as First Lord of Trade and Plantations, was responsible for its establishment.

Before summer was over, the streets were laid out and the fortifications of the city begun. England sent her best engineers to plan the defenses and so well was this done that in its history the city was never seriously challenged. These same engineers laid out the streets and the settlers drew lots for their property. Soon houses were built and they prepared to spend their first winter in Canada. Joining these new arrivals from the Old World were New Englanders who had been swayed by the eloquence of Governor Shirley and given up their comfortable existence to pioneer the rugged Nova Scotian wilderness.

As a temporary defense a palisade was built around the settlement manned by British regulars who had been sent to relieve the New Englanders who had garrisoned Louisbourg before its return to France.

Succeeding years brought more immigrants until, in 1752, the population reached four thousand. The English now had a firm base from which patrols could keep an eye on Cape Breton Island and Louisbourg.

Cornwallis next had to face the thorny problem of the Acadians and their loyalty or lack thereof. The Acadians, as usual, were caught between the two titans struggling for supremacy in the New World.

EPILOGUE

With the founding of Halifax the British served notice that they were in Nova Scotia to stay. The governor at Quebec saw the danger and took steps to make the English presence in Acadia as difficult as possible.

The decade of the 1750's was to be the most critical for the survival of Canada. Despite overwhelming odds, the Canadians held their own in the early stages, even gaining ground on the British and Americans arrayed against them.

In **Canada's Story, Book Three, The War of the Conquest**, we will see the expulsion of the Acadians and the last desperate struggle to save New France from extinction.

Other Books in print
by Robert J. Foley
Illustrated by George Balbar

ISBN 1-895528-05-4 **Canada Story Book One, The Dawn of Time** , Robert J. Foley, The Haunted Press 1997/stock Retail: $21.95
Format: TP 8 1/2 X 11 120 pages, Illustrated by George Balbar
Beginning with the last Ice Age, The Dawn of Time tells the story of Canada from those first humans to cross the Siberian/Alaskan land bridge who struggled to survive in a savage land. With the coming of the Europeans the search for the route to Cathay drove Cabot, Cartier and Champlain and those that followed them in a centuries long search for a route to the western sea. Book One takes us up to the destruction of the Hurons in 1649

ISBN 1-895528-02-X **The War of 1812, Niagara. Story Vol. 2**, Robert J. Foley, The Haunted Press 1994/stock Retail: $19.95
Format: TP 8 1/2 X 11 Illustrated by George Balbar
 This lively account of the War of 1812 not only tells of monumental events, from the Battles of Queenston Heights & Lundy's Lane to the wilds of Michilimackinac; but also of the extraordinary and the ordinary men and women who lived and died as a result of this important war in the building of the Canadian Nation.

ISBN 1-895528-01-1 **The Welland Canal, Niagara. Story Vol. 3**, Robert J. Foley, The Haunted Press 1995/stock Retail: $19.95
Format: TP 8 1/2 X 11 Illustrated by George Balbar
The Welland Ship Canal is one of the engineering marvels of Canadian History. Follow the human sacrifices that made the canal possible, from the illusive dreams of William Hamilton Merritt to the backbreaking work of the Irish immigrants who fought, loved and died to make those dreams a reality.

ISBN 1-895528-03-8 **Niagara Story Vol. 4, The Canadians**, Robert J Foley, The Haunted Press 1995/stock Retail: $16.95
Format: TP 8 1/2 X 11 Illustrated by George Balbar
This is the story of our epic march to Confederation. The struggles of a pioneer society to open up the wilderness first by canoe, then on to corduroy roads, steamships and railways. They survived droughts, and pestilence in their fight to wrest a living from the land. Here we explore some of the day to day labours of these courageous people. Finally the Rebellion of 1837 and the Fenian Raids made our ancestors realize the value of what they had fought for so long and so hard. Thus Canada was born.
This is also the story of the freedom seekers fleeing the slavery of the American south. Their courage and perseverance helped mold this great country.